The King's Arms.

RATCLIFFE HIGHWAY CIRCA 1811

MARR'S SILK MERCERY, LACE.
PELISSE, MANTLE & FUR WAREHOUSE.

29 MARR

The Marr Residence.

BENTON HUGHES

THE MAUL and THE PEAR TREE

John Williams, drawn in the prison cell
by Sir Thomas Lawrence soon after he was cut down

THE MAUL and THE PEAR TREE
The Ratcliffe Highway Murders 1811

P. D. JAMES &
T. A. CRITCHLEY

THE MYSTERIOUS PRESS • New York

First published in 1971 by Constable & Company Ltd,
10 Orange Street, London WC2H 7EG.

Copyright © 1971 *by* T.A. Critchley and P.D. James
All rights reserved.

The Mysterious Press, 129 West 56th Street, New York, N.Y. 10019

Printed in the United States of America

Library of Congress Cataloging-in-Publication Data

Critchley, T. A. (Thomas Alan), 1919–
    The maul and the pear tree.

    Reprint. Originally published: London : Constable,
c1971.
    Bibliography: p.
    1. Mass murder—England—London—Case studies.
2. Homicide investigation—England—London—Case
studies. I. James, P. D.   II. Title.
HV6535.G6L634 1986   364.1'523'094215   85-43163
ISBN 0-89296-152-X

'Mr. Williams made his *début* on the stage of Ratcliffe Highway, and executed those unparalleled murders which have procured for him such a brilliant and undying reputation. On which murders, by the way, I must observe that in one respect they have had an ill effect, by making the connoisseur in murder very fastidious in his taste, and dissatisfied by anything that has since been done in that line. All other murders look pale by the deep crimson of his.'

Thomas De Quincey,
On the Knocking at the Gate in Macbeth

CONTENTS

ILLUSTRATIONS

THE MAUL and THE PEAR TREE

FOREWORD

During the dark nights of December 1811 in the vicinity of Ratcliffe Highway, in the East End of London, two households, comprising seven people, were brutally clubbed to death within a period of twelve days. From the first the murders, in their barbarity and ruthlessness, powerfully gripped the public imagination. Never before, even at the time of the Gordon Riots, when London was brought to the edge of anarchy, had there been such a national outcry against the traditional means of keeping the peace, or a more vigorous and persistent demand for reform. The Government advertised the highest reward ever offered for information that might lead to the discovery of the murderers; for three weeks *The Times* gave the crimes pride of place over almost every other news; in De Quincey's mind they inspired one of the great essays in the English language, *On Murder considered as one of the Fine Arts,* with its immortal version of the butchery of the Marrs and Williamsons added, years afterwards, as a *Postscript.* For decades legends of the brutalities continued to circulate until, three-quarters of a century later, Jack the Ripper set to work on a neighbouring East End stage to steal the limelight from his only competitor for the sanguinary laurels of the British criminal calendar.

Horror and mystery, as well as a similarly squalid location, were common to the authors of both these outstanding crimes, but in one respect the circumstances of 1887 were very different from those of 1811. Some 14,000 Metropolitan policemen, aided by hundreds of detectives, were available to hunt the Ripper; and although they never caught him, the police were at least able to spread reassurance to a terrified populace. But in 1811 Britain had no police force, and panic was unbridled. One of the most fascinating aspects of the study of these crimes is the insight they afford into the way in which the moribund parish system, aided by the innovation of 'police magistrates', rose to the challenge of a major murder investigation – and apparently, despite the public clamour, met with ultimate success. But when we ranged beyond the printed accounts of the murders it became obvious that the case was a great deal more involved than anyone but a handful of men then living has ever appreciated. From unpublished sources and newspaper reports we reconstructed the actual events; and as the story developed it became clear that the system of 1811 had done no more than pronounce a confident, convenient and ghoulish judgement on a corpse, while leaving the core of the Ratcliffe Highway murders wrapped in continuing mystery.

Of all the published accounts of the murders we have been able to trace only two that have any value. The most important comprises three contemporary (and now rare) pamphlets published at sixpence each by John Fairburn. They are undated, but from internal evidence it is clear that they were printed in December 1811 or early 1812. The pamphlets narrate the circumstances of the murders and include a useful amount of evidence taken before the magistrates and, at three successive inquests, by the Coroner. The other published source of value is Sir Leon Radzinowicz's *History of the English Criminal Law,* vol. 3, where the outline of the story is briefly told, but without the supporting evidence; Radzinowicz, however, makes some use of the Home Office papers, obviously not available to Fairburn. Most of the remaining accounts appear to derive either from Fairburn or from De Quincey's fanciful essay; consequently they have not been useful for our purpose. However, because of the enormity of the crimes the contemporary newspaper reports of the proceedings are remarkably full, and we have relied particularly on those in *The Times,* the *London Chronicle,* the *Morning Post* and the *Morning Chronicle,* supplemented by the *Courier, The Examiner,* and the *Gentleman's Magazine.*

Our other principal source has been the Home Office papers (Domestic Series) now in the Public Record Office. Before the Metropolitan Police were set up, the Middlesex magistrates maintained a regular correspondence with the Home Secretary on criminal matters, and the bundles of papers for December

1811 and the early part of 1812 contain a wealth of material on the Ratcliffe Highway murders that has never before been assembled or, with the exception of a few documents referred to by Radzinowicz, published.

Two sources of material, either of which might contain a final clue to the mystery, have eluded our searches. The most serious loss is that of the original depositions of evidence taken before the Shadwell magistrates. They were sent to the Home Office by order of the Home Secretary on 10 January 1812, and returned by him to the Clerk to the Shadwell bench on 7 February. We have not been able to trace them since. The magistrates themselves told the Home Secretary in December 1811 that the newspaper reports of the hearings were 'pretty accurately given', so the loss may not be great. Nevertheless it seems likely that small additional details contained in the original transcripts, set against what we now know, might confirm what must otherwise be tentative conclusions about the true authors of the crimes. The other lost source seems once to have lain among the records of the East India Company. We believe that particulars of a mutiny that broke out on board the East Indiaman the *Roxburgh Castle* early in 1811 would shed light on the events that occurred in Ratcliffe Highway a few months afterwards; and we think that the circumstances of that mutiny, could they now be traced, would bear out our own hypothesis.

We are grateful to many people who have helped us to collect material for this book, and in particular it is a pleasure to acknowledge the always courteous, and often enthusiastic, assistance we have received from the following: the staffs of the Public Record Office, the British Museum, the London Museum, the Archives Department of the Greater London Council, and the Library and Print Room of the Guildhall; Mr. Douglas Matthews, Deputy Librarian of the London Library; the Librarians of the Home Office, New Scotland Yard, the London Borough of Tower Hamlets and the Port of London Authority; the Curator of the Museum of the River Thames Division of the Metropolitan Police; the Rev. A. M. Solomon, the present Rector of St. George's-in-the-East, who kindly produced for us early parish documents bearing on the case; and Mr. Benton Hughes, to whom we owe a particular debt of gratitude for his work in preparing the illustrated street plan printed on the endpapers. The plan is based on a map engraved by Richard Horwood in 1807; the drawings of Marr's shop, the King's Arms and St. George's church are from contemporary prints; that of the Pear Tree is imaginary.

For the illustrations we thank the following: the drawing of John Williams is reproduced by courtesy of Madame Tussaud's Ltd.; the print of the funeral procession of the Marrs by courtesy of the London Borough of Tower Hamlets Library Committee; for permission to reproduce the handbill issued by the Parish of St. George's and the account of rewards paid, we are indebted to the Keeper of the Public Record Office; the drawing of Marr's shop together with the Maul is from the Guildhall Library, and that of John Williams's body on the cart outside Marr's shop from the Greater London Council Print Collection. The prints of the nightwatchmen of St. Paul's, Covent Garden, Riverside Wapping and Coldbath Fields Prison are reproduced by permission of the British Museum.

Finally it is a pleasure to record our thanks to Professor Keith Simpson, MA, MD, Professor of forensic medicine at Guy's Hospital, London, for kindly agreeing to read the medical evidence given at the inquest, and for answering our questions arising out of it.

T.A.C.

April 1971   P.D.J.

A little before midnight on the last night of his life Timothy Marr, a linen draper of Ratcliffe Highway, set about tidying up the shop, helped by the shop-boy, James Gowen. Lengths of cloth had to be folded and stacked away, rough worsted, dyed linen, canvas for seamen's trousers and serge for their jackets, cheap rolls of printed cotton at fourpence a yard, and bales of silk and muslin laid in to attract the wealthier customers from Wellclose Square and Spitalfields. It was Saturday, 7 December 1811; and Saturday was the busiest day of the week. The shop opened at eight o'clock in the morning and remained open until ten o'clock or eleven o'clock at night. The clearing up would take the pair of them into the early hours of Sunday.

Marr was twenty-four years old. He had been a seafaring man, employed by the East India Company, and had sailed on his last voyage in the *Dover Castle* three years earlier, in 1808. It was also Marr's most prosperous voyage. He did not sail before the mast with the crew, but was engaged by the captain as his personal servant. He seems to have been an agreeable young man, conscientious, anxious to please and ambitious to better himself. During the long return voyage this ambition took shape. He knew precisely what he wanted. There was a girl waiting for him at home. Captain Richardson had held out the promise of help and patronage if Marr continued to serve him well. If he came safely home he would take his discharge, marry his Celia, and open a little shop. Life on shore might be difficult and uncertain, but at least it would be free from danger; and, if he worked hard, it would hold the sure promise of security and fortune. When the *Dover Castle* docked at Wapping Marr was signed off with enough money to start him in a modest way of business. He married, and in April 1811 the young couple found what they were

looking for. Property in the riverside parishes of East London
was cheap, and Marr understood the ways of sailors. He took
a shop at 29 Ratcliffe Highway, in the parish of St. George's-
in-the-East, on the fringes of Wapping and Shadwell.

For two centuries the Highway had had an evil reputation.
It was the chief of three main roads which ran out of London
to the east, following a ridge of firm ground above Wapping
Marsh. There had been a road along this bluff since the days
of the Romans, and the point where the strand of reddish
gravel came closest to the water's edge ('red cliff') had been
a harbour from earliest times. But already, by 1598, the year
when Stowe published his *Survey of London*, Ratcliffe Highway
had become a 'filthy strait passage, with alleys of small
tenements, inhabited by sailors' victuallers'. The degeneration
had come about in Stowe's own lifetime. Forty years earlier
the Highway had run between 'fayre hedges, long rows of
elme, and other trees' to the hamlet of 'Limehurst, or Lime
host, corruptly called Lime house'. Wapping, and all the land
bordering the river had been green fields and orchards, much
as the Romans had established it, with 'never a house standing
within these forty years'.

There was a particular reason why nobody wanted to build
at Wapping, despite the growth of shipping in the Pool of
London in Elizabethan times. The hamlet 'was the usual
place of execution for hanging of pirates and sea rovers, at
the low water mark, and there to remain, till three tides
had overflowed them'. For years superstition and dread had
held back the builders, and it was not until the gallows were
shifted a little farther down river that the first slums came.
Then they spread rapidly over the marshy ground, reaching
out to the gallows and beyond, to Shadwell, Ratcliffe, Limehouse and Poplar. Life in these eighteenth-century hovels was
savage, and the rattle of a dead man's chains when the waves
surged in on a rising tide was just a reminder of its realities.
So too was the twisted street plan of Wapping. The piers
and causeways and flights of tide-washed stone steps that led
down to the river – Pelican Stairs, King James's Stairs,
Wapping New Stairs – still revealed the skeleton of an ancient
maritime village, but it was rapidly disappearing. Dr. Johnson
witnessed something of the early transition. 'He talked today,'

Boswell recorded in March 1783, 'a good deal of the wonderful extent and variety of London, and observed that men of curious enquiry might see in it such modes of life as very few could ever imagine. He in particular recommended us to explore Wapping.'

The whole district was bounded to the south by London's dark blood stream, the Thames, a wide, busy thoroughfare, alive with shipping.[1] There were the great vessels of the East India Company, bulky and formidable as men-of-war, bearing cargoes of tea, drugs, muslin, calicos, spices, and indigo; West Indiamen bringing sugar, rum, coffee, cocoa and tobacco from the Americas; colliers down from Newcastle; whalers from Greenland; coastal vessels; packets; brigs; lighters; barges; ferries and dinghies. The parishioners of Wapping lived their lives against a constant accompaniment of river sounds; the sighing of the wind in sail or mast, water slopping heavily against the wharves, the raucous shouts of bargees and ferrymen. The rich summer smell of the Thames, its sea winds and autumn mists, were part of the air they breathed. Even the shape of the waterfront was created by its manifold associations with the river, and the names of many of the streets expressed their function. Old Gravel Lane brought sand for ballast from the pits of Kingsland to the wharves of Wapping, while Cable Street was the home of rope makers who twisted their cables in the fields through which it ran.

It was from the bustling trade of the river that nearly all the inhabitants, rich and poor alike, drew their life. There were the stevedores, or lumpers, who humped the cargoes from hold to lighter; the watermen, who worked the lighters and other craft which provisioned the vessels as they rode at anchor; the suppliers of rope and tackle; ships' bakers; marine store dealers; instrument makers; boat builders; laundresses who lived by taking in the sailors' washing;

---

[1] Every year 13,000 vessels from all parts of the world dropped anchor in the port of London – then the world's greatest port in the world's greatest city. Before the London Dock opened in 1805 some 10,000 thieves preyed on the cargoes of thousands of vessels moored in the open river. The losses ran to about £500,000 a year, but such was the astonishing wealth pouring into London that this amounted to less than one per cent of the total value of goods handled.

carpenters to repair the ships; rat catchers to rid them of vermin; lodging house and brothel keepers; pawnbrokers; publicans and others who made it their business to relieve the returning sailors as speedily and completely as possible of their accumulated pay. All, in their different ways, served the needs of the ships and seamen; and it was the sailors, a swaggering, disreputable aristocracy, coming and going with the tides, who lorded it over all. They lodged in cheap houses by the river, sleeping on straw mattresses four or five to a room, their sea-chests stowed between. After months at sea under harsh discipline men came home rich, with thirty or forty pounds in their pockets, and spent it fast – a cosmopolitan breed, thugs as well as gentlemen in the making, one-eyed, one-legged, ex-mutineers, heroes, pirates, Empire builders homing to the greatest city on earth. There was endless brawling between the English and foreign seamen. In October 1811 the Home Secretary wrote to the local magistrates warning them to stop the fighting before someone was killed. Soon afterwards, as if to emphasise this warning, a Portuguese was stabbed to death.

Marr evidently emerged from his encounters with these ruffians of the Merchant Navy as a well-disciplined man. In the few months since he had been in business he had already gained a reputation for industry and honesty. Trade was brisk, and for the past few weeks he had been employing a carpenter, Mr. Pugh, to modernise the shop and improve its layout. The whole of the shop front had been taken down and the brickwork altered to enlarge the window for a better display of goods. And on 29 August 1811, a son had been born to increase his joy and fortify his ambition. He could look forward to the day when his shop front – perhaps the front of many shops, stretching from Bethnal Green through Hackney, Dalston, the Balls Pond Road to Stamford Hill and beyond – would bear the inscription 'Marr and Son'.

The first shop, though, was a very modest start. It was one of a terrace of mean houses fronting on to Ratcliffe Highway. The shop, with its counter and shelves, took up most of the ground floor. Behind the counter a door led into a back hall from which ran two flights of stairs – downwards to the kitchen, in the basement, and upwards to a first-floor landing

and two bedrooms. A second floor served as a warehouse to
store silk, lace, pelisse, mantles and furs. It was a plain house,
saved from drabness by the fine new bay window, freshly
painted in olive green. The terrace in which the shop stood
was one of four similar terraces that formed the sides of a
square. Within the block each house had its own fenced-in
back yard, accessible by a back-door in the hall. The ground
inside the square was common to the inhabitants of the whole
block. The terrace on the side of the square opposite to Marr's
shop faced Pennington Street, and here the houses were
overshadowed by a huge brick wall, twenty feet high. This was
the wall of the London Dock, built six years earlier, and
designed like a fortress by the architect of Dartmoor Prison
to protect the hundreds of vessels moored inside. To build the
dock eleven acres of shacks and hovels had been levelled and
their inhabitants crammed into the slums alongside. Most of
them were cut off from the only living they knew, since the
ships they had once plundered were now protected by the
monstrous black wall of the dock. Baulked of this easy living
they preyed on the inhabitants of the riverside parishes, and
added to London's growing army of thieves and beggars. The
wall that made London's shipping more secure did nothing
to increase the safety of Ratcliffe Highway.

And it was a bad time, as well as an unsavoury district, in
which to set up shop. In 1811 Napoleon's blockade of the
continental ports had almost halted European trade. In the
industrial midlands the activities of machine-breakers fed
fears of revolution. The harvest had been a disaster; and,
appropriately for a year of violence and confusion, it was in
1811 that the old king was finally pronounced by his doctors
to be irrevocably mad, and the Prince of Wales became
Regent.

Now though, as he tidied his shop at the end of a busy week,
Marr's mind would be occupied with more personal worries:
the health of his wife, who was recovering only slowly from
her confinement; the wisdom of the alteration of the shop –
had he perhaps over-reached himself? the irritating matter
of a lost ripping chisel which Pugh, the carpenter, had been
loaned by a neighbour and now insisted was still in Marr's
shop – but which a thorough search had failed to recover;

his own hunger at the end of a long day. The draper paused in his work and called to the servant girl, Margaret Jewell. Late though it then was (about ten minutes to midnight, as Margaret Jewell afterwards told the Coroner) he gave the girl a pound note and sent her out to pay the baker's bill and to buy some oysters. At a penny a dozen, supplied fresh from the oyster boats from Whitstable, they would be a cheap, tasty supper after a long day. And they would be a welcome surprise for Marr's young wife, Celia, who was then in the basement kitchen, feeding her baby. Timothy Marr junior was three and a half months old.

As she closed the shop door and went out into the night Margaret Jewell saw her master still at work, busy behind the counter with James Gowen. The girl turned left into Ratcliffe Highway.

Here, it seems, she was unafraid to walk alone at night; but this sense of security, about to be shattered for a generation, was comparatively new. The parish vestries of a few Queen Anne churches had brought the first civilising influences – paving stones, oil lamps and parish watchmen – but the principal changes had come about in Margaret Jewell's own lifetime. People never wearied of recalling the fire of 1794, the most destructive since the fire of London, when the flames had consumed hundreds of wooden houses and shacks on both sides of the Highway. A kettle of pitch boiled over in a boat-builder's yard, and the fire spread to a barge loaded with saltpetre. The tide was out, and neighbouring vessels lay helpless in the mud. The barge blew up and ignited the salt-petre warehouses of the East India Company. Fire rained on Ratcliffe Highway, as it was to do again 150 years later. But it was a cleansing fire. The wooden shacks were replaced by little brick houses, of which Marr's shop was one, and pockets of respectability grew up. The opening of the London Dock in 1805 brought others, as wealthy merchants moved into the parish, evincing their quality every Sunday with a line of carriages drawn up outside the church gates of St. George's-in-the-East. On a wild winter night the Highway could still be a fearful place for the superstitious, when the bowsprits and booms juddered and creaked against the quays of the London Dock and the wind moaned through old rigging like the last sigh of a pirate swinging by the river. But most nights were now peaceful, and by day the Highway had become a cheery, vulgar, boisterous street, brilliant with the colours of scores of painted signs hanging outside inns and shops, and permeated everywhere by enticing smells of the sea and river: of fish, tarred twine, new ropes and sails, resinous timbers for ships' spars. And on a Saturday night, especially, when men were paid their week's wages in the public houses and the shops stayed open late, the Highway had a glittering life of its own, sustained by the comparatively new sense of security that enabled a servant girl to walk out safely alone at midnight.

Margaret Jewell made her way along Ratcliffe Highway to Taylor's oyster shop, but she found it shut. She retraced her steps to Marr's house, glanced through the window, and saw her master still at work behind the counter. It was the last time she saw him alive. The time would then be about midnight. It was a mild, cloudy night, following a wet day, and the girl may have been glad of an excuse to stay out longer. She continued past Marr's shop and turned off the Highway down John's Hill to pay the baker's bill.

And now she was turning her back on safety. Round the corner from John's Hill ran Old Gravel Lane, the historic land link with Wapping shore, winding down to the river seventy yards east of Execution Dock, where the pirates swung. Between the wharves the water heaved under a scum of sludge and sewage; behind them the tides of centuries had washed up deposits of old decaying hovels like barnacles on a ship's hulk. They conformed to no plan. The old custom had been to build in courts and alleys at right angles to the roads. Courts were built within courts, alleys behind alleys. And more recently the girl had seen whole areas walled in, dwarfed and darkened even in daylight by the eyeless walls of warehouses, the bleak soaring walls of sailors' tenements, and the cliff of the London Dock, sheltering its alien floating city. She would have heard chilling tales of life in the dark labyrinths taken over by squatters, men and women crammed into derelict property that offered a perpetual fire risk to the dens and warrens where Old Gravel Lane twisted down to the Thames – Gun Alley, Dung Wharf, Hangman's Gains, Pear

Tree Alley. The starving people were quiet for the most part, with the sullen fortitude of despair, but to respectable Londoners they constituted a perpetual menace. Occasionally it erupted into reality, when savage mobs surged West to riot and plunder, or roared out for the festival of a public hanging.

'The baker's shop was shut,' Margaret Jewell later told the Coroner. 'I then went to another place to get the oysters but I found no shop open. I was out about twenty minutes.' She did not venture down towards riverside Wapping, but returned to the familiar safety of Ratcliffe Highway.

But now it was past midnight, and the street noises were dying down. Public houses were closing, shutters were being fastened, bolts shot. And as the street fell silent Margaret Jewell would begin to hear her own footsteps echoing on the cobblestones. Overhead, the rickety parish lamps of crude fish-blubber oil cast a flickering light on the wet pavement, animating and deepening the shadows; and between the lamps were pools of total darkness. Nor, when Margaret Jewell reached 29 Ratcliffe Highway, was any light shining in Marr's shop either. It, too, was dark, the door shut tightly against her. The girl stood alone in the silent street and pulled the bell.

Immediately the jangling seemed unnaturally loud to the waiting girl. There was no one about at this late hour, except George Olney, the watchman, who passed by without speaking on the other side of the street, taking a person in charge to the lock-up. Margaret Jewell rang again, more loudly, pressing herself close to the door, listening for any sound from within. She was not yet seriously worried. The master was taking his time. Probably he was with her mistress, in the comfort of the downstairs kitchen. Perhaps the family, despairing of their oysters, had even made their way to bed. The girl hoped that her master would not chide her for taking so long on a fruitless errand; that her ringing wouldn't waken the child. She pulled again, more vigorously; listened: and this time heard a sound which, to the end of her life, she would never recall without a *frisson* of horror. For the moment, though, it brought only relief, and the comforting assurance that she would soon gain the warmth of the familiar kitchen. There was a soft tread of footsteps on the stairs. Someone – surely her master? – was coming down to open the door. Then came another familiar sound. The baby gave a single low cry.

But no one came. The footsteps ceased and again there was silence. It was an absolute silence, eerie and frightening. The girl seized the bell and rang again; then, torn between panic and frustration, began to kick the door. She was cold and beginning to be very frightened. As she rang and kicked a man came up to her. His drunken senses irritated by the noise, or imagining the girl was causing a nuisance, he began to abuse her. Margaret Jewell gave up knocking. There was nothing to be done but wait for the next appearance of the watchman. To continue with her useless ringing now would only expose her to fresh insults.

She waited about thirty minutes. Promptly at one o'clock George Olney came calling the hour. Seeing the girl at Marr's door and not knowing who she was he told her to move on. She explained that she belonged to the house, and thought it very strange that she should be locked out. Olney agreed. He said he had no doubt but that the family were within. He had passed when calling the hour at twelve o'clock, and had himself seen Mr. Marr putting up his shutters. A little after midnight he had examined the window, as was his custom, and had noted that the shutters were not fastened. He had called out to Marr at the time, and a strange voice had answered, 'We know of it'. Now, holding his lantern high against the window, he examined the shutter again. The pin was still unfastened. Seizing the bell he rang vigorously. There was no reply. He rang again, pounded on the knocker, then bent down and called through the keyhole, 'Mr. Marr! Mr. Marr!'

The renewed ringing, rising now to a crescendo, roused John Murray, pawnbroker, who lived next door. He was not a man to interfere with his neighbours, but he had been disturbed by Margaret Jewell's earlier assault on the door. Now, at a quarter-past-one, he and his wife were ready for bed, and hoping for sleep. There had been mysterious noises earlier in the night. Shortly after twelve o'clock he and his family had been disturbed at their late supper by a heavy sound from next door, as if a chair were being pushed back. It had been followed by the cry of a boy, or of a woman. These noises had made little impression at the time. Probably Marr, irritated and tired at the end of the longest and busiest trading day, was chastising his apprentice or his maid. This was his business. But the continued din was another matter. Murray made his way out into the street.

The situation was rapidly explained in a confused babble from Margaret Jewell of oysters, baker's bills and baby's cries, and George Olney's quieter explanation of the un-fastened pin, and the fruitless knocking. John Murray took charge. He told the watchman to continue pulling hard at the bell, and he would go into his backyard and see if he could rouse the family from the back of the house. He did so, calling out 'Mr. Marr', three or four times. Still there was no answer. Then he saw a light at the back of the house. Returning to the street he told the watchman to ring yet louder, while he tried to get into the house by the back door.

It was easy enough to get over the flimsy fence dividing the two properties, and he was soon in Marr's backyard. He found the door of the house was open. It was very quiet and very still inside, but there was a faint light from a candle burning on the landing of the first floor. Murray made his way up the stairs and took the candlestick in his hand. He found himself opposite the door of the Marrs' bedroom. Then, inhibited by delicacy, as habit sometimes does impose itself against all reason, he paused irresolutely at the door and called softly, as if the young people, oblivious of the clamour from the street, were sleeping quietly in each other's arms. 'Marr, Marr, your window shutters are not fastened.'

No one answered. Murray, still reluctant to invade the privacy of his neighbour's bedroom, held the candle high and made his way carefully down the stairs and into the shop.

It was then that he found the first body. The apprentice boy, James Gowen, was lying dead just inside the door which led to the shop and within six feet of the foot of the stairs. The bones of his face had been shattered by blow after blow. His head, from which the blood was still flowing, had been beaten to a pulp, and blood and brains splattered the shop as high as the counter, and even hung, a ghastly excrescence, from the low ceiling. Petrified with shock and horror Murray for a moment could neither cry out nor move. The candle shook in his hand, throwing shadows and a soft fitful light over the thing at his feet. Then, with a groan the pawnbroker stumbled towards the door, and found his path blocked by the body of Mrs. Marr. She was lying face downwards with her face close against the street door, blood still draining from her battered head.

Somehow Murray got the door opened and gasped out his news incoherently. 'Murder! Murder! Come and see what murder is here!' The small crowd outside, swollen now by the arrival of neighbours and a second watchman, pressed into the shop. They stood aghast with horror. Margaret Jewell began to scream. The air was loud with groans and cries. It took only a moment for fresh tragedy to be revealed. Behind the counter, and also face downwards, with his head towards the window, was the body of Timothy Marr. Someone called out 'The child, where's the child?' and there was a rush for the basement. There they found the child, still in its cradle, the side of its mouth laid open with a blow, the left side of the face battered, and the throat slit so that the head was almost severed from the body.

Sickened by the horror and brutality and almost fainting with fright, the little group in the kitchen staggered upstairs. The shop was becoming crowded now and there was light from many candles. Huddled together for protection they looked around the room. There on that part of the counter which was free of Gowen's blood and brains they saw a carpenter's ripping chisel. With shaking and reluctant hands they took it up. It was perfectly clean.

PERSON OR PERSONS UNKNOWN

The sudden springing of watchmen's rattles spread instant alarm. Bedroom windows flew open and night-capped heads emerged. People hurriedly dressed, and a small crowd gathered outside Marr's shop. Some had heard Murray's terrible cry 'Murder!', others flocked by instinct to a scene already half familiar in nightmare. But there was nothing to see; only the half-open door, the unfastened shutters and the white, terrified faces of the few who had seen inside.

Within minutes the news reached the River Thames Police Office at Wapping, where Police Officer Charles Horton was on duty. He raced up Old Gravel Lane, forced his way through the crowd in Ratcliffe Highway and entered Marr's shop. As the first policeman on the scene it was his duty to search the premises. He was lucky to be on duty that night. Two months afterwards, when the Home Secretary authorised the distribution of reward money, Horton received ten pounds for what he was to find.

The policeman surveyed the corpses by the dim light of his lantern. Already the air seemed tainted with a sickly sweet smell of blood and brains. He searched systematically, thrusting the lantern under the counter, behind the door, into shelves, in every dark place where the murderers might have flung their terrible weapons. But apart from the ripping chisel he found nothing. Nor, it seemed, had anything been stolen. In Marr's pocket Horton found five pounds, and there was loose money in the till. Then he went downstairs to the kitchen, where the dead child lay in his blood-soaked cradle. But that search, too, was fruitless. Whoever had sliced through the baby's throat had taken the knife away with him.

It remained to search the upper floors. Joined by Olney, Horton crept cautiously upstairs and stood on the landing, alert and listening, where Murray had so recently called to the young couple in their bedroom. Their door was still open. Taking a firm grip on his truncheon, Horton went in. The bed was undisturbed. Beside it stood a chair, and resting against the chair, the handle upwards, was a heavy iron mallet, or maul, such as ship's carpenters used. The handle was covered with blood, and on the iron head the blood was still wet, with hairs sticking to it. The murderers must have dropped the weapon and fled, disturbed by Margaret Jewell's ringing. Nothing had been stolen from the bedroom either. A drawer contained £152 in cash.

Horton carried the maul downstairs gingerly. The sight of it caused the crowd in the shop to shrink back. Setting his lantern on the counter the policeman examined the weapon. The iron head was shaped rather like an anvil, the thick end, now horrible with blood and hair, flattened to drive nails into ships' timbers. The narrow end, which tapered to a point about the diameter of a sixpence, was used as a punch for driving the nail in deeper beneath the surface of the wood. Here was the first clue. The end was seen to be broken at the tip.

Someone else, meanwhile, had discovered other clues. Two distinct sets of footprints led away from the back of Marr's house. The carpenters had been at work in the shop that day and the impressions contained traces of blood and sawdust. Evidently the murderers had escaped over the fence at the rear and made their way across the enclosed ground at the back. A man from Pennington Street confirmed it. He lived next door to an unoccupied house at the corner of Pennington Street and Artichoke Hill. Soon after the first alarm was given he had heard a rumbling in the empty house, and 'about ten or twelve men' were heard to rush out of it down Pennington Street. It was a fair inference that the gang had fled down Old Gravel Lane, where they disappeared.

Sometime before dawn Horton returned to the River Thames Police Office with the maul; and there he discovered three men already in custody. They were Greek sailors, seen loitering near Marr's house, and one had spots of blood on his trousers. These were the first of many to be arrested in similar circumstances, picked up on the slightest suspicion, or none. The sense of horror, and especially a feeling of outrage at the murder of the baby, rapidly infected the whole community with a sort of mass hysteria which at first battened on foreigners. The Greek sailors were brought before the River Thames Police magistrate, John Harriott, but they were able to produce an alibi to prove that they had just come up from Gravesend and were discharged.

So already, soon after daybreak on Sunday morning, within a very few hours of the murders, much had been accomplished. A police officer had searched Marr's house and found the blood-stained maul with its distinctive mark; it had been established that nothing had been stolen; two sets of footprints had been discovered; the likely route of escape had been plotted; and three men had been arrested and brought before the magistrate. The impression gained is that there existed in London eighteen years before the Metropolitan Police were established, in 1829, an organised, if rudimentary police force, trained and equipped to react swiftly to events. Such an impression would be false.

The primary responsibility for the fight against crime in the parish of St. George's-in-the-East was saddled firmly on the Churchwardens, Overseers and Trustees of the parish vestry, who were required by laws going back to the Middle Ages to go through the annual ritual of conscripting persons to the part-time, unpaid offices of High Constable and Constable. These offices, though honourable, were irksome. The constables, up to a dozen of whom might be appointed every year, were responsible for setting the nightly watch, inspecting it, charging prisoners, and bringing them before a magistrate in the morning. After a hard day's work tradesmen and artisans had neither energy nor inclination for arduous and unrewarded public service; and by long custom they could avoid it, either by paying a ten pound fine to the parish or by paying a deputy to act for them. Most of these deputies were corrupt, and many served on for years.

Under the control of the constables (or their paid deputies) the parish of St. George's–in–the–East also employed thirty-five night watchmen at two shillings a night, together with a Night Beadle to supervise them. The watchmen's duty was to call the half-hours from nine o'clock at night until four in the morning, and to 'apprehend, arrest and detain, all malefactors, rogues, vagabonds, disturbers of the peace, and all persons whom they shall have reason to suspect have any evil designs, and who shall be loitering or misbehaving themselves'. That is what the local Act said, but the watchmen saw their job differently. For them it was the easiest way they knew of earning fourteen shillings a week plus perquisites. Between their rounds they sheltered in little watch-boxes which, according to a contemporary account in *The Examiner*, were 'only a common piece of charity, considering what poor, superannuated creatures inhabit them, and what fogs and rains will often last a whole night'.

These parish watchmen were invariably old. Most were employed on other work during the day, but were no longer physically strong enough to undertake hard manual labour; so they took on the night work to supplement a necessarily low wage. According to a Mr. Jenkinson, of Charterhouse Square, there was a further reason of public – or rather, parish – policy why only old men were employed. 'I have heard that some years ago the parish of Covent Garden tried the effect of employing young men as watchmen,' he confided delicately to the Home Secretary, 'but were obliged to abandon it on account of the connection which subsisted between them and the Prostitutes, who withdrew them from their Duty while Depredations were committing.' But the old men were little more effective. They may have been too senile to be tempted by prostitutes, but they were also too weak and ineffectual to be a threat to burglars. What was evidently required was a body of strong, energetic and honest young men impervious to the sexual wiles of women, a species which, even had it existed, was unlikely to be attracted to the job or the pay of a parish night watchman.

The Home Office papers contain a description of the job as one watchman saw it at the time. Thomas Hickey had been employed in five metropolitan parishes, and the rackets he reported were the same in each. A favourite trick was for a watchman to accept a bribe from a burglar (often a close friend) to arrest some stranger for a trifling matter such as loitering, take him to the watchbox, and keep up an argument long enough to enable the burglar to rob the chosen house and get away. Then when the constable came along to charge the arrested person he and the watchman would undertake to drop the charge for an agreed sum. 'Then Mr. Watchman and Mr. Constable, to give you, Sir, the Phraise, divide the Bit.' Hickey and his friends also had experience of the wiles of prostitutes. 'Another Great Evil is the Unfortunate Females who from Actual Necessity parade the Streets late at Nights, they poor Creatures for their Personal Safety are obliged – I say obliged – to have a Protector, better known by the name of a Bully or a Flash Man – pardon this Language Sir – who are Noted Thieves – the Unfortunate Female from meeting with interruption from the Watchman is obliged, and is often planned, to Call him from his Bait to treat him with some Gin – this is never refused and answers the double purpose of giving her Freedom to prowl about and her *Pall* an opportunity of Breaking open a House or robbing the Unwary Passinger.'

A watchman was not allowed to stray from his parish without permission from a neighbouring constable, and stories are common of old men looking benignly on while burglars ransacked a house across a road that formed a parish boundary. Frequently, however, they simply dozed through the night in a drunken stupor. The tools of the trade, beloved by generations of cartoonists, were a lantern (or 'lanthorn') and a rattle. The lantern was a heavy iron contraption encrusted with layers of tar and grease. The rattle served as little more than a rallying call to criminals, a fortissimo accompaniment (to quote *The Examiner* again) to the 'old time-cracked and weather-cracked voice that seems to call the thieves together to rob where they please'.

No one could expect this meagre parish force, even when supplemented in winter by twenty-four 'night patrols', to prevent murder; and the idea of using it as a detective agency would have been ludicrous. However, it was not the only agent of the law in the parish where Marr lived. Behind it (though not in charge of it) was a local bench of three magistrates at their Public Office at Shadwell. This was one of seven such Public Offices created in 1792. The statute might have been called the Anti-Corruption Act, for it finally swept away from Middlesex the disgrace of the old 'trading justices', who for upwards of a century had run justice as a highly profitable business. Having bought their way on to the bench they openly took whatever bribes they could get to buy thieves out of trouble, ran protection rackets with brothel keepers and blackmailed with the threat of imprisonment any who dared to oppose them. Sometimes they encountered rascals more clever than themselves. A confidential report to the Lord Chancellor spoke of 'One Sax, a justice near Wapping; very poor and scandalous; lately a prisoner of the King's Bench for debt; now skulks about in blind alehouses about Tower Hill and Wapping and takes affidavits at a little ale house near the Victualling Office'. But few justices sank as low as this. They had only to open up shops near their courts to make an excellent living by imposing surcharges of ten or twenty per cent on all goods sold to thieves and prostitutes as the price of immunity from prosecution. The object of the 1792 Act had been to replace these enviable little businesses by courts modelled on the pattern Henry Fielding had established fifty years earlier at Bow Street, where for half a century justice had been administered fairly. The magistrates in the seven new Public Offices were each paid £400 a year (later raised to £500) – enough, it was hoped, to put them beyond the reach of temptation.

But the solution of one problem created another. The only qualification laid down for the appointments was one that applied to the magistracy generally: a person had to have a private income of at least £100 a year, so that he need not be a tool of government. The new jobs were filled, as was usual at the time, by patronage. By 1811 (to quote *The Examiner* again) 'A number of persons, with whom their patrons are at a loss what to do, and who have neither time nor inclination nor any one requisite for the duties which they ought to perform, are seated in the Public Offices, to the great annoyance of themselves and injury of their fellow-subjects. . . . One of them would be writing novels, another studying politics, a third immersed in divinity, a fourth speculating on the girls that went by, a fifth gnawing his pen for an unfinished couplet and a sixth playing the fiddle over a life of Dr. Johnson.' The Poet Laureate himself ('The poetical Pye,' said Walter Scott, 'was eminently respectable in everything but his poetry') was one of the magistrates, and all were enthusiastic literati – 'An offender might be taken up at a theatre conducted by one Magistrate, for creating a riot at a play written by another, and be brought before a third who criticises it in a magazine.' The magistrates might be considered by day, the writer summed up, 'what the watchmen are to us by night – poor creatures entirely out of their places, and of no use but to those who plunder us'.

The three Shadwell magistrates, Robert Capper, Edward Markland and George Story, had their Public Office in Shadwell High Street, and from there they were supposed to cover the six densely populated parishes of Shadwell, Wapping, St. Anne's (Limehouse), St. George's-in-the-East, Ratcliffe and Poplar. To help them they (like each of the other Public Offices) were authorised to employ not more than eight police officers. These men wore no uniform and had no badge of office or equipment of any kind. They formed, in effect, a tiny, isolated police force of which the magistrates were in personal command. Each police officer was paid twenty-two shillings a week, but this was in the nature of a retaining fee. It was expected that the men would undertake jobs for private individuals, track down suspected criminals and recover stolen goods for an agreed reward. By these means the police officers earned as much as £100 a year over and above their nominal salaries. Relations between them and the parish constables and watchmen were deeply hostile; the parish force regarded the little band of police officers as spies, whom they were reluctant to help in any way. They were animals of the same genus, a magistrate declared, but 'the one is the natural enemy of the other'. This was inevitable, as they were competing for the same perquisites, and they served different masters.

Charles Horton, the police officer who searched Marr's shop, was not one of the Shadwell men. He belonged to yet another organisation, and one more recent, even, than the Public Office at Shadwell. The River Thames Police Force, with its Police Office at Wapping New Stairs, had been set up by statute in 1800. Its purpose was to protect the valuable cargoes and ships at anchor in the Pool of London, and although it was authorised to employ five 'land constables', as well as forty-three water men, its operations were ordinarily confined to the river. But the man who had been in charge of the force ever since its inception, John Harriott, was no ordinary man. To understand his part in investigating the crime it is necessary to glance at his background.

Harriott joined the Navy as a boy and sailed to the West Indies. He was shipwrecked off the Levant, then served under Admiral Pocock at the taking of Havana and again at the capture of Newfoundland. When peace came he enlisted as first mate in the Merchant Navy, lived for some time with the American Indians, then suddenly re-appeared in the East as a soldier, where he was acting chaplain and Deputy Judge Advocate. Sent to quell a refractory rajah, he sustained a matchlock wound in the leg, sailed off to Sumatra and the Cape, then after a spell in the wine trade settled down to farm in Essex, where he became a magistrate. In 1790 the farm was destroyed by fire. Harriott emigrated to the United States, returned after five years to England, and then (in 1798) helped Patrick Colquhoun to plan the River Police, with its headquarters at Wapping. He had been the magistrate in charge of the force ever since its inception. In 1811 he was sixty-six; a flamboyant, brave, crafty old buccaneer, a founding father of the first British Empire, type-cast for the pages of Robert Louis Stevenson.

Yet Harriott's memoirs show him to have been more than the conventional buccaneer. He was a man of astonishing energy and versatility. No subject was alien to his fertile and inquiring mind. He was something of an amateur theologian, always ready to speculate in print on the existence of God and the efficacy of the Sacraments; an inventor of considerable engineering ability, although some of his schemes were more ingenious than practical; a humanitarian who was one of the first to expose the evils of private lunatic asylums, and a philosopher whose mind, speculating on death, was 'elevated to a mental satisfaction far beyond what language can express by the experience of transferring the putrefying remains of his first two wives, his father and a number of his infant children to a tough oak coffin', while tidying things up for his own reception. Moreover, he was a practical moralist whose advice to his sons embarking for the East Indies, 'at a time when the passions will become strong and the warm climate will increase a desire for gratification', deserve better than to be buried in the now rare pages of *Struggles through Life* (3 vols. 1815).

These, then, were the arrangements for policing London in 1811. Out of a total population of just over one million, about 120,000 people lived in the City; and here alone in the Metropolis was a properly organised system of government, and the money to pay for an efficient nightly watch. The urban sprawl outside the City boundaries was divided into fifty separate parishes, each like a tiny independent state, whose only common rulers were, remotely, the King and Parliament. Each parish was governed by its own vestry, comprising the church wardens, overseers, and trustees; and between them these parishes employed about 3,000 parish constables and watchmen. Scattered among the parishes, but in no way set in authority over them, were the seven new Public Offices, each with its quota of three magistrates and eight police officers. These, too, were independent units. Down by the river there was the Thames Police Office to look after the shipping. And finally, *primus inter pares,* there was the prestigious Bow Street Office, where there were also three magistrates and a *corps d'élite* of sixty Bow Street Runners, whose operations, however, were normally confined to patrolling the main highways that led into London. Under this system – or rather lack of it – there was no regular focal point, and no one was answerable to anyone for anything. Animosities and jealousies were endemic, and it was a point of honour not to exchange information.[1] The Home Secretary could use his authority to order the temporary loan of Bow Street or Thames police in an emergency, but any other mutual aid was inconceivable.

[1] When John Gifford, a magistrate at the Worship Street Office, was asked by a Parliamentary inquiry (in 1816) whether there was any 'regular correspondence' between his and the other Offices, he replied firmly: 'Certainly not. . . . Different Police Offices keep their information to themselves, and do not wish to communicate it to others, that they may have the credit and advantage of detecting offenders.' (Gifford's real name was Green. By the age of twenty-three he had run through a large fortune, fled to France and changed his name. He returned to edit political and literary magazines and was rewarded by the appointment of the Worship Street Office after writing the history of Pitt's political life in six vols., 1809.)

Nearly eighty years later, when Jack the Ripper set about his midnight butchery a little to the north of Ratcliffe Highway, some 14,000 Metropolitan policemen drawn from all over London failed to solve the crimes. In 1811 the forces available in Ratcliffe Highway to detect and apprehend the murderers of the Marrs comprised: one Night Beadle, one High Constable, one Constable, thirty-five old night watchmen and twenty-four night patrols employed by the vestry of St. George's-in-the-East; three magistrates at their Public Office in Shadwell, with their eight police officers; and an inquisitive old adventurer, Harriott, with a force of River Police and five land constables.

The parish vestry was next in action after Harriott, and it acted in the only way open to it. Good detection depended on reliable information, and information had to be paid for. It was an old, well-proven formula; the only question was, how much to offer? Not a penny more than was needed, for the parish of St. George's-in-the-East was as poor as any in London. Yet the enormity of the crime and the danger that would still hang over the parish so long as it remained unsolved, both pointed to a considerable sum. Having viewed the bodies, the Churchwardens, Overseers and Trustees held an urgent, anxious meeting in the vestry of St. George's. The clerk, John Clement, drafted a hand-bill and rushed it round to Skirven, the printer of Ratcliffe Highway. Skirven put it in the press at once, and the same afternoon it was pinned up on the church door and on the doors of all the churches and public houses in the neighbourhood.

Poor James Gowen was the least regarded of the victims. His short life must have held more toil than pleasure, and he died brutally in an agony of terror. Now, when it came to issuing the reward bill, no one seems to have known his real name. But there was someone who remembered him. A week later an anonymous letter arrived at the Home Office from 'a distant Relation of the poor apprentice who was so barbarously murdered in Ratcliffe Highway', observing that 'the lad's name was not James Biggs but James Gowen'. 'Query?' a disbelieving Home Office clerk wrote on the letter; but the point was perhaps not without interest, and might be followed up some time – 'Mr. Capper, speak,' he added.

FIFTY POUNDS

REWARD.

Horrid Murder!!

WHEREAS,

The Dwelling House of Mr. TIMOTHY MARR, 29, Ratcliff Highway, Man's Mercer, was entered this morning between the hours of Twelve and Two o'Clock, by some persons unknown, when the said Mr. MARR, Mrs. CELIA MARR, his wife, TIMOTHY their INFANT CHILD in the cradle, and JAMES BIGGS, a servant lad, were all of them most inhumanly and barbarously Murdered!!

A Ship Carpenter's Pæn Maul, broken at the point, and a Bricklayer's long Iron Ripping Chissel about Twenty Inches in length, have been found upon the Premises, with the former of which it is supposed the Murder was committed. Any person having lost such articles, or any Dealer in Old Iron, who has lately Sold or missed such, are earnestly requested to give immediate Information.

The Churchwardens, Overseers, and Trustees, of the Parish of St. George Middlesex, do hereby offer a Reward of FIFTY POUNDS, for the Discovery and Apprehension of the Person or Persons who committed such Murder, to be paid on Conviction.

By Order of the Churchwardens, Overseers, and Trustees,

JOHN CLEMENT,

Ratcliff-highway,
SUNDAY. 8th, DECEMBER, 1811.

VESTRY CLERK.

SKIRVEN, Printer, Ratcliff Highway, London.

The Shadwell magistrates, meanwhile, assembled in their Public Office in Shadwell High Street. But what to do? Little but wait: the vestry's offer of a fifty-pound reward for information was bound to bring rapid results. Moreover they learned that Harriott's man Horton had found a blood-stained maul; so they sent a message to the River Thames Police Office inviting Harriott to join them in examining Margaret Jewell, John Murray and George Olney.

Already on Sunday morning, therefore, three separate authorities were active in the case: the Churchwardens, Overseers and Trustees of the parish, with their offer of a reward; Capper and his fellow magistrates at the Shadwell Public Office, waiting for any information the offer might throw up; and Harriott at the River Thames Police Office. During the succeeding days, as news of the crime spread, this confused situation grew worse. Suspicious characters were rounded up all over London and brought before the magistrates at the other six Public Offices and at Bow Street itself. Each bench worked largely in isolation from the others, sending messages to Shadwell only when they felt inclined to do so. Nevertheless, there existed one central point at which, in theory at all events, the various threads could, exceptionally, be pulled together.

The magistrates in the Public Offices were appointed by the Home Secretary and they acted under his direct authority. In the case of Bow Street the relationship was intimate: the Chief Magistrate, Sir Richard Ford, was constantly in and out of the Home Office with plans for capturing enemy agents; and William Day, a Home Office clerk, played a leading part in operating the Bow Street Runners. The Thames Police, too, were strictly controlled, as Harriott was soon to be reminded. The other seven Public Offices, by contrast, were relatively independent (except for their staff and annual budgets) but they were encouraged to draw the Home Secretary's attention to anything of importance. This explains why, from the beginning, detailed reports flowed into White-hall describing every new suspicion, almost every prisoner examined, and every fresh turn, until eventually the Home Secretary was obliged to take a very close personal interest in the case himself.

But that came later. At first the Home Office treated the Ratcliffe Highway murder as it would have treated any other – with bland indifference. The Right Hon. Richard Ryder, a pompous man of forty-five, lacking in humour (Harrow and St. John's, Cambridge, Lincoln's Inn, Judge Advocate General before being appointed to the Home Office) had been Home Secretary for two years, but he seems to have taken little interest in the Department's affairs. In his office in Dorset House – a building on the site of Henry VIII's old tennis court, on the north corner of Whitehall and Downing Street – he employed two under-secretaries, a law clerk, a précis writer and a private secretary, supported by eighteen clerks; and at the end of 1811 public business was pressing. The Peninsular War was at a critical stage, and Napoleon's Continental System was beginning to take effect; much of the Department's time was occupied with subversive activities at home. In November 1811, too, the Luddites' frame-breaking in Nottinghamshire had risen to a peak, and it was the Home Secretary's duty to supervise a full-scale military campaign against the saboteurs. So when the first letters from the magistrates came in little notice was taken of them.

Harriott, characteristically, was the first to get in touch with the Home Office. He wrote at once, on Sunday. The startling account he had heard from Margaret Jewell and Murray deepened his interest. Directly the preliminary examination at Shadwell was over he elbowed his way through a vast crowd outside 29 Ratcliffe Highway and inspected the house himself. Then he returned to the River Thames Police in Wapping to write to John Beckett, the senior of the under-secretaries.

'For the information of Mr. Secretary Ryder,' he began, 'I deem it necessary to lose no time in acquainting you with the following account of the extraordinary inhuman Murder of four persons.' The letter went on to summarise what Margaret Jewell and Murray had told the magistrates that morning, and already Harriott had his ideas. 'It is pretty evident,' he wrote, 'that at least two persons were concerned, and most probably had planned their operations for a Saturday night as the shops are then kept open so late, when watching the master's putting up the shutters, and leaving the door open when he went in to fasten the Bolts. They rushed in and perpetrated the horrid Murders; but being disturbed by the girl's returning and ringing for admittance, they made their escape at the back door.'

What of the prospect of detection? Harriott was optimistic. There were two points to follow up. First, he would discover whether any of the dozen or so young women Marr employed part-time would know that he had money in the house, and had been concerned in planning the murders; the offer of a reward and a free pardon might induce someone to come forward. Second, a 'singular mark' on the maul should enable it to be traced. The reference to Marr's 'dozen or so young women' is curious. Marr was in a small way of business in modest premises, and was a man's mercer not a tailor. It seems unlikely that he employed any labour other than James Gowen and one female servant. It may be that Harriott, in his zeal and enthusiasm, too readily accepted rumours as truth or misunderstood an informant. Certainly no servant other than Margaret Jewell and her predecessor gave evidence, and we hear no more of the dozen or so young women.

Harriott was restless, eager to strike fast while clues were fresh. Having dispatched his letter he made further inquiries, and soon additional information came to light. It could be vital. Three men had been seen outside Marr's shop for half an hour, one of whom kept looking through the shop window. Their descriptions had been obtained. One was dressed in 'a light coloured sort of Flushing Coat, and was a tall, lusty Man'. Another was wearing 'a Blue Jacket, the sleeves of which were much torn, and under which he appeared to have also Flannel Sleeves, and had a small-rimmed Hat on his Head'. No description of the third man had been given. Such promising clues had to be followed up without delay; and on Monday, 9 December, Harriott had his own hand-bill printed, setting out the men's descriptions and offering twenty pounds for their arrest.

This was the day on which the murders ceased to be local news and became a national event. 'Horrid and Unparalleled Murders', announced Monday's *Morning Chronicle;* and *The Times* reported: 'We almost doubt whether, in the annals of murders, there is an instance on record to equal in atrocity those which the following particulars will disclose.' The account was gruesome enough, but 'the magistrates are making every exertion to find out the murderers'. Certainly this was true of Harriott.

But the Shadwell bench, having carried out their preliminary examinations the day before, seem to have lapsed into a sort of baffled resignation. Throughout Monday they waited for suspects to be brought in, but none came. Markland sat down to write his own account of the case for the Home Secretary, declaring bleakly, 'We have no clue which promises to lead to a discovery.' The broken and bloody maul, the footprints, the ripping chisel, it seems, were scarcely relevant. When they spoke of 'clues', the magistrates meant first-hand information that would lead directly to a conviction; and information had to be bought. 'The parish of St. George have issued hand Bills offering a Reward of £50 on Conviction of the Offenders,' Markland concluded, adding delicately: 'Permit me to suggest the propriety of His Majesty's Government taking notice of it in the *Gazette* in such manner as to them may seem most proper.'

Little can be discovered about this Shadwell bench of magistrates except that, in contrast to that of the impetuous Harriott, their behaviour throughout was that of well-meaning dilettantes. Story, the senior, had been one of the original stipendiaries appointed in 1792. He would have been an old man now, and took no part in the correspondence with the Home Secretary or, so far as can be discovered, any interest in the case. His colleagues were much junior, and both were new to stipendiary office. Markland, formerly an unpaid magistrate in Leeds, had only been on the Shadwell bench since February 1811; and Capper, a Hertfordshire magistrate, since March. They would both know a great deal about rural crime – poaching, sheep stealing, vagrancy – and Markland might well have punished some of the men the Industrial Revolution had soured, and who were now enrolling in the armies of King Ludd. But neither would know anything of the life of East London slums or understand the ways of sailors. Nor is it likely that either man had the slightest experience of a major criminal investigation. They merely waited for the information that never came, and it is scarcely surprising that on Tuesday *The Times* was obliged to report, 'Every effort of the police, and of every respectable inhabitant of the parish of St. George's-in-the-East has hitherto proved unavailing.'

Harriott's initiative, meanwhile, in offering twenty pounds for information about the three men who had been seen outside Marr's shop on the night of the murder, had produced nothing – except a reprimand for his zeal. The Home Office could tolerate inefficiency, but not a breach of regulations. The Home Secretary tartly reminded the old man that he had no discretion to offer such a reward. His job was to get on with policing the river, and Ryder demanded an explanation. Harriott's reply was a nice compromise between dutiful submission and pained reproach. 'Feeling vexed with myself that I should suffer my zeal for discovering the atrocious Murderers to run me into an error,' he began, and not knowing that the discretionary powers of police magistrates 'on such an extraordinary occasion' were limited, he had thought it best to issue the hand-bill without delay. But for the future, 'I will take special care to keep my zeal within proper bounds'. Unfortunately for the progress of the investigation Harriott seems subsequently to have done so.

Meanwhile the bodies of Marr and his wife with the child beside her were laid out on their bed. James Gowen's body was placed in another room, probably the one normally occupied by Margaret Jewell. There they were left until it was time to coffin them for the funeral. They were no doubt guarded – at least in the sense that there was a Shadwell police officer in the house – but there was no restriction on sightseers and little control of the stream of neighbours, acquaintances and the curious and morbid from all over London, who passed endlessly up the narrow staircase into what was virtually a morgue. Fine ladies drew their skirts to one side as they brushed against the artisans of Ratcliffe Highway and the seamen and their women who had surged up Old Gravel Lane from the lodging houses near the river. The narrow landing was a crush of bodies as the visitors pushed their way from the mean room which held James Gowen's pitiably mangled corpse, to view the even more poignant scene in the Marrs' bedroom. There was a constant buzz of conversation broken by exclamations of horror, while the stench of the mob, the strong and ever-present smell of nineteenth-century Wapping, overlaid the first sickly-sweet intimation of decay. There lay the bodies, drained of all blood, their unsutured wounds gaping like those of butchered animals, yet wearing on their waxen faces the secret and committed look of human dead.

Such visits to the houses of the bereaved to view the bodies of the dead were nothing new or strange to early nineteenth-century Wapping, particularly among the Irish immigrants who flocked into East London to escape the greater poverty and misery of their homeland, and who supplied a considerable part of the casual and unskilled labour of the metropolis – as well as of its army of professional beggars. Few of their domestic habits were acceptable to their more respectable and prosperous neighbours, and the custom of the Irish Wake was particularly disturbing. The corpse, no matter what was the cause of death, was laid out on the only bed, and burial was delayed until sufficient money had been collected from visiting neighbours to provide drink and food for the Wake. Wakes always led to drunkenness and often to violence, illness and death; although the worst case did not arise until 1817, when a Mrs. Sullivan, whose prostitute daughter had died in the workhouse, persuaded the parish authorities to release the girl's body for what she described as 'decent burial'. This they unfortunately did. Mrs. Sullivan raised three separate subscriptions for the Wake, all of which were spent in drink and feasting, and delayed the decent burial so long that twenty-six people who had viewed the decaying corpse were stricken with fever. Six of them died, and the parish was obliged to bury the girl in the end. We are not told whether Marr's brother took the opportunity of raising some cash for the funeral expenses, although it may be significant that burial was deferred for a week. It is not unlikely that one or two visitors, particularly if they were Irish, moved by pity as well the high level of horror and interest of the spectacle provided, dropped a coin or two in a cup on their way out. They would not have been unacceptable. The bill for the recent alteration to the shop had still to be met, and it transpired that Marr had left only sufficient capital to pay his creditors nineteen shillings in the pound.

Among the sightseers who came up from the slums close to the river to view the bodies was a German sailor called John Richter, who lodged with a Mr. and Mrs. Vermilloe at the Pear Tree public house. He pushed his way up the narrow staircase, saw what he had come to see and went unobserved away, telling no one at the Pear Tree where he had been.

The inquest on the four victims was arranged for Tuesday, 10 December, at the Jolly Sailor public house in Ratcliffe Highway, nearly opposite to Marr's shop. While his wife bustled from taproom to kitchen preparing for an unusual influx of customers, the landlord suitably arranged his largest room. An imposing table was set ready for the Coroner, bearing candles to lighten the gloom of a December afternoon; two longer tables were placed together for the jury; a chair was set in place for witnesses. The fire was banked high. Outside could be heard the muttering and movements of a vast crowd.

Early in the afternoon the jury began to assemble, and soon after two o'clock the Coroner, John Unwin, made his appearance. He and the jury first crossed the road and inspected Marr's premises and the four corpses. Then they returned, visibly shaken and stern faced, to the Jolly Sailor, and the inquest was opened.

The first witness called was Walter Salter, the surgeon who at the request of the Coroner had examined the bodies. There was something of self-importance in his manner as, with no concessions to the education or vocabularies of the locals of Shadwell and Wapping, he translated into Latinate obscurity the brutal realities of battered skulls and slit throats which many of his hearers had seen for themselves. *The Times* reported:

Timothy Marr the younger had the left external artery of the neck entirely divided; from the left side of the mouth, across the artery the wound was at least three inches long, and there were several marks of violence on the left side of the face. Celia Marr, the wife, had the left side of the cranium fractured, the temple-bone totally destroyed and a wound about the articulation of the jaw extending two inches to her left ear, and another at the back of the same ear. Timothy Marr the elder had his nose broken, the occipital bone was fractured and the mark of a violent blow was over the right eye. James Gowen, the apprentice boy, had several contusions of the forehead and nose. The occipital bones were shattered dreadfully and the brains were partly protruding and partly scattered about. Mr. Salter swore that these violences were all in themselves a sufficient cause of death.

Margaret Jewell was examined next. She described how her master had sent her out with a pound note to buy oysters, her fruitless search along Ratcliffe Highway and in the surrounding streets, her return after about twenty minutes to find the house locked against her, the arrival of the watchman and the subsequent appearance of Murray. She described how Murray had got into the house at the back and opened the street door. At this point in her evidence the girl was so much overcome by shock that she fainted away, and every effort to restore her was used for a considerable time without effect. She was not examined further.

John Murray next took the stand. He testified that he was a pawnbroker and resided in the next house to that in which the murders were committed. About ten minutes past twelve on Sunday morning he was sitting at supper when he heard a noise in the shop floor of the next house which resembled the falling of a shutter or the pushing of a chair; he also heard the sounds of a human voice as if arising from fear or correction. The voice he thought to be that of a boy or a woman. All this happened in one minute. A little before one o'clock he heard the continued ringing of Mr. Marr's bell; this ringing continued until nearly half past one and at last he went to the door to know what was the matter. The watchman said that the pin was not fastened and that the girl was shut out. Murray then described how he had succeeded in making his entry from the back, his brief visit upstairs and his subsequent discoveries of the bodies. He testified that after the child had been found dead he had seen a mallet or maul in the hands of a police officer which was covered in blood and hair. Mr. Marr had been living in Ratcliffe Highway only since last April. He was twenty-four years of age, his wife about the same. The child was only fourteen weeks old.

George Olney next took the stand. He said that he was a watchman belonging to the parish of St. George. His evidence entirely corroborated the testimony of the girl. When he got into the house the bodies were dead but not cold. He described how he had seen Mr. Marr about twelve o'clock putting up his shutters. He had been present in the backroom when the police officer found the maul. The head of it was on the ground and the handle standing against a chair. The blood was running from it on the ground. He also saw the chisel which was found but there was no blood upon it.

These were the only witnesses examined before the Coroner.

The examinations being closed, the Coroner stated to the jury that having now before them the melancholy statement of the facts unassisted by a particle of testimony calculated to point out the perpetrators of the atrocious and wicked act of murder to which their attention had been so painfully directed, their verdict unfortunately must be given generally on the imperfect evidence before them. He trusted, therefore, that they would not suffer their verdict to be influenced by the passing reports originating from the laudable anxiety of everyone to trace out and detect the wretches, whose future existence must evidently be marked with remorse and conscious guilt, and who perhaps in a little time, by the hand of providence, the prayers of humanity, and the exertions of the police, would be brought to detection and merited punishment.

The jury, after a short deliberation, gave a verdict on each of the bodies of wilful murder against some person or persons unknown.

THE MAUL

'The sensation excited by these most ferocious murders,' reported *The Times* on Wednesday, 11 December, 'has become so general, and the curiosity to see the place where they were committed so intense, that Ratcliffe Highway was rendered almost impassable by the throng of spectators before ten o'clock yesterday morning.' The account of the inquest occupied a whole column, and the report concluded:

We were ourselves indefatigable in our enquiries; but we could hear nothing save the vague rumours of the crowd which sprung from no authentic source. At one time it was said that Mr. Marr had been an evidence at the Old Bailey against a Portuguese who was lately hanged for murder, and that it was some of this man's friends who from revenge were determined to shed his blood. It is, however, to be hoped that the race of the ruffians will be short, and that justice and humanity will soon be avenged.

There followed an intriguing postscript. It was reported that on the Monday evening a man named Ashburton, who lived in Gravel Lane, Ratcliffe Highway, was discussing the Marrs' murders with some friends in a public house, when he was overcome 'with such powerful sensations of horror and guilt' that he was compelled to confess that he had himself witnessed a murder some eighteen years previously. He had been to Gravesend to see an East Indiaman set sail, and on coming home up the river he was present at a quarrel between a sergeant of marines and a gentleman who was now living in a most respectable way in Prince's Square. The dispute was about a boy plying the ferry at Gravesend whom the sergeant had attempted to enlist. Ashburton saw the sergeant of marines fall back while the other man leaped on his body three times and stabbed him to death. He saw the sergeant's sword thrown overboard but did not know what had become of the body. He said he had often mentioned the circumstances before but only when he was thrown off his guard by liquor, and then what he said had always been imputed to drunkenness. Now, however, he spoke soberly and *The Times* reported that the person accused was taken into custody and was to be brought up on Saturday before the magistrates of the Shadwell Public Office for further examination, thus adding to the congestion in the prison and to the exertions of Messrs. Capper, Markland and Story. The unfortunate gentleman, a Portuguese named Fansick, was examined at the Shadwell Office on 14 December and granted bail, the magistrates, perhaps feeling that they had more immediate problems than an alleged eighteen-year-old murder.

It is not surprising that Mr. Ashburton of Gravel Lane was so affected by the Marrs' murders that he was compelled under their strong and remarkable influence to break the silence of eighteen years. The murders from the first exercised a unique power over the hearts and minds of Londoners. The emotion was compounded partly of horror at the cruelty and ruthlessness of the deed, and partly of pity at the helplessness and youth of the victims, all under twenty-five years of age, and one a baby in arms. It was to be expected that the wealthy and powerful should attract envy and be at the risk of robbery or worse. They knew the danger and had the means to combat it. It was equally understandable that prostitutes, informers and thieves should be exposed to violence and vengeance. But Timothy Marr had been poor, hard-working and respectable, living at peace with his neighbours, a good husband and father. Nothing had saved him; neither virtue nor poverty. He and his whole family had been annihilated in a brutal holocaust as if they were of no account, either to heaven or man.

The times were certainly hard, ungentle and sometimes barbarous. Justice was cruelly administered. Yet there was justice, there was public order, however arbitrarily enforced. The people of East London were poor, uneducated and often violent, yet atrocious murder was comparatively uncommon, and England had an enviable reputation in Europe for the lowness of its murder rate. In 1810, for example, the first year for which returns were made to the Home Office, broken down by offences, there were sixty-seven executions, but only nine of these were for murder. Eighteen were for burglary and eighteen for forgery. The figures reflect the low rate of murder detection, but the ratio is significant. Offences against property were far more common and were as ruthlessly punished as offences against the person. Murder, however, was still the unique, the horrifying crime. The wiping out of the whole Marr family seemed to strike at the very foundations, not only of public order but of morality and religion themselves. If this could happen, who could be safe? If decency and humbleness could not protect a man, what could? The fact that the murders were apparently irrational and motiveless added to the terror. The poor and respectable were particularly vulnerable. They worked long hours. Shopkeepers and publicans could not bar their doors against prospective customers if they were to make a living at all. But how could they carry on their business if every face at the door after dusk might be that of a murdering devil, if their wives and families refused to leave their sides once dark had fallen, if customers were afraid to venture out alone?

The three ineffectual magistrates of Shadwell and the indefatigable Harriott were well aware of the unrest, now almost mounting to panic. But so far their exertions, such as they were, had borne little fruit. However, on Wednesday, 11 December, some progress was made. A carpenter who had been engaged in work at Marr's premises was taken into custody at the Shadwell Office and questioned about the ripping chisel. *The Times* reported:

Mr. Marr's premises had been undergoing repairs for some time. A Mr. Pugh was engaged to superintend the carpenter's work; he employed a man who altered the shop windows. This man applied for an iron chisel already described as twenty inches in length. Mr. Pugh had no such tool but borrowed one from a neighbour. After the man had completed his work he was discharged, but did not return the chisel. Mr. Pugh asked the man what he had done with it, as he had borrowed the tool from a neighbour. The man replied that it was on the premises and he could not find it; this happened three weeks ago. Mr Pugh called on Mr. Marr and begged he would search for the instrument in order that it might be returned. A few days after, Mr. Marr informed Mr. Pugh that he had examined his house and could not find such an article; and no tidings were had of the chisel until the morning of the fatal massacre when it was found lying by the side of Mr. Marr's body. Mr. Pugh gave information of the circumstances and the carpenter was brought up for examination. Mr. Pugh and the person who lost the chisel swore to the identical marks being similar to the one delivered to the prisoner, who was committed for further examination in order that the servant girl (whose life was so providentially preserved) might be brought forward to recognise this person as having been employed on the premises.

So by Wednesday one of the weapons found in Marr's house had been positively identified, and a carpenter who was known to have handled it was in custody. The next person charged was a man, secured by the police in a public house, who was heard to boast on Tuesday night that he knew the parties who had committed the murders. He was questioned and confined on suspicion. However, his story before the magistrates was so incoherent that it was apparent that he had spoken in his cups, and he was discharged with a severe reprimand for uttering such improper and unfounded language. At the same time another subject taken into charge on equally slender and unsubstantiated evidence was examined and subsequently discharged.

It was on the following day, Thursday, five days after the murder, that the Home Secretary yielded to pressure in *The Times* and elsewhere, and advertised the offer of a reward by the Government. Such a step was virtually unprecedented – at all events for half a century. It was common enough for the Government to offer rewards for information that led to the conviction of an offender against the public good, but requests relating to crimes against individuals, even murder, were invariably refused. The following hand-bill posted up in Ratcliffe Highway and other parts of the town, must therefore be regarded as a sign of the Government's exceptional concern:

> Whitehall, December 12th, 1811. Whereas it has been humbly represented to His Royal Highness the Prince Regent, that the dwelling house of Mr. Timothy Marr, No. 29, Ratcliffe Highway, in the parish of St. George, Middlesex, man's mercer, was entered on Sunday morning last between the hours of twelve and two by some person or persons unknown, and that the said Mr. Marr, Mrs. Celia Marr, his wife, Timothy, their infant child, in the cradle, James Gowen, a servant lad, were all of them most inhumanly and barbarously murdered; His Royal Highness, for the better apprehending and bringing to justice the persons concerned in the atrocious murders is hereby pleased to offer a reward of £100 to any one of them (except the person or persons who actually perpetrated the said murders) who shall discover his or their accomplice or accomplices therein, to be paid on the conviction of any one or more of the offenders by the Right Honourable The Lords Commissioners of His Majesty's Treasury.
>
> R. Ryder

The reward was substantial, but not excessively generous. As always it had regard to the probabilities. The carpenter was still in custody. He might yet prove to be concerned in the murders and in this case the reward of £100 to his accomplices might well prove sufficient to induce one of them to turn King's evidence.

But the case against the carpenter also collapsed. *The Times* of 13 December reported:

> Yesterday (Wednesday) morning the carpenter, Mr. Pugh's man, who had been employed about three weeks ago in furnishing Mr. Marr's shop, underwent another examination. Mr. Marr's servant and a bricklayer attended to identify the man. Many respectable housekeepers, his landlord and others appeared in favour of his character, and to the satisfaction of the magistrates, proved an alibi. The chisel was proved to be that which Mr. Pugh's man had

borrowed, but a young man swore he found it in the cellar at the time he accompanied the watchman in Mr. Marr's house immediately after the murders were committed. The magistrates discharged the man, there not being sufficient evidence for another hearing.

There are several odd points about this report. The chisel was not found in the basement of Marr's house. All the magistrates when reporting to the Home Secretary stated that it had been found on the shop counter. Even had it been found in the basement its presence there would hardly exonerate the carpenter. The chisel was positively identified by Pugh and the man from whom he borrowed it. It was undeniably found in the Marrs' house following the murders. The actual place is in this context immaterial. So either Marr had succeeded in finding the chisel in his shop some time after Margaret Jewell had gone for the oysters, despite his earlier thorough but fruitless search, or it had been brought into the house by one of the murderers, either as a potential weapon or as a means of breaking into or out of the house. It was clearly of the greatest importance to discover what had happened to this chisel from the time it was first missing and who could have gained possession of it. The first and obvious step was surely to question Margaret Jewell on this point. She must have known the chisel was missing and that Marr had been asked by Pugh to return it. She probably helped to look for it. The premises were small and the chisel, unless deliberately and cunningly hidden, must surely have come to light. Margaret Jewell could have testified to the thoroughness of the search and her master's conviction that the chisel could not have been left on his premises. We can probably safely assume that the chisel was not on the counter when the girl left to buy oysters. Marr would have called out to his wife that he had found it even if Margaret did not notice it lying on the counter before she left the shop. The magistrates would probably have paid more attention to the chisel had it been matted with hair and blood. Yet, if it were not in the shop before Margaret Jewell left, nor discovered by Marr during her absence, then it was almost certainly brought into the house by one of the murderers, and it was as important, if less spectacular, a clue to their identity as was the blood-stained maul.

But the magistrates were apparently unimpressed by the chisel's significance. They were a great deal more impressed by the excellent testimonies to the carpenter's character. In the absence of any scientific method of detection, evidence of character was held in particularly high regard, and the carpenter was able to produce gratifying accounts of his industry and good conduct. He was also able to provide an alibi, and without any apparent effort of the magistrates to verify it, he was discharged.

What is also odd, and particularly frustrating, is the careful avoidance by *The Times* of the carpenter's name. It was later to transpire that there were two men who worked for Pugh – Cornelius Hart and a joiner, variously referred to in the evidence as Towler or Trotter. A third man, Jeremiah Fitzpatrick, also a joiner, was an associate of Hart, and may have been another of Pugh's men. It is likely that Hart was the one questioned about the chisel, since it was he who had been mainly concerned with the recent adaptations to Marr's shop. But we are not specifically told this. The identification of the ripping chisel was a discovery of the first importance, but it was treated as just one more minor incident in the unrewarding routine of the magistrates' inquiries.

On the same day, Wednesday, a girl named Wilkie, who had been servant to Mrs. Marr for six months, and had left her only six months ago, presented herself to the magistrates to clear her name. Immediately after the murders, when the magistrates were interrogating Margaret Jewell, she had described how Mrs. Marr had discharged Wilkie because of a suspicion of dishonesty. There was a quarrel and the accused girl threatened her mistress with murder. Margaret Jewell reported that Mrs. Marr gently rebuked her for using such intemperate language and requested that she would not alarm her in her advanced state of pregnancy. The threats and emnity could hardly have been serious since Wilkie subsequently visited the Marrs, dressed 'in a white gown, black velvet spencer, cottage bonnet with a small feather and shoes with Grecian ties'. It is possible of course, that these visits were more to show off her new finery and demonstrate her

independence than to inquire after the health of the family,
but they seem to have been amicable. Margaret Jewell said
that Mrs. Marr often remonstrated with Wilkie on her loose
character and hasty temper, but assured the girl of her friendship and her readiness to serve her if she would reform her
prostituted life and return into honest service. Not surprisingly,
Wilkie had declined to exchange 'a white gown and shoes
with Grecian ties', and her freedom, for the drudgery of a
general servant and the confines of a small basement kitchen
at 29 Ratcliffe Highway. Now, however, she turned up to
protest her innocence and to give the magistrates what help
she could. She was quickly exonerated. No one thought it
likely that a common servant girl, however disenchanted
with her late employers, would have had the means, capacity
or physical attractions to procure from her male protectors
such wholesale and barbaric vengeance, and it was obviously
ridiculous to suppose that she had wielded the maul and the
knife herself. The magistrates examined her and she was
discharged, but not before she had testified to the affection
and amity existing between Marr and his wife's relations,
and to the happiness of the Marr ménage. It may all have been
true, but one suspects that the young Marrs were already
sanctified by the pity and horror of their deaths into paragons
of virtue, archetypes of the innocent and good to set against
the villainy of their destroyers. We know so little about them
beyond the superficialities that they were respectable, hard-
working and ambitious. It is only John Murray's evidence,
that he assumed the cry which he heard at midnight to have
arisen from the fear of correction, which makes one wonder
whether such cries were perhaps not uncommonly heard
from 29 Ratcliffe Highway, whether Marr, raised by his
own exertions from servitude to the power of being another's
master, may not have been a hard as well as an ambitious
man.

The rumours, allegations and snippets of information continued to pour in. One hopeful lead led to great excitement,
and *The Times* reported that the police officers 'were despatched in every direction'. It appeared that about half-past-
one on the Sunday morning of the murders a man in the
employ of Messrs. Sims of Sun Tavern Fields, having received

his pay of eight shillings, returned to his lodgings wearing a smock frock which was seen by the woman of the house to be very dirty. She inquired where he had been, and he replied that an oil cask had burst over him and that he had endeavoured to wash off the oil. The woman pointed out that cold water would not take away the oil and said that she could not smell it. Shortly afterwards the man went to bed with his fellow lodger, but very early the next morning he had made an escape from his lodgings, and had not been heard of since. He was thought to have taken the Portsmouth Road. He was described as being about middle stature, thirty years of age, with only one eye and wearing a smock frock which was much washed in the front, and dark trousers. This exciting news provoked a great deal of activity which was surprisingly effective. On the following Sunday an express message arrived in town from Lord Middleton, a magistrate at Godalming, to the magistrates at Shadwell Public Office, informing them that the man they sought, whose name was discovered to be Thomas Knight, had been taken and safely lodged in Guildford Gaol. Two police officers were immediately dispatched from Shadwell to bring him back to London.

Meanwhile news of the missing one-eyed lodger in the stained frock coat quickly spread, and before Thomas Knight had been identified and taken into custody a number of unfortunates were arrested on suspicion. Information was received at Bow Street from a cook shop in St. Giles, stating that a one-eyed man answering Knight's description, and wearing a smock frock and dark trousers, was there. He was arrested and brought to Bow Street, where he said he was a journey-man carpenter residing in Shy Lane. However, he was unable to give a satisfactory account of himself at the time of the murders, so the magistrates committed him for further examination. When he was again brought before the magistrates his landlord proved that he did indeed lodge with him in Shy Lane, and that he had been at home and in bed at the time of the murders. So he was discharged, although *The Times* tartly notes that it was his stupid manner of giving an account of himself that resulted in this inconvenience to himself and his betters.

On Saturday morning yet another report arrived at Bow Street of a man wearing a smock frock with blood, who had been seen with some soldiers in Windmill Street. It is apparent that, at this stage, the police in their confusion were busily hunting for anyone in a blood-stained smock who bore the least resemblance to Thomas Knight. An officer was sent to bring the new suspect to the Office. He found the man with some marines, who said that he had enlisted with them and had taken seven shillings in part of the bounty. This they considered to be a fraud, since he must know he was not fit to serve as he had a bad leg. However, he was taken to the Office, where he accounted for the blood on his smock frock by saying that he had been carrying a sheep's head. So he too was discharged; but at the same time a further significant find was reported. A man named Harris, with a friend, evidently Quakers, had been on their way to a Penn Street meeting on Sunday morning, when – they now remembered to tell the Shadwell magistrates – they had seen a guernsey frock shirt and a handkerchief, all very bloody, lying in the middle of Ratcliffe Highway near the watch house of St. George; so the magistrates had yet another hand-bill posted up:

MURDER!

WHEREAS, certain information has been received at this office that on Sunday morning last, about quarter-past eight-o-clock a Guernsey frock (or shirt) very bloody, and also near it a handkerchief in the same state, were observed lying in the middle of Ratcliffe Highway near Watch House in the parish of St. George, Middlesex.

Any person or persons, having picked up, or may be in possession of such shirt or handkerchief are earnestly requested to bring the same without delay to this office, it being conceived that this may afford a clue to the discovery of the late horrid murders in Ratcliffe Highway. Also any person or persons who may be able to give any information respecting the said shirt and handkerchief are desired immediately to communicate the same to the magistrates of this office by whom they will be handsomely rewarded for their trouble. By order of the magistrates.

J. J. Mallett
Chief Clerk.

The rewards offered were indeed handsome. By this date they totalled over £600, a considerable fortune in the days when the weekly wage of an artisan could be as little as one pound. On 14 December the Government had increased their reward from £100 to £500 – an unprecedented sum; in addition there was fifty pounds by the Overseers of St. George's-in-the-East, twenty pounds by the Thames Police and a personal reward of fifty guineas offered by The Honourable Thomas Bowes, and advertised on 14 December.

On the next day, Sunday, almost exactly a week after their deaths, the Marr family were buried. A single grave was prepared in the churchyard of St. George's-in-the-East. The week had been bitterly cold and the spades of the grave diggers struck earth as ringing hard as iron. But the day of the burial was milder and the breath of the waiting crowd, who had lined Ratcliffe Highway from early morning, rose like a thin mist, through which one could hear the stamping of frozen feet on the cobbles, the murmur of hushed voices, the whine of an impatient child. Promptly at half past one the bodies were borne up the steps, under Hawksmoor's splendidly individual tower with its coronet of columns, and into the church of St. George's-in-the-East, where the Marrs had worshipped and where only two months earlier they had stood proudly at the font for the christening of their child. The weeping figures of Mrs. Marr's mother and sisters, heavily veiled in black, were greeted with groans of pity as the crowd recalled how they had come up from the country on the Sunday of the murders to spend the day with the young family, and had known nothing of the tragedy until their arrival.

John Fairburn's contemporary pamphlet describes the scene:

This day the neighbourhood of Ratcliffe Highway presented a scene of mournful sorrow and lamentation, and perhaps there was never an occasion in which general

A, the body of M.ʳ Marr. | THE FUNERAL of THE MURDERD Mᴿ. AND Mˢ. MARR AND INFANT SON | B. The Bodies of Mˢ. Marr and Son

The Interment of this Murdered Family was at Sᵗ Georges in the East on Sunday Dec: 15. 1811. the deceased were attended to the grave by Mᵉ Marrᵉ father Mother and brother and Mᵉ Marrᵉ four Sisters and other relatives - this Shocking Murder was committed Dec: 7ᵗ 1811

Published Apr: 7ᵗ 1811 by G Thompson Nᵒ 43 Long Lane West Smithfield.

melancholy was impressed with stronger feelings of dejection than on the awful scene of this family being conveyed to the dreary mansion of mortality. It is almost impossible to give an adequate idea of the solemnity observed by all ranks on this occasion. The people formed a complete phalanx from the house to the door of St. George's church, waiting with patience for some hours.

The crowded congregation in the church that attended Divine Service remained in their stations to witness the afflicting spectacle. At half-past-one the procession entered with some difficulty. The Reverend Dr. Farrington officiated and performed the funeral rites almost overwhelmed with his impressive duty. The procession entered the aisle of the church in the following order:

> The body of Mr. Marr;
> The bodies of Mrs. Marr and infant;
> The father and mother of Mr. Marr;
> the mother of Mrs. Marr;
> the four sisters of Mrs. Marr;
> the only brother of Mr. Marr;
> the next in relationship to the deceased;
> the friends of Mr. and Mrs. Marr;

in the whole, eighteen mourners, among who, was the servant girl.

The affliction of the aged parents, and the brothers and sisters of the deceased was the most heart-rending spectacle; and the tears of the crowded congregation universally mingled in compassion. After the church ceremony the corpses were conveyed into the burial ground and deposited in one grave. Notwithstanding the immense crowd the spectators conducted themselves with the utmost decorum, although they could not restrain from the impulse of strong language in the universal prayer for the vengeance of heaven upon the heads of the unknown murderers.

There is a small and pathetic postscript. After the verdict of the Coroner's inquest the relatives of the servant lad removed his body from Marr's house and had it buried at another place. The Marrs were buried in the south side of the graveyard and a tall tombstone was erected over them:

Sacred to the memory of Mr. Timothy Marr, aged twenty-four years, also Mrs. Celia Marr his wife, aged twenty-four years, and their son Timothy Marr, aged three months, all of whom were most inhumanely murdered in their dwelling house, No. 29 Ratcliffe Highway, Dec. 8, 1811.

Stop mortal, stop as you pass by,
And view the grave wherein doth lie
A Father, Mother and a Son,
Whose earthly course was shortly run.
For lo, all in one fatal hour,
O'er came were they with ruthless power;
And murdered in a cruel state –
Yea, far too horrid to relate!
They spared not one to tell the tale:
One for the other could not wail
The other's fate in anguish sighed:
Loving they lived, together died.
Reflect, O Reader, o'er their fate,
And turn from sin before too late;
Life is uncertain in this world.
Oft in a moment we are hurled
To endless bliss or endless pain;
So let not sin within you reign.

So, a week after the Marrs' murders, nothing had been accomplished but their burial. Wapping was unchanged. The murderers were still at large. The great vessels still sailed out of the marvellous new London Dock, majestically with the tides, their horizons infinite, their crews indifferent to local gossip, their affairs encompassing the world. And London's poetical magistrates, too, had had an opportunity that week of voyaging beyond their own familiar shores. Bemused as they might be by examining Portuguese and Irish, beset by idiots and drunkards, busy perhaps (as it is tempting to suppose that Pye had been) with the composition of the Marr's epitaph, all might have found time during the week to attend a series of lectures delivered in Fleet Street by a true poet. Coleridge, tormented during the week that followed the murders by the overmastering power of opium, had been delivering a series of lectures on Shakespeare's plays; and all week the *London Chronicle* had offered its news in adjacent, incongruous columns. While one headline shrieked, 'Murder of Mrs. Marr and Family', the next announced, 'Mr Coleridge's Lectures'. Readers aghast at lurid stories of battered brains and spilt blood could turn to gentler, more lasting themes. The 'orations on Shakespeare', the journal declared, 'are advancing rapidly in public favour, and the poetic Lecturer is taking effectual means to render them delightful to those whom we presume him particularly anxious to please – the Fair.'

On Monday afternoon there was a renewal of excitement when Thomas Knight was brought up from Godalming in a post-chaise to the Public Office at Shadwell. The circumstances of suspicion alleged against him were reiterated. 'On Saturday fortnight he had retired to his lodgings apparently very much dejected. He had taken off his smock frock and began to wash and dry it before the fire; it had upon it stains a good deal resembling blood, and on the following morning he had left his lodging early without telling his landlady where he was going.'

The prisoner denied all but the last allegation, and told a consistent story from which he never subsequently deviated. He said that he was a Portsmouth man born and bred who had come to London about six weeks ago, and remained in the service of Messrs. Sims & Co. rope-makers, as a hackler, until Saturday fortnight. His wife had been ill for some time and he determined to go down to Portsmouth where she was living with her father and bring her up to town. On the evening of Saturday fortnight he went to the King's Arms public house kept by Mr. Edwards to get paid his weekly wages which amounted to twelve shillings. He remained at Mr. Edwards's until about eleven o' clock, drinking with some of his fellow workmen. He then went home to his lodgings and soon to bed. He denied that he had washed his smock frock, or even that he took it off until he went to bed. He had not been dejected; on the contrary he had been rather merry in consequence of the liquor he had drunk and had laughed with his landlady, who bantered him for keeping such late hours at night during the absence of his wife. Next morning he rose about half past seven and went to Mr. Dodds, the overseer of Mr. Sim's work, and told him he was going down to Portsmouth to bring up his wife, and requested that he would take care of his tools until his return. He then went to the King's Arms public house in hopes of getting one and sixpence halfpenny which Mr. Edwards owed him, and he remained there a short time with some of his work-mates. After that he walked about Shadwell for about an hour, when he met two men named Quinn, father and son, and went with them to a wine vault for some gin. He remained with them until ten o'clock on Sunday morning when he started for Portsmouth. He rode for only twelve miles of the journey, and arrived in Portsmouth on Monday evening, where he remained with his wife and child at Gosport until Thursday morning when they set off, all together, for London. On Thursday night they arrived at Peats Field, where they slept together. The next day, when he was walking through Godalming, he was apprehended by two officers 'on a charge of which he protested to God he was as innocent as an unborn child'. The reason why he did not tell his landlady of his intention to go to Portsmouth was because he owed her three shillings, and having only twelve shillings in the world, he was afraid that she would insist on being paid if he told her he was going to leave the lodgings.

The Shadwell magistrates cross-examined Knight rigorously, but he adhered to the first statement and they quickly concluded that he had no connection with the Marrs' murder. However, they decided to remand him for further examination, apparently in the belief that having brought him at public expense all the way from Godalming, it would be extravagantly generous to let him go after so little inconvenience.

The magistrates at the different Public Offices were keeping the Home Secretary informed of any developments as and when it seemed necessary to them, although there was no organised system of exchanging information, and no evidence that John Beckett or anyone else at the Home Office collated the reports or attempted either to direct the investigation or to co-ordinate the various activities. On the Monday, while the Shadwell bench were examining Thomas Knight, the magistrates at the Queen's Square Public Office (now Queen Anne's Gate) offered Beckett yet a further promising lead: 'Under

cover I send you for the information of Mr. Ryder an information upon Oath of a private in the Guards, subjecting two
persons unknown to a considerable degree of suspicion. I have
sent copies of the information by this post to the Chief
Magistrates at Southampton, Newport, Isle of Wight, and
Plymouth, requesting their attention to the description of the
two men and to have them apprehended and arrested.'

The enclosure was as follows:

The deposition of George Judd, a corporal in Lieutenant
Colonel Cook's company of the Second Battallion of Cold-
stream Guards. On Saturday evening the 14th instant, about
half-past six o' clock I was passing by the Old White Horse
cellar, Piccadilly, and was accosted by two men in great-
coats. Each had a bundle and a stick. One of them was
about 5' 10" in height who was a few yards distant in the
dark. The other man was middle aged, about 5' 5" with a
scar on the right cheek who came up to me and asked
if I knew of any coach that was going to Plymouth. I
answered him no. He desired me to go into the coach office
and make the enquiry and he would give me something to
drink. I did so and communicated to him the answer that
there would be no coach to Plymouth until the next morning at four o' clock. He then went to his companion who
still stood at a distance as if he was afraid to come to the
light, and spoke to him, and returned to me and gave me the
price of a pint of beer, and said that will not do, we must
take the Mail. On his turning his back to me I saw a paper
drop from him which I picked up and put in my pocket.
They then went away together towards Hyde Park Corner.
Taken by James Bligh, Officer of Police, Queen's Square,
Westminster, December 15th, 1811.

A copy of the mysterious paper is attached to the deposition.
The note is unpunctuated, and was obviously written by
someone almost illiterate. The first word is undecipherable.
. . . To the Isles of Wight

After I have settle my affairs her, My Dear Frands,
proceed home by Monday morning as I hear the rumour is

great of our transaction to leave England imedty is the best way. The dead is greatly done Dont fail come if you will meet me at Air Old Van de Vose your sworn friend, M M Mahoney.[1]

These two men were never identified and we hear no more of them. It seems probable that they had been involved in some criminal enterprise, but if they had murdered the Marrs, it is unlikely that they would have lingered in London for a week before making their escape to the Isle of Wight. Subsequent events proved that if they did, indeed, leave London on 15 December, they were most unlikely to have been concerned in the Ratcliffe Highway murders. At the time, however, this deposition by a corporal of the Guards, his unexpected meeting, and the mysterious paper so fortuitously dropped at his feet, suggested that providence might at last be taking a hand in bringing the murderers to justice, and it was with considerable hope that the magistrates awaited from their colleagues at Southampton, Newport and Plymouth the news that never came.

The magistrates at Whitechapel were having no better luck. Two Portuguese sailors named Le Silvoe and Bernard Govoe were brought into the Public Office, and with considerable difficulty on both sides were examined for two hours. They had been seen drinking at the Artichoke public house[2] near Marr's home at half-past-eleven on the night of his death, and had been seen in the street adjoining as late as one o'clock. Le Silvoe alleged that he came home for admittance at one, knocked at the door, and was let in by his wife just as the watchman was crying half past one. His landlord supported his story. Mrs. Le Silvoe offered to prove that her husband was at home at eleven o'clock, but her testimony was not admitted. A woman who lived with Govoe wanted to prove his alibi but her evidence was regarded as

---

[1] The *Morning Post* obligingly translated this for the benefit of its readers: My dear friends, the rumour is great, and the deed we have done is great. I think it expedient we should leave England as soon as possible, of course you will meet me at the old rendezvous. I remain your sworn friend, Patrick Mahony.

[2] A public house bearing the name still stands in Artichoke Hill.

very doubtful. The magistrates, in some frustration and perplexity, committed both the Portuguese for another hearing.

Meanwhile John Harriott had not been idle. His officers searched the ships in the river and at Gravesend to see if any suspicious characters had lately come aboard, and made enquiries 'at all the old iron shops along the shore as well as at shipwrights' yards and other places' in an attempt to trace the maul. All was without success.

And still the hunt went on. On Wednesday, 18 December, a man named Thomas Taylor was charged at the Shadwell Office with having uttered expressions at a public house at Deptford tending to excite suspicion that he knew something important. The prisoner, while drunk, had sworn that he could prove that Marr's brother had employed six or seven men to commit the barbaric murders, that he knew one of the men so employed, who had told him that he could not find it in his heart to cut the throat of the child, that he had since felt remorse even being present on the occasion and that he was prepared to go before a magistrate and confess all he knew of the transaction. Here indeed was surely some hopeful evidence at last; but again it fell to the ground. The prisoner protested that he was unconscious of the language attributed to him, that he had been wounded in the head in His Majesty's service, and was sometimes so deranged, particularly when drunk, that he did not know what he said. He was totally ignorant of the murder, and if he did make the observations imputed to him, he must have heard the words in idle conversation at some public house. He brought forward his landlady and other persons acquainted with him to prove that he was home in his lodgings on the whole of Saturday fortnight, and that in consequence of his irregular and incoherent conduct at different times, he had acquired a reputation for insanity. Having examined the man at some length the magistrates took the view that the reputation was richly deserved and let him go.

He was not the only madman nor the only drunkard who was taken up and brought before the magistrates. Wapping richly abounded in vagrants, eccentrics, psychotics and minor criminals, and all were now at risk. It needed only a word

The Nightwatchmen of St. Paul's, Covent Garden

The Residence of the late

Mr. MARR,

RATCLIFFE HIGHWAY.

where he was dreadfully murderd with his Wife, Infant Child,
& Apprentice, on the 7th Day of December 1811.

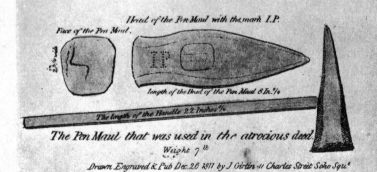

Head of the Pen Maul with the mark I.P.

Face of the Pen Maul.

length of the Head of the Pen Maul 8 In. ¾

The length of the Handle 22 Inches ¾

The Pen Maul that was used in the atrocious deed.

Weight 7 lb

Drawn Engraved & Pub Dec. 26 1811 by J Girtin 11 Charles Streit Soho Squ.

from a disgruntled neighbour, a keen glance from a police officer avid for reward, a blood-stained shirt or an Irish accent, and yet another suspect was on his way to the Watch House. There was an unfortunate engraver named Simmons, for example. He was taken up on no better evidence than that 'he evinced a strong disposition to drink, frequently coming home inebriated, was very much in the habit of skylarking, and in such freaks did many improper things. He was very industrious when sober, but when drunk there was no depending upon him.' Happily for him Simmons had been going through one of industrious spells on the night of the Marrs' murder, and had been heard all night working at his engraving. His landlord testified that he could not have left the house without being heard either by himself or his wife. The magistrates accepted that this seemed a good alibi, but were reluctant to let such an unsatisfactory character loose without at least attempting to scare him into sobriety, and he too was remanded in custody.

And then, on Thursday, 19 December, after all the false starts and disappointments, a discovery of crucial importance was made concerning the maul. It seems incredible that it was not made earlier. The weapon had been in Harriott's possession at the River Thames Police Office since the day of the murders, and one hand-bill describing it had already been issued. Its identification was obviously essential to the success of the investigation, as the hand-bill and Harriott's searches and inquiries among the river shops and warehouses bore witness. The significance of the broken tip had been appreciated, yet it was evident that the maul had not been carefully scrutinised. We are not told who made the discovery. It may have been one of Harriott's officers, or even the old man himself. It may have been a visiting magistrate, the Captain of an East Indiaman come to pay his respects to the celebrated John Harriott, or a gentleman of the town who, less squeamish than his fellows, and concealing his interest beneath an air of fastidious distaste, raised his eye-glass to the weapon and observed something which caused him to exclaim in excitement. A handkerchief was produced and the caked blood and hairs carefully scraped from the head of the maul. There, faint but now clearly discernible, were the initials **I. P.**[1] punched in dots on the face. The importance of this discovery was immediately recognised and next day Harriott put out yet another hand-bill:

THAMES POLICE OFFICE
WAPPING

WHEREAS it is most particularly necessary that any person who may possess any knowledge of the

MAUL

with which the late barbarous murder in Ratcliffe Highway appears to have been committed, should come forward and make the same known.

The magistrates have caused the same to be again described, and do most solemnly and urgently require that every person who may be enabled to give even the slightest information respecting it, do immediately acquaint the magistrates therewith.

The maul may be seen by any such person, on application to this office.

DESCRIPTION

The handle of the maul is 23 inches long – the head, from the face to the extremity, of the pin-end, is eight inches and a half. It has a flaw on the face, and the pin-end has been broken off in flakes. It is marked faintly with the letters **J.P.** in dots on the crown near the face, and appears to have been marked with a coppering punch.

By order of the magistrates,

E. W. SYMONS, chief clerk.

December 20th 1811.

It was on the same day that the initials were discovered on the maul, Thursday 19 December, that Aaron Graham, one of the Bow Street magistrates, began to take an active interest in the investigation – probably at the request of the Home

[1] Some newspapers reported that the initials stamped on the head of the maul were 'J.P.', others 'I.P.' On the drawing reproduced opposite page (55) they are clearly 'I.P.'

Secretary. He was the antithisis of the flamboyant Harriott, a quiet and intelligent bureaucrat with a logical and inquiring mind, a just appreciation of facts, and a patient tenacity in discovering them. He was bred in the tradition of Henry Fielding who some fifty years earlier had established Bow Street in its pre-eminence, had published the first index of wanted criminals, and had set up the first Bow Street thief-takers. At the time of the Marrs' murders Aaron Graham was fifty-eight, and he was to enjoy only one more year of good health until the onset of the illness which caused him to give up his post at Bow Street, and which killed him in December 1818. He shared the interest in the theatre of more famous Bow Street magistrates, and for a number of seasons superintended the concerts at Drury Lane. His only son was a naval officer and through him Graham had some insight into the lives and ways of seamen; Ratcliffe Highway was less alien to him than it was to Capper and his colleagues.

Apart from his official position as a Bow Street magistrate, with all that implied of probity and zeal, Graham had won a high personal reputation for his conduct, six years earlier, of a murder investigation which in 1806 led to the conviction and execution of one Richard Patch, for the murder by shooting of his partner Mr. Blight. The Patch case aroused extraordinary interest at the time and is noteworthy as an example of Graham's logical and deductive way of working, his insistence on verifying facts and his capacity, rare at the time, to see himself as an active investigating officer rather than the passive recipient of information which might or might not be relevant to the crime. The case also proved to have small but interesting points of similarity with the otherwise very different murders in Ratcliffe Highway.

Richard Patch, who was the son of a respectable Devon yeoman, was born in 1770, and was thirty-five at the time of the murder. He had come up to London in 1803 after a series of litigious disputes about the payment of tithes and had taken service with Mr. Blight, a former West India merchant, who at that time was successfully engaged in the ship-breaking business. Patch and Blight agreed to enter a partnership and Patch sold his Devon property to obtain the necessary capital. Details of their agreement are obscure, but it was brought to a sudden end by the murder on 23 September 1805 of Blight, who was mortally wounded by a pistol while sitting in his own house. Patch attempted to provide himself with an alibi by feigning a 'bowel disorder' and making a hurried and ostentatious retreat to the outside privy shortly before the fatal shot was fired. A few days earlier he had prepared the ground by faking an attack, by shooting, on himself.

He was at once suspected and taken into custody. Circumstantial evidence piled up against him. A number of respectable persons were brought forward who had been passing Mr. Blight's residence, either on the occasion of the first shot on 18 September or at the time when Mr. Blight was killed. They testified that had the murderer fled from the house by the front door they could not have failed to see him. Graham ordered an examination of the privy. It was apparent that it had not recently been used by anyone suffering from diarrhoea but the search did reveal the ramrod of a pistol. In Patch's bedroom the police officers discovered a pair of apparently unworn stockings which when unfolded were found to have dirty soles, as if the wearer had crept about outside in his stockinged feet. Patch had suggested to the first outsider on the scene that the murderers had escaped to a ship lying off the wharf. It was low water, and the ship was discovered to be lying some sixteen feet from the wharf in thick soft mud, which showed no signs that anyone had escaped through it. The final and damning piece of evidence was that Patch was carrying out a system of systematic fraud against his partner.

The trial on 5 April 1806 was a sensation. Three Royal Dukes attended in a box specially fitted up for their accommodation, while the peerage was liberally represented, and even the Russian Ambassador and his secretary saw fit to attend. The evidence was circumstantial, but the jury found it good, and Patch was condemned to death. The execution was deferred until the following Tuesday as it was thought more convenient that he should hang with a man and his wife, (Benjamin and Sarah Herring, who had been convicted of coining), in order, as the *Newgate Calendar* points out, 'to obviate the inconvenience of having two public executions following each other so closely'.

As sometimes happens between an interrogator and the

accused, Patch seems to have respected and even liked Graham, and the magistrate was the last person to see him in his cell on the night before he was executed. Before they parted Patch took Graham by the hand and said emphatically, 'We shall, I trust, meet in heaven.'

By 1811 this pious hope had not been realised and Aaron Graham was still very much alive to apply his talents and enthusaism to the case of the Marrs. He was obviously puzzled by the apparent lack of motive; the savage butchery of an entire family, including even the baby, who could have been a danger to no one, suggested a personal vendetta rather than murder for gain, particularly as nothing had been stolen. He cast his mind around to discover where this malice might lie. There were rumours that Marr's only brother was at enmity with him, vague talk of a lawsuit between them, in which Timothy Marr had been successful; it was said that the brothers had not spoken to each other for years. He felt that the other Mr. Marr could bear investigation. It is unlikely that he knew of Wilkie's evidence, owing to the absence of any regular system of communication between magistrates, and equally unlikely that he would have been particularly impressed by it had he heard.

He was puzzled, too, by the behaviour of Timothy Marr on the night of the murder. It was strange that he had sent Margaret Jewell to buy oysters and to pay the baker's bill at so late an hour. There was every chance that both shops would be closed by midnight and, in fact, she had found them closed. Graham wondered whether Marr had wanted the girl out of the house, perhaps because he had an assignation or was expecting a visitor, someone whom he did not wish his servant to see. An errand to buy oysters should keep her away for at least half an hour, longer if he were lucky. She was a dutiful girl; he could rely on her to search from shop to shop before she returned empty-handed.

Marr had been a seaman; he had lived in Ratcliffe Highway for only eight months. He might be expecting an unwelcome reminder of the old days at sea, a blackmailer perhaps with some knowledge of some disreputable incident in Marr's past which could blight his present hopes and modest prosperity. But, in such a case, would the blackmailer have killed his victim? Was it not much more likely that a conspiracy was afoot and that the visitors, in a passion of rage, or suspecting perfidy, had killed their accomplice?

But why should Marr have sent out his only female servant? Surely he would have been equally anxious to get young Gowen out of the way? The sharp eyes and ears, the lively curiosity of a fourteen-year-old boy would be equally dangerous to a secret purpose. There would have been no difficulty in getting rid of him. There was every excuse at that late hour for providing Margaret Jewell with a male escort, however young. Saturday night could still be a notoriously riotous time in Ratcliffe Highway.

It is likely that the magistrate's mind moved logically to a possible explanation of the whole mysterious business of the midnight errand. There was now only one person who could testify to its truth, Margaret Jewell herself. No one else was alive to confirm her story of Marr's instructions. Suppose the whole tale was untrue? That might explain the different stories Graham had heard about who actually sent the girl for oysters, Marr or his wife. At the inquest, Margaret Jewell had testified that it was her master. But Graham was able to verify that the magistrates, in reporting the facts to the Home Secretary, had written that it was Mrs. Marr. That seemed to be the general belief and it was certainly more natural that the wife should concern herself with the family's food. But Margaret Jewell might have given two different accounts, one to the magistrates at her first examination, and one to the Coroner. It was this kind of small and apparently unimportant lie which could catch a murderer.

Suppose that Margaret Jewell had herself made some excuse to leave the house that night, that someone had warned that her life depended on her leaving by midnight? Suppose that someone had instructed her in the elaborate pantomime of trudging from shop to shop in a pretended search for oysters? Who could have had a motive for destroying the whole of the Marr family whilst preserving the girl? Was it possible that the other Marr was motivated as much by love of Margaret Jewell as hate for his brother? Was there any evidence of a guilty connection between them?

Graham recalled the description of the girl's behaviour at

the finding of the body, and how she had swooned so deeply
while giving evidence at the inquest that all efforts to revive
her had proved unsuccessful. Was that the behaviour of an
accomplice or of a girl with guilty knowledge? He decided
that it could be. It was one thing to plan or to acquiesce
in an evil enterprise; another to witness its results in flowing
blood and protruding brains. But there was no reason to
suppose the girl depraved. She might have acquiesced in no
more than robbing her master. True that was a hanging matter
for her. The penalty was the same as for murder if the theft
was over five pounds. But she might have been technically
innocent. She might have been given her instructions to get
out of the house by midnight, but with no explanation of why
it was necessary, or with the wrong reason. The degree of her
complicity must remain at present a matter of doubt.

Aaron Graham, a true detective, would have turned his
attention to the timing of the crime. John Murray had
testified that he had heard the noise of a chair being pushed
back and a cry of fear at about ten minutes past twelve.
Margaret Jewell had left her master's house 'when it wanted
a few minutes to the hour' and had stated that she was away
for about twenty minutes. If she started off on her journey
at five to twelve and returned to the house at quarter past,
it was probable that the murderers were still in the house
when she was at the door; indeed the mysterious feet on the
stairs could only have been those of the killers, while the soft
wail she heard from the child must have been its last cry.
So it was all accomplished in the short time she was absent.
The murderers could even have been watching from a safe
distance to see her leave the house. It was too great a coincidence to believe that the girl had just happened to be sent
on an errand at almost the exact time that the murder of her
master and his family was planned. It was surely through the
design of sinful man, and not through the inscrutable wisdom
of Almighty God, that this one comparatively unimportant
life had been signalled out for preservation. Graham, gratified
by the strength and logic of his impressive edifice of conjecture,
determined to lose no time in putting it to the test. He took
Marr's brother into custody and subjected him to forty-eight
hours of rigorous cross-examination.

And brick by brick the case was demolished. Marr was able to produce a number of the most respectable acquaintances to prove that he was in Hackney at the appropriate time. He was able to satisfy Graham that so far from lusting after Margaret Jewell, he had never even known the girl. At the end of forty-eight hours he was released. Neither then nor later was any further accusation made against him or against the servant girl, and subsequent events proved only too dramatically that they were most unlikely to have been concerned. The husband of one of Mrs. Marr's sisters was later examined. He was a hackney driver by trade and, by an extraordinary coincidence, had driven a fare to the Ratcliffe Highway on the night of the murder, although he had not seen his sister-in-law for many years. He too was exonerated. Graham was satisfied that there had been no murderous family feud, no conspiracy. Margaret Jewell was indeed one of those lucky few who are perennially interesting to their fellows, because through some seemingly miraculous intervention, they live while others die.

Marr's ordeal was unfortunate and the conduct of the police, though not of Graham by name, was subsequently criticised in the House of Commons on 18 January 1812 by Sir Samuel Romilly in language which is sometimes echoed today by those who feel they are the victims of an over-zealous constabulary:

He did not wish to speak harshly of the police, but he did think it a most monstrous evil that so many persons had been taken up on that occasion upon such slight ground of suspicion, among them the nearest relative of one of the murdered persons, who on no ground whatever, had been apprehended and kept for forty-eight hours in custody on the dreadful charge of having murdered his brother. One way and another no less than forty or fifty persons had been apprehended on bare suspicion.

The theory that the murders were a private vendetta against Marr was comforting. The alternative struck cold in the hearts of every humble and defenceless family in East London. As De Quincey wrote:

With this mighty tide of pity and indignation pointing backwards to the dreadful past, there mingled also in the thoughts of reflecting persons an undercurrent of fearful expectation for the immediate future. All perils, especially malignant, are recurrent. A murderer, who is such by passion and by wolfish craving for bloodshed as a mode of unnatural luxury, cannot relapse into inertia. . . . But, apart from the hellish instincts that might too surely be relied on for renewed atrocities, it was clear that the murderer of the Marrs, wheresoever lurking, must be a needy man; and a needy man of that class least likely to seek or find resources in honourable modes of industry. Were it, therefore, merely for a livelihood, the murderer whom all hearts were yearning to decipher, might be expected to make his resurrection on some stage of horror, after a reasonable interval. . . . Two guineas, perhaps, would be the outside of what he had obtained in the way of booty. A week or so would see the end of that. The conviction, therefore, of all people was, that in a month or two, when the fever of excitement might have cooled down, or have been superseded by other topics of fresher interest, so that the newborn vigilance of household life would have had time to relax, some new murder, equally appalling, might be counted upon.

But if there were any who could comfort themselves with the hope that they would gain at least a few months of safety in which to secure their houses against a fresh outrage, or who could even persuade themselves that the murderers were foreign sailors now far off on the high seas, or convicts released from the hulks who had passed on their annihilating way through London and were now remote in the country or in Ireland, they were speedily to be disillusioned. 'Such,' De Quincey continues, 'was the public expectation. Let the reader then figure to himself the pure frenzy of horror when in this hush of expectation, looking, and indeed waiting for the unknown arm to strike once more . . . on the twelfth night from the Marr murder, a second case of the same mysterious nature, a murder on the same exterminating plan, was perpetrated in the very same neighbourhood.'

The parish adjoining St. George's-in-the-East was St. Paul's, Shadwell, comprising a community of 9,000 people, most of them mariners, shipwrights and dock-workers. Circumstances had squeezed them into a warren of alleys and yards between Ratcliffe Highway and the squalid reaches of the river at Wapping. In its composition and way of life St. Paul's was indistinguishable from St. George's, but a formal boundary divided the two parishes down New Gravel Lane – some 300 yards to the east of Old Gravel Lane and roughly parallel to it. New Gravel Lane was lined with the familiar conglomeration of ship's chandlers, lodging houses, pawnbrokers, and public houses packed out at night with brawling sailors. In the Lane there was one public house to every eight other houses.

But one of these houses stood out from the rest for its quaint air of respectability. Mr. and Mrs. Williamson were a genteel couple. They had held the licence of the King's Arms, at number 81 New Gravel Lane, for fifteen years, and so were well known in the area. They were also highly regarded. Williamson was a man of fifty-six and his wife Elizabeth was sixty. The remainder of the household consisted of their fourteen-year-old grand-daughter, Kitty Stillwell, and a servant in her fifties, Bridget Harrington, who worked in the tap-room. For the past eight months the Williamsons had taken in a young lodger, John Turner.

The couple liked to get to bed early, and they imposed their own strict habits on the household. There were no late night gambling parties or cock-fights in the King's Arms. Punctually every night at eleven o'clock Williamson began to put up the shutters, and if there were trouble with late drinkers he was well able to handle it; a big, burly man, tall and strong. There was a watch-box just opposite; and, as it happened, one of this year's parish constables, a man named Anderson who was a particular friend of Williamson, lived next door but one.

The King's Arms had two upper stories and hence stood literally, as well as morally, higher than the houses on either side. The ground floor comprised the tap-room, a private kitchen behind, and a parlour. Underneath, with a flap-door opening on to the pavement for the delivery of barrels of beer, was a cellar. The Williamson's bedroom and that of Kitty Stillwell took up most of the first floor, from the landing of which a further flight of stairs led up to a couple of garrets. These were occupied by Bridget Harrington and the lodger. Behind the house was a plot of enclosed ground, where in fine weather the inhabitants of the King's Arms and the neighbouring houses played Bumble-puppy, a variant of skittles; and behind this ground were acres of waste land belonging to the London Dock Company.

The night of Thursday, 19 December was fine and mild, but apart from roaming gangs of seamen the streets were nearly empty. Twelve days had gone by since the murder of the Marrs, and it was terrifyingly clear to everyone who lived in Shadwell that the magistrates were in despair. Every night thirteen frightened and lonely watchmen employed by the Churchwardens, Overseers and Trustees of the parish of St. Paul's staggered drunkenly from their watch-boxes to call the half-hours and lurched back to safety again for another swig to drown their fears. Very occasionally one – or more usually two, for now they preferred company – of the five police officers from Wapping or the eight from Shadwell would patrol in the parish, but with a population of about 60,000 to protect in all the six parishes they were supposed to cover these heartening appearances were rare. The only real safety lay behind bolts and bars, especially after nightfall, and this week was bringing the longest nights of the year. Sixteen hours of darkness gave a murderous gang sixteen hours of silent cover. In the streets, outside the tight-shut doors, the oil-lamps guttered unnaturally loud. When a wind blew up from the river their twisted cotton wicks flared up and as suddenly died down, scarifying and multiplying the shadows. To shatter so troubled a silence with the half-hour's call a watchman had to nerve himself with something more potent that prostitutes' gin.

But social life had not been brought completely to an end. As it neared eleven o'clock Mr. Lee, the landlord of the Black Horse, the public house opposite the King's Arms, went from time to time to his door to look out for his wife and daughter. They had been to the Royalty Theatre in Wellclose Square, and Lee was concerned for their safety, his mind dwelling darkly on the murders. Then, at ten minutes to eleven, Anderson, the constable, slipped out into New Gravel Lane, braving the shadows, and made his way to the King's Arms, two doors away, for a pot of beer.

Williamson welcomed his old friend. He was in a mood to talk. 'You shan't carry it home,' he insisted, 'I'll send it.' While Mrs. Williamson drew the beer her husband sat back in a favourite armchair in the kitchen, warming himself by a low fire. Only one thought can have been in his mind. Suddenly he sat up. 'You're an officer,' he said. 'There's been a fellow listening at my door – with a brown jacket on. If you should see him take him immediately into custody. Or tell me.'

'I certainly will,' Anderson replied; adding grimly, 'for my own safety as well as yours.'

Bridget Harrington carried the pot of beer the few yards to Anderson's house, then returned to the King's Arms. Anderson was certain, when he said good night, that the only people then in the public house were Mr. and Mrs. Williamson, Bridget Harrington, Kitty Stillwell and Turner, the lodger.

It took Anderson little more than twenty minutes to finish his beer. Although his neighbour always reckoned to close the tap-room to casual drinkers at eleven o'clock sharp, he would never turn away friends until he finally locked up for the night and went to bed. Thirsty again, Anderson decided to fetch another pot. He opened the street door and, immediately, was swept into turmoil. People were shouting and running, and above the din, repeated again and again, came the terrible cry, 'Murder! Murder!' A small crowd stared up at Williamson's house and Anderson followed their gaze. A man, nearly naked, was suspended in mid-air, clutching sheets knotted together. Hand over hand he was making

ESCAPE of **IOHN TURNER,** by the **SHEETS** Knotted together, after he had seen one of the Murderers plundering the dead bodies.

his way down from an open garret window, shrieking and crying incoherently. A watchman, Shadrick Newhall, stood helplessly on the cobblestones, lantern in one hand, rattle in the other, gaping as though he saw a ghost. Anderson rushed indoors for his constable's sword and staff, rushed out again, and was in time to see the man drop the last eight feet into the arms of the watchman. It was John Turner, the lodger.

The crowd acted by instinct. Some began beating down the street door. Anderson found himself with three or four others prising open the pavement flap that led down to the cellar. One was armed with a poker, another, the butcher, wielded an axe. Lee, the landlord of the Black Horse, joined them. They broke the flap open. Steps led down into darkness, but there was light enough to reveal Williamson's body. It lay stretched out on its back, head downwards, the legs splayed out grotesquely on the stairs that led up to the tap-room.

Alongside the corpse lay an iron bar, smothered with blood. The old man's head had been beaten in cruelly. His throat was cut to the bone and the right leg fractured. But he must have put up a brave fight. One hand had been dreadfully hacked about, as though in the last frenzied moments he had clutched at the knife that finished him. A thumb dangled loosely in a spreading pool of blood.

As the little party gazed, frozen with horror, a cry came from above. Someone shouted down: 'Where's the old man?'

They had to climb over Williamson's broken and bleeding body to get up to the kitchen, where half an hour earlier the old man had been warming himself by a dying fire. The first corpse they saw was Mrs. Williamson's. It lay on the left side, the skull terribly shattered, the throat slashed through. Blood poured from a great, gaping wound. Bridget Harrington was not far away. She lay on her back, her feet under the grate, and near to the dead fire she must already have been laying for the morning when the murderers struck. Bridget's skull was more dreadfully fractured, even than Mrs. Williamson's. But it was the throat that held Anderson's horrified gaze. It had been sliced through to the neckbone.

Little bands of men armed with axes and pokers searched the house, but the murderer had fled. Miraculously Kitty Stillwell, the grand-daughter, was still in her bed, fast asleep, unharmed. She was carried out into the street. Someone sent a message to Shadwell Public Office and a couple of police officers rushed to the scene. They had been scouring Shadwell parish that very night, carrying cutlasses and pistols, but had been taking supper in a tavern opposite the Public Office at the moment the murderer broke in.

Now, according to a report in *The Courier,* 'All Wapping was immediately in uproar. The drums of the volunteers beat to arms, and fire-bells were rung, and every person flew in consternation to the spot. The police searched every house around and every boat in the river, while every cart, wagon and carriage was stopped.' This seems an exaggerated account, considering the paucity of police available. Nevertheless, it is true that London Bridge was sealed off and a suspect picked up. And towards morning, to hearten the terrified populace, a detachment of Bow Street Runners came canter-

ing along Ratcliffe Highway, streaking the drab streets of
Shadwell and Wapping with a sudden flash of colour from
their bright blue coats, scarlet waistcoats, blue trousers,
Wellington boots and black hats. Then, *The Courier* reported,
'The bodies were removed from the shocking position in which
they lay, undressed, washed, and laid out on boards, in the
back parlour, where the old couple sometimes used to sleep;
and the little girl, who was found asleep above stairs, was
removed to a place of safety.'

Several clues were quickly discovered. Anderson reported
that a tall man in a long Flushing coat had been seen outside
the King's Arms that evening. The lodger, when they could
get some sense out of him, stammered out that he had actually
seen a tall man so clad bending over Mrs. Williamson's body –
though anything Turner said was at that time highly suspect,
since he had been the first to be taken in charge by the watchman. A window at the back of the King's Arms was found
open, and there were bloodstains on the sill. Outside was a
high clay bank in which a footprint was found. The clay was
wet, and whoever had escaped that way must have had to
drop down eight feet and then scramble up a slippery bank.
He would have clay on his trousers, and perhaps on the front
of his jacket too, and clay was not easy to wash off. It seemed
that the murderer had made his escape over the waste land
belonging to the London Dock Company. So also, someone
recalled, had the gang who murdered the Marrs. A man with
a claim to forensic ability – perhaps the butcher? – put it
out as his opinion, considering the nature of the wounds, that
the murderer was left-handed.

Before it was yet midnight a huddle of terrified men
gathered in the vestry of St. Paul's, Shadwell. The Churchwardens, Overseers and Trustees, despite their impressive
titles, were simple folk. They were local tradesmen and
artisans, shopkeepers, butchers, biscuit bakers and victuallers,
who had known the Williamsons for years. They would have
gossipped with them in the tap-room of the King's Arms about
the catastrophe that had struck Marr's family: at first in
incredulous horror, later, perhaps, in an attempt to keep their
spirits high, exchanging ghoulish jokes. Now though, sickened
by the sight of three more dreadfully mangled corpses, they

had suddenly to adjust to a frightening new reality. They were caught up at the centre of events so chillingly macabre that ordinary folk could only shudder in disbelief. But these men, holding office, were not permitted to act as ordinary folk. They constituted authority; and stunted and dwarfed as it now was by stupendous events, they had a clear responsibility to discharge. So, with their clerk Thomas Barnes, they assembled near midnight in the familiar vestry, where the normal calendar ran to marriages, tithes, christenings and the poor-rate, to deliberate, so to speak, at Cabinet level. They passed hurried resolutions; entered up the Minute Book; sacked all the watchmen; and sent Barnes hurrying off to Skirven the printer of Ratcliffe Highway. Less than an hour after the murders another hand-bill appeared in the streets.

100 Guineas

REWARD

MURDER!

WHEREAS,

On **THURSDAY NIGHT**, 19th December, 1811, between the hours of Eleven and Twelve o' Clock, Mr. WILLIAMSON his WIFE, and the MAID SERVANT, were all of them most barbarously MURDERED in his house, the Sign of the

KING's ARMS
NEW GRAVEL LANE
SAINT PAUL, SHADWELL.

The Churchwardens, Overseers, and Trustees of the Parish of St. Paul, Shadwell, do hereby offer a Reward of ONE HUNDRED GUINEAS, to any Person or Persons who shall discover and apprehend the Perpetrator or Perpetrators of the said HORRID MURDER, on Conviction.

By Order of the Churchwardens, Overseers, and Trustees

THOMAS BARNES,

VESTRY CLERK

SHADWELL
19th December, 1811.

But the motive? What terrible appetite for gain or passion for revenge could conceive malignity on such a scale, could account for seven victims in less than a fortnight, with brains beaten out and throats butchered? It was beyond all experience, irrational. The parish vestry was stupified. Those who sought a simple motive of robbery pointed out that both Marr and Williamson were relatively rich. Although nothing had been stolen from Marr it was discovered that Williamson's watch was missing. Perhaps the gang, surprised in the one case by Margaret Jewell's ringing and in the other by the cries of the lodger, had on each occasion been foiled in the act of plunder, and turned coward? It was a theory that left too much unexplained. Why was money left in Marr's pocket and in the shop till? Why stop at taking Williamson's watch? Why not at least grab the loose money in his till? Was it in character that so brutal a gang should turn tail so swiftly, empty-handed, with only the pointless murders accomplished?

But if there was no prime motive of robbery, was it a case of multiple vengeance? Some sort to establish a connection between Marr and Williamson that might provide a clue, but none was apparent. Marr was young, and had been in the neighbourhood for only a few months; Williamson was fifty-six and had been settled in Shadwell for years. Yet the parishioners must have tried desperately hard to find a common link between the two families: for the alternative – if no rational motive for private vengeance could be found – was too horrible to contemplate. A maniac, or a gang of maniacs was at large, cunning, pitiless, inhuman, who might strike again at any moment during the long December nights.

What use was the offer of 100 guineas reward likely to be, when the Government's offer after the Marrs' murder of 500 guineas had evidently failed? A gesture only: yet the parish owed it to the Williamsons to make it. They also needed to do everything possible to reassure their terrified families and neighbours. So, too, did the Churchwardens, Overseers and Trustees of the next parish, to the east of Shadwell. The vestry of the hamlet of Ratcliffe met next morning; and their meeting, understandably, seems to have been conducted more rationally than the midnight gathering of the panic-striken folk of Shadwell. They took time to think, and someone who

had been inside the King's Arms described the iron bar that
had been found beside Williamson's body. It was about thirty-
five inches long, and similar to the weapon found on Marr's
counter. Perhaps it was not a crow-bar, as at first thought,
but a ripping chisel. The same perhaps that had been found
in Marr's shop? But that was impossible, for the first was now
held by the magistrates, and this seemed new. Mystified, the
vestry drew up their own hand-bill carefully, and the principle
on which they acted was an old and logical one. Although they
were not directly concerned, the fact that a gang of monsters
could roam the area with impunity obliged them to look to the
security of their own parish. Their duty was first to assess
the risk and then settle the size of the reward in proportion
to it. They followed the example of Shadwell and offered
100 guineas. But, in addition, they offered a further twenty
guineas to anyone able to prove to whom the new ripping
chisel had been sold. To the parish of Ratcliffe, clearly, this
ripping chisel was a most important clue to the mystery.

No one could reasonably expect the parish authorities to
do more; but what of the magistrates? Criticism welled up.
For all their apparent activity during the twelve days since
the murder of the Marrs they had accomplished nothing –
worse, they had failed, even, to prevent the monsters from
striking again. It was not enough to sack a few watchmen,
people muttered; the magistrates themselves should go.

To Harriott this situation was intolerable. With no help
coming from the Home Office and a trio of incompetent
amateurs in charge at Shadwell, he resolved to take matters
into his own hands. A man who had sailed the world, conquered fresh territories for Britain and subdued an Indian
rajah was not to be foiled by a gang of thugs. After breakfast
he called on Capper and Markland at the Shadwell Public
Office, then hurried back to Wapping to issue an imperious
message:

The Magistrates of the Thames Police present their
compliments to the Magistrates of Shadwell requesting
their meeting them at the Thames Police Office this day at
2 o'clock – to consult together on the most effectual
measures for discovering the atrocious midnight murderers

that infest the neighbourhood of their respective Offices, which from the murder of three people in a house in New Gravel Lane last night, gives an appearance of a gang acting on system.

A similar message went to the magistrates at the White-chapel Public Office. Had they been challenged, the magistrates would have strenuously claimed that they were, in fact, already co-operating fully. Was not every policeman and watch in East London, no matter what his parish allegience, on the look out for suspects? Were they not keeping each other and the Home Secretary informed of progress? Had not the Shadwell magistrates invited Harriott to be present when they first interviewed Murray, Olney and Margaret Jewell? But the only kind of co-operation which could have been effective, the central control of the whole investigation by one bench, including the deployment of a united force, the interrogation of all the suspects and the custody of all exhibits, together with a system for the prompt receipt by the investigating magistrate of all information, was as much beyond their comprehension as it was beyond their ability to organise.

The meeting took place that Friday afternoon, the day following the murders, in an atmosphere of rising tension and excitement. An angry mob surged outside, gripped by raw, seething emotions that might turn to sudden panic, hysteria, blind vengeance. The magistrates' responsibility stared them starkly in the face. If the murderers were not quickly dis-covered the people would arm themselves – many were already doing so – and nobody would be able to answer for the safety of the Portuguese, or Germans, or Irish, or any other foreign community the mob might turn on in their rage. Yet the means available to the magistrates were pathetically small in relationship to their responsibility: eight police officers at Shadwell, eight more at Whitechapel, five at Wapping and the temporary loan of a *posse* of Bow Street Runners.

To Harriott all this – the angry crowd, the challenge, the danger – would have a curiously familiar ring. He had seen it before, in the very same setting, at the Wapping Police Office, and would relish once more being called upon to play a leading role. One October evening soon after the River

Thames Police had been set up, an army of half-savage Irish coal-heavers, incensed at the way the new police were interfering with their pilfering on the river, massed outside the Office. Some of their mates had been caught and were under examination; the rest were determined to release them. They attacked the door, then tore up paving stones and smashed the windows. 'I believe,' Harriott exulted in his memoirs, 'I was the only person in the office, at the time, who had ever smelt gunpowder burnt in anger before.' The riot spread, and it seemed that the office would be overwhelmed. One City merchant fled from his business to the attic; others, to Harriott's disgust, 'made a prudent retreat by getting into a boat and rowing away'. Harriott, meanwhile, had given orders for firearms to be loaded; and 'their loading, and giving necessary directions, seemed to electrify and make me young again'. The Riot Act was read, and it was enough for Harriott to shoot one rioter for the mob to disperse. Had the murderers of the Marrs and Williamsons come charging down Old Gravel Lane armed with cutlasses, mauls and ripping chisels, Harriott would have known how to deal with them, and would have gloried in the chance. Unhappily this investigation required more subtle methods and, for all his experience, enthusiasm and courage, Harriott was no more effective than were the less flamboyant magistrates of the Shadwell and Whitechapel benches.

No record exists of the discussion behind the shuttered windows of the Police Office, and probably no minute was taken. Harriott was no slave to bureaucracy. The meeting was, in any case, the last, as well as the first of its kind. With it, co-ordination lapsed. Each bench went home and proceeded to give its own account of the Williamsons' murder to the Home Secretary.

Harriott was brief, as befits a man of action. He took credit for calling the conference on the fresh 'atrocious murders', at which the magistrates had considered 'the most effectual measures to be adopted, and of co-operating and exerting their joint endeavours'. But he gave no hint of what these measures might be. The confidence he had shown after the Marrs' murder, when he had allowed his zeal to outrun his discretion, was abating. He now gives the impression of an angry, frustrated old man, grappling with somebody else's problem for no better reason than that it presented a challenge, and becoming uneasily aware that the challenge was beating him.

The Whitechapel bench had hitherto been little involved, although like every other Public Office in the Metropolis they had examined suspects brought in after the murder of the Marrs. Harriott's conference seems to have jerked them out of apathy. Perhaps, with reason, they feared dismissal unless they, too, showed the Home Secretary evidence of less than usual sloth. 'With deep regret,' they wrote, 'we feel it our duty to state that a horrid murder was last night committed at the King's Arms Public House in New Gravel Lane. . . . Every exertion is making (*sic*) to trace the Perpetrators of this alarming and most atrocious deed.' There is no indication at this or any other time that the Whitechapel magistrates exerted themselves to the point of inconvenience, or even interested themselves in the case once they had got away from Harriott's conference.

But it was, after all, the Shadwell bench who were primarily concerned, for it was in their area that all the victims had lived. Here, at least, the Home Secretary had a right to look for enthusiasm. The letters from both the Thames and the Whitechapel Offices arrived at the Home Office during the course of Friday, but as the day wore on there was still no news from Shadwell. Ryder sent by hand a message of inquiry, and learned the reason for delay: immediately on their return from Harriott's conference Capper and his colleagues had proceeded to examine a suspect, a cheerful Irishman named Sylvester Driscoll, who was unlucky enough to lodge near the King's Arms, in New Gravel Lane. On his arrest the prisoner was found to be in possession of what he protested to be 'only a drop he was laying in, as usual, before the holidays' – a gallon of brandy, for which he had paid thirteen shillings and sixpence, a quart of whisky and a sample of British brandy. Searching his room, a police officer then discovered a pair of white canvas trousers, still damp from recent washing, and with evident traces of blood on them. Driscoll insisted that the marks were paint but a 'medical gentleman' confirmed that they were blood stains. Thereupon, 'the prisoner said that a milkwoman slept in the same room where he lodged, and that the trousers were found under her bed'. Mrs. Driscoll hopefully offered an alibi, but the magistrates seem to have been unimpressed by either explanation, and Driscoll was committed. Then, this important business concluded, Capper turned his attention to the Home Secretary's inquiry; and late in the day the messenger brought back his reply. The handwriting betrays the magistrate's weariness and agitation. Towards the end it resembled that of an old and sick man.

Shadwell 20th Dec. 1811.

Sir,

In answer to your letter I beg leave to inform you of the following circumstances of the case of murder that took place last night in New Gravel Lane, Shadwell, at the Public house called the King's Arms, and kept by a man named John Williamson. At Eleven o'clock the Watchman whose Box is immediately opposite left his Box to go his round, when all was safe, in ten minutes time he returned, and observed a young man who was a Lodger in the house, lowering himself down by two Sheets from a two pair of stairs window, on catching him, he told him the family were murdered, the door was immediately broken open, and Catherine (*sic*) Williamson, and her Maid Servant, Bridget Harrington, were found Murdered in the Tap Room, their throats cut etc. and the man in the cellar in the same state.

There is every reason to suppose the murderers of Mr. Marr's family are the perpetrators of this atrocious act also. The circumstances in very many respects corroborate this idea. The same description of a man was seen about the house. The print of a nailed shoe was also discovered, at the back of the house, where they *also* made their escape. We are much in hopes that we have obtained some clue, tho' I cannot speak with any certainty, but you shall have the first information. Pardon any inaccuracy, as I have been writing in very great confusion.

I am Sir Your Very Obt. & Hble. Servt.,

B. C. Capper.

'We are much in hopes that we have found some clue'. Capper was nothing if not cautious. Already there were at least five clues: a new iron crow-bar – or was it another ripping chisel? – covered with blood; Williamson's missing watch, bearing the name James Catchpole, of which a description had been circulated; Turner's description of the man he claimed to have seen bending over Mrs. Williamson's body; a footprint discovered in the clay bank outside the back window where the sill was stained with blood; and Anderson's description of a man seen during the evening to be lurking outside the King's Arms.

Nor was this all. During the course of Friday, *The Times* reported:

> Mr. Henry Johnson, a person of respectability in St. Paul's parish, Shadwell, and two women of the town deposed, that just at the time the alarm of murder was given, they saw two men running up the lane towards Ratcliffe Highway. One of them appeared to be lame, and could not keep up with his companion. He appeared to be exhausted, either by running or by some violent exertion. This man was the shortest of the two. They heard the tallest man say, 'Come along Mahoney (or Hughey) Come along,' or words to that effect. They made their way towards the Bluegate Fields.

In ignoring all these clues Capper was, indeed, writing in great confusion.

What effect these various accounts had on the Home Secretary it is impossible to say, nor is there any reason to think that he made any use of them; although it is likely that Beckett would have communicated their contents to Graham, at Bow Street. Once again, however, the Home Secretary acted exceptionally in offering the Government's own reward for any information that led to the conviction of the murderer or murderers, and as in the case of the Marrs, the reward was again pitched at the extraordinarily high sum of £500. Coupled with the offer was the usual promise of a free pardon to anyone, other than the villains themselves, who might be prepared to come forward.

The Government's proclamation came out on Saturday,

21 December, the same day that the national newspapers
were reporting the second 'Horrid Murders'. The tone set by
The Times was typical: 'On Thursday night, between the
hours of eleven and twelve, another scene of sanguinary
atrocity was acted in New Gravel Lane, Ratcliffe Highway,
equalling in barbarity the murders of Mr. Marr and his family.'
To the *London Chronicle,* it was 'with equal horror and concern
we have to state that three more persons have lost their lives
by the hands of midnight murderers, within two minutes
walk of the very spot where the family of the late unfortunate
Marr perished a few days ago by the same means.'

Within hours a fresh thrill of horror convulsed the capital.
'It is almost impossible,' a Mr. Johnson of Fenchurch Street
told the Home Secretary, 'to conceive the fear and dismay
these dreadful occurrences have made on the public, particularly at the East End of the Town.' Dreadful reports circulated,
building up fresh panic. It was rumoured that another publican had been murdered on Friday night in the City Road,
and that Mr. Corse, landlord of the White Rose[1] in Ratcliffe
Highway, was next on the death list. An armed guard was
placed outside the public house all night. Then a story circulated that two policemen had been massacred in Limehouse
while trying to arrest a suspicious character. The truth was
that the policemen had chased the suspect, taken him in
custody and bundled him off. But before they had got far
they were attacked by 200 angry Irishmen, who rescued the
prisoner. The policemen obtained help and got their man
again, but he was released a second time. Finally the man
disappeared, when it turned out that the rioters had believed
the policemen to be part of a press-gang. The man eventually
surrendered himself, as *The Times* put it, 'with his shirt
completely stained with the blood of his antagonists and
accounted satisfactorily for his opposition in this unfortunate
affair.' Similar scenes were occurring all over London. No
one knew where the murderers would strike next. 'Many of
our readers,' Macaulay wrote years later, 'can remember
the state of London just after the murders of Marr and

[1] Probably identical with the *Old* Rose, still standing in Ratcliffe Highway near the site of Marr's shop, and bearing the inscription, *Established
in 1666.*

Williamson – the terror which was on every face – the careful barring of doors – the providing of blunderbusses and watchmen's rattles. We know of a shopkeeper who on that occasion sold three hundred rattles in ten hours.'

Three hundred miles away, in Keswick, Southey (according to De Quincey) was following every turn in the saga with the deepest interest; it was, he declared, a rare case of 'a private event of that order which rose to the dignity of a national event'. De Quincey himself was even more enthralled. Having known London as a youth, his opium-stimulated imagination took in every detail that years afterwards he was to work over and over again. In 1811 De Quincey was living at Dove Cottage (which he had taken over from Wordsworth three years earlier), and even in Grasmere:

> the panic was indescribable. One lady, my next neighbour, whom personally I knew, living at that moment, during the absence of her husband, with a few servants in a very solitary house, never rested until she had placed eighteen doors (so she told me, and indeed satisfied me by ocular proof), each secured by ponderous bolts, and bars, and chains, between her own bedroom and any intruder of human build. To reach her, even in her drawing room, was like going, as a flag of truce, into a beleagured fortress; at every sixth step one was stopped by a sort of portcullis.

The account may be exaggerated, yet there is no doubt that the panic De Quincey describes was widespread. The Home Office papers contain letters from all parts of the country testifying to the 'general alarm' caused by the murders, and calling for the urgent reform of the police and the magistracy.

If it had been generally realised just how paltry, confused and disjointed the local efforts were that week-end, just a fortnight after the murder of Marr's family and forty-eight hours after the killing of the Williamsons, the public alarm would have been even greater.

Three adjacent parish councils had each posted up its own

hand-bill advertising different rewards for different purposes. The parish of St. George's was still offering fifty pounds for information that might lead to the conviction of the Marrs' murderers, and their hand-bill described the broken maul and ripping chisel about twenty inches long; it appealed to dealers in old iron or anyone who had lost such articles to come forward. The parish of St. Paul's, concerned with the Williamsons, held out a promise of 100 guineas for information leading to a conviction of *their* murderer, but advertised no clue or lead that might be followed up. The parish of Ratcliffe, not directly concerned with either crime, was offering 100 guineas in respect of the Williamsons and a further twenty guineas to anyone who could point to a person who had recently bought a ripping chisel about thirty-five inches long.

The magistrates were similarly at odds. The Thames Police Office had offered a reward of twenty pounds for information about three suspicious characters seen outside Marr's shop, but had been rebuked for doing so. Subsequently they had appealed for information relating to the maul, which they were now able to advertise as being definitely identifiable by the initials J.P.; but this time no reward was offered. The Shadwell magistrates had offered an unspecified reward for information about a bloody shirt and handkerchief, and had then again lapsed into baffled impotence. All they had been able to do, after being prodded by the Home Secretary, was to express the not surprising opinion that both crimes must have been committed by the same ruffians, and this on no better grounds than that both gangs escaped by the back of the house and that 'the same description of man' was seen about both houses. This was one of the men, presumably, whose description Harriott had advertised a fortnight earlier with his irregular offer of a reward. The Home Office meanwhile, took delivery of a great deal of paper and said nothing, resting on the two vast offers of 500 guineas each with which they hoped to bring information to light bearing on both crimes. It seems incredible that no one in authority even attempted to pull the various strings together, build up a theory or work out a consistent line of investigation that would take account of all the important clues that were now available. But at that time it was no one's duty to do so, and affairs continued to run their haphazard course. Meanwhile the whole country waited eagerly for the report of the Coroner's inquest on the bodies of the Williamsons and their servant.

The custom was to hold the inquest as near as possible to the scene of the crime, so on Saturday, Unwin, the Coroner, took over the Black Horse, just across the road from the King's Arms. Vast crowds swarmed outside, some curious, some awestruck, all avid for sensation, pushing and jostling up New Gravel Lane to Ratcliffe Highway and round the corner to Marr's shop less than half a mile distant. Inside the Black Horse witnesses, jury, pressmen and a few lucky spectators struggled for space. Then, promptly at two o'clock, the Coroner called for silence and addressed the jury:

The frequent instances of murder committed in the eastern part of the metropolis, which no vigilance has been successful to detect; in a vicinity where the population of the lower classes preponderates, increased by the number of strangers and seamen discharged from time to time at the East and West India, and London Docks, and the influx of foreign sailors from all parts of the globe; imperiously call for the solemn attention of those more immediately entrusted with the administration of Government; for the late and present murders are a disgrace to the country, and almost a reproach on civilisation: while the exertions of the police, with the ordinary power of the parochial officers, are found insufficient to protect men's persons from the hand of violence; and the Coroner has to record the most atrocious crimes without the possibility of delivering the perpetrators to justice and punishment; our homes are no longer our castles, and we are unsafe in our beds. These observations, strong as they are, will be found warranted by the events which have lately taken place within a short distance of the spot where we are now met, and by the numerous verdicts of wilful murder, which, during the last three months, have been returned by Juries against persons unknown, not one of which has yet been discovered. Until some more appropriate remedy be pointed out, it appears advisable, in the present agitation of the public mind, that parties of the military, under the direction of the civil power, selected from Militia or Guards, should patrol this district during the night. Your verdict, I am sorry to say, will, in these cases, be given generally on the evidence, as the perpetrators are unknown; but it may be hoped, by the aid of the Divine Providence which seldom permits murder, in this life, to go unpunished, with the exertions which will be used, these inhuman monsters may be discovered and brought to justice. Your verdict will be wilful murder against some persons unknown.

The first witness to be sworn was John Turner. He said he was in the employ of Messrs. Scarlett & Cook and had lodged with the Williamsons for about eight months. His room was in the front garret, two floors from the ground. He boarded at his brother's house near by. Turner went on:

I went from my brother's to Mr. Williamson's on Thursday evening last, about twenty minutes before eleven o'clock, as near as I can say. When I went in, Mrs. Williamson was standing at the front door. She followed me. Mr. Williamson was sitting in the middle room, in his great chair: the servant was in the back room. I saw no other person in the house but those three. Mr. Williamson told me to sit down. I stood by the fire. A little man came in, whose name I understand to be Samuel Phillips – he came in according to his usual custom for a pint of beer, and told Mr. Williamson that there was a stout man with a very large coat on, peeping in at the inner glass door in the passage. Mr. Williamson, catching up the candlestick, said: 'I'll see what he wants.' He went out with the candle in his hand and returned saying, 'he could not see him, but if he did see him, he would send him where he ought or would not like to go.' Phillips went out with his beer, and Mr. Anderson came in directly afterwards – he did not stay above two or three minutes. Shortly afterwards the servant raked out the fire and I went to bed; at which time Mrs. Williamson followed me upstairs to her own room with a watch and silver punch ladle. This was the last time I saw either of them living. I heard Mrs. Williamson lock the bedroom door and go downstairs again. There was no fastening to my room door. I went to bed, and had not been there above five minutes before I heard the front door being banged to: very hard. Immediately afterwards I heard the servant exclaim 'We are all murdered' or 'shall be murdered' two or three times; I cannot exactly say which of the expressions she made use of. I had not been asleep. I heard the sound of two or three blows, but with what weapon I cannot say. Shortly afterwards I heard Mr. Williamson cry out, 'I'm a dead man.' I was in bed still. About two minutes afterwards I got out of bed, and listened at the door, but could hear nothing. I went down to the first floor, and from below I heard the sound of three heavy sighs. I heard some person walk across the middle of the room on the ground floor very lightly. I was then half way down the last pair of stairs, and naked. I went to the bottom of the stairs, and the door stood a little on the jar. I passed through the opening, and by the light of a candle which was burning in the room, I saw a man, apparently near six feet high, in a large rough Flushing coat, of a dark colour, which came down to his heels. He was standing with his back towards me; apparently leaning over some person, as if in the act of rifling their pockets, as I heard some silver rattle, and saw him rise and open his coat with his left hand and put his right hand on to his breast, as if to put something in his pocket. I did not see his face, and I only saw that one person. I was fearful and went upstairs as quick but as softly as I could. I thought first of getting under the bed, but was fearful I should be found. I then took the two sheets, tied them together, tied them to the bed post; opened the window, and lowered myself down by the sheets. The watch-man was going by. I told him there was murder in the house and he assisted me in getting down. I had nothing on but my nightcap, my shirt and a Jersey waistcoat. The watch-man sprang his rattle. Mr. Fox then came up, and said, 'break the door open'. Mr. Fox went over the way and came back again with an hanger. I have frequently seen Mr. Williamson's watch. It is a small thick silver watch, with a glass. It had a gold coloured chain, and a large seal with a stone in the bottom. I saw Mr. Williamson playing with the chain on Thursday night, when I was standing at the fire. I never saw an iron crow in the house to my knowledge.

As Turner finished his evidence, white and tense with the remembered shock of what he had seen, the silence of the taproom would have been broken only by the scratching of the quill pens of the journalists and coroner's clerk, the crackling of the fire and the subdued murmuring from the crowd in the street. It was impossible to doubt that Turner had told the truth. Although someone had instantly given him in charge to the watchman on the night of the murder he had quickly been released. But what sort of man was he to abandon Williamson's grand-daughter, Kitty Stillwell, to her fate? In his desperate anxiety to get out of the King's Arms alive he had apparently given her no thought. But De Quincey, painting his picture in stark black and white, with one character portrayed as villain, and the rest ennobled to provide an effective contrast to his depravity, contrived an ingenious defence of the unfortunate lodger:

'But courage! God by the proverb of all nations in Christendom, helps those that help themselves. . . . Were it only for himself that he worked, he could not feel himself meritoriously employed; but this is not so; in deep sincerity, he is now agitated for the poor child, whom he knows and loves; every minute, he feels, brings ruin nearer to her; and as he passed her door, his first thought had been to take her out of bed in his arms, and to carry her where she might share his chances. But, on consideration, he felt that this sudden awakening of her, and the impossibility of even whispering any explanation, would cause her to cry audibly; and the inevitable indiscretion of one would be fatal to the two. – No; there is but one way to save the child; towards her deliverance the first step is through his own. And he has made an excellent beginning; for the spike, which too fearfully he had expected to see torn away by any strain upon it stands firmly when tried against the pressure of his own weight. He has rapidly fastened on to it three lengths of new rope, measuring twelve feet. He plaits it roughly;

so that only three feet have been lost in the inter-twisting;
he has spliced on a second length equal to the first; so that,
already, sixteen feet are ready to throw out of the window, –
To his sixteen feet, of which seven are neutralised by the
distance of the bed, he has at last added six feet more
which will be short of reaching the ground by perhaps
ten feet – a trifle which man or boy may drop without
injury – and at this very moment, whilst desperate agitation
is nearly paralysing his fingers, he hears the sullen, stealthy
step of the murderer creeping up through the darkness. –
Never perhaps in this world did any man feel his own
responsibilities so cruelly loaded and strained, as at this
moment did the poor journeyman on behalf of the slumber-
ing child. Lose but two seconds, through awkwardness or
through self-counteractions of panic, and for her the total
difference arose between life and death. Still there is a hope:
and nothing can so frightfully expound the hellish nature
of him whose baleful shadow at this moment darkens the
house of life, than the simple expression of the ground on
which this hope rested. The journeyman felt sure that the
murderer would not be satisfied to kill the poor child whilst
unconscious. This would be to defeat his whole purpose
in murdering her at all. To an epicure in murder . . . it
would be taking away the very sting of the bitter cup of
death without fully apprehending the misery of the situation. – But all considerations whatever are at this moment
suddenly cut short. A second step is heard on the stairs,
but still stealthy and cautious; a third – and then the child's
doom seem fixed. But just at that moment all is ready. The
window is wide open; the rope is swinging free; the journeyman has launched himself and already is in the first stage
of his descent.

De Quincey's account, like the whole of his essay, is a powerful evocation of fear and suspense, but it bears little relation
to the truth.

George Fox was next sworn:

I reside in New Gravel Lane, opposite the house of the
deceased. On Thursday night, as the watch was going

eleven, I came to the top of New Gravel Lane, on my way home, and I saw two watchmen standing at Mr. Williamson's door; when I came up to them and asked them what was the matter? Mr. Lee the landlord of the Black Horse, was along with the watchmen. I was told the house was being robbed if not the people being murdered in it. Several other persons coming up soon after, I begged of them to knock hard. If there was no answer, I proposed to break open the door, and I would be answerable for the consequences. They did knock and received no answer. While they were breaking open the door I ran across to my own house for an hanger,[1] which the servant immediately gave me with my going indoors. The door and the front cellar window were immediately broken open. Three or four persons went down the cellar window while myself and three or four others went in at the door. We looked in at the fore-room which was in darkness. We went into the middle room, occupied as a kitchen, where there was a light burning on a table. There I saw Mrs. Williamson, lying with her face along the hearth, with her head towards the door; with her throat cut, and the blood flowing from the wound, apparently dead. She had her clothes on. Some keys and a box were lying by her side, and it appeared to me that her pockets had been rifled. The servant, Bridget Harrington, was lying between Mrs. Williamson and the fireplace, in the same direction. Her throat was cut and the blood was flowing from it: the fire was out; and materials laid ready to light it in the morning. She was also completely dressed, and appeared to have received a violent blow on the head. I immediately called out, 'Where is the old man, Williamson?' I was answered from those in the cellar: 'Here he is, with his throat cut.' I went part of the way down, and saw him lying upon his back in the cellar. I immediately with the others, proceeded to search the house. I went into the back room, next to that in which I had found the bodies of Mrs. Williamson and the servant. I found that the inside shutter of one of the back windows had been taken down and the sash thrown up. In about half an hour afterwards I examined the window most

[1] A short sword, originally hung from the belt – O.E.D.

Riverside Wapping, 1791

The Docks, Night Scene, by Gustave Doré

closely, and saw that the window shutter, which had been taken down, was marked with blood, apparently with the print of a hand. There was also blood upon the inside iron bar. When I first saw the window open I begged somebody would go upstairs and search the house, while I remained at the window. I stopped at the window to stop any retreat. Mr. Mallett, the Chief Clerk of the Shadwell Police, and two Police Officers, went with me to search for the offenders, but without effect, at different houses; in consequence of information that two suspicious persons had gone along Shadwell High Street. Soon after I got into the house I saw John Turner, who had, as I was informed, made his escape out of the window; and gave him in charge to the watchman.

Next the surgeon, Walter Salter, was sworn. He testified that he had inspected the bodies of the several parties deceased by the direction of the Coroner, and had found the following marks of violence on their bodies:

John Williamson – has a wound extending from the left ear to within two inches of the right, penetrating through the trachea or windpipe, and down to the vertebrae of the neck; and the tibia, or large bone of the left leg, fractured a little above the ankle, apparently from a fall, as if downstairs, because, had it been done by any other means, I think there must have been a laceration of the integuments; no marks of violence upon any other parts.

Elizabeth Williamson – the right temporal and parietal dreadfully fractured; apparently from a large poker, or some such instrument, comprehending nearly the whole of the right side of the head; the throat cut from ear to ear, through the windpipe etc; no marks of violence upon any other part.

Anna Bridget Harrington, the woman servant – the right parietal bone laid open about four inches in length and two inches in width, with the bones exposed; and the throat cut about four inches in length through the windpipe; no other marks of violence appear.

I conceive their throats to have been cut with a razor; as none but a sharp instrument could have cut so deep without tearing the parts; which is not the case in this instance; their throats being cut by one incision. On each of their bodies there is sufficient cause of death appearing.

The jury retired and at seven o'clock that evening, returned the expected verdict: wilful murder against some person or persons unknown.

The Williamsons and their maid were buried at twelve o'clock on Sunday 22 December, at St. Paul's Church, Shadwell.

The service [Fairburn reports] was read by the Reverend Mr. Denis in a most impressive manner and the feelings of the multitude were expressive of the deepest sorrow. The feelings of the Reverend Divine were so much overpowered that both in the church and at the grave the service was suspended for some minutes until he could recover himself. All the shops in the neighbourhood of the church were closed and the magistrates, having very judicially stationed a considerable number of officers in the churchyard, the service was conducted with the utmost solemnity and without the slightest disorder.

But all through Sunday the atmosphere of fear, suspicion and panic intensified. One of its victims was a young solicitor's clerk named Mellish, who worked in Old Jewry. He was sitting in the back parlour of the Three Foxes public house in Fox's Lane and talking about the murders with the nephew of the landlord, when they heard a watchman's rattle and a cry, 'Stop the murderers!' Mellish cried out, 'My God, there is more murder!' and each arming himself with a poker, they ran out into the street and joined in the pursuit of the suspects. Mellish could not keep up with his companion but followed as fast as he could. At the street corner he met three men running, 'two of whom were remarkably ill-looking fellows, and the third a very short man'. Supposing they were the men against whom the hue and cry had been raised, he said, 'You are the villains and I shall have at you' – a remarkably courageous defiance, considering he believed himself to be facing murderers, and the odds were three to one. He instantly levelled a blow with a poker at the head of the little man, but it had no effect other than to stun him for the moment. The man quickly recovered his feet and discharged a pistol of small shot into Mellish's face. His assailant made his escape and Mellish was carried back to the Three Foxes public house, his face appallingly disfigured and both eyes completely blinded. *The Times* reported that he remained in a very precarious state. We are not subsequently told whether he died or, less mercifully perhaps, survived the crude methods of early nineteenth-century surgery to eke out an existence as a blind and mutilated dependent. Either way he was a victim of the hysteria which was spreading like an infection among the dark alleys and courtways of Wapping and the neighbouring parishes.

On Monday morning the Shadwell Public Office again opened early for the examination of suspects. One of them was a young seafaring man named John Williams who lodged with Mr. and Mrs. Vermilloe at the Pear Tree public house in Old Wapping, by the river. He was arrested there on the Sunday by Hewitt and Hope, two of the police officers at Shadwell, who were acting on private information received – though from what source there is no record. Williams was taken to the watch house and searched. In his possession were two pawn tickets of eight shillings and twelve shillings for shoes, fourteen shillings in silver and a pound note. The date on the pawn tickets was not apparently thought worth noting.

The two police officers probably picked up this new suspect with no great hope that here at last was the man they sought. There had been so many suspects, so many false alarms, so many sanguine expectations that had come to nothing. They must by now have been carrying out their duties with dogged persistence but with diminishing hope of success. As they laid their hands on Williams's shoulders they could not have foreseen that the commonplace name of this somewhat frail and shabbily elegant young seaman would, in a few days time, be on the lips of all London.

John Williams was twenty-seven at the time of his arrest. *The Times*, a few days later, described him as 'about 5 feet 9 inches in height, of an insinuating manner and pleasing countenance'; and added, 'he is not lame'. He was an ordinary

seaman who had once sailed with Marr in the *Dover Castle,*
had returned from his last voyage in the East Indiaman the
Roxburgh Castle early in October 1811, and had gone immediately to stow his sea chest and take up his old lodgings
at the Pear Tree. This was his home in England and may
well have been the only home he had. He returned there after
all his voyages, paid over his earnings to Mr. Vermilloe as
banker, and was welcomed by Mrs. Vermilloe as an agreeable
and honest lodger, tidy about the house, considerate to her
personally and affable to her acquaintances, particularly the
females. He was superior in education and dress to the
ordinary seaman, wrote a good hand, and was fastidious
about his clothes and appearance. Not surprisingly he was
occasionally mistaken for a gentleman, an impression he did
nothing to dispel. He was a foppish young man, with a slim
figure and an abundance of fair hair of a remarkable and
unusual sandy colour which curled about a handsome, if
rather weak, face. He had an open manner, described as
agreeable by those susceptible to his attractions, usually
women, and as insinuating by those, usually men, who judged
by other criteria. Williams was extremely hot-tempered,
easily provoked into fights and brawls, and invariably he got
the worst of them. Men delighted to tease and incite him;
his reaction, particularly when he was in drink, was predictable
and to them, highly entertaining. Not surprisingly, perhaps,
he had an abundance of female acquaintances but few men
friends. Nothing was known of his family and antecedents,
but it was generally agreed that a young man so superior in
person and in education to an ordinary seaman must have
some secret in his past to account for his present way of life.

No doubt Williams considered life at the Pear Tree to be
somewhat beneath him, but a bed in a room shared with two
other seamen was all he could afford. The Pear Tree was a
typical riverside house catering for sailors. Its raucous life
centred on the tap-room; its yard was alive with the comings
and goings of riverside Wapping. There was a back room in
which the lodgers ate, and much of their personal washing was
done under the pump in the back yard, although Mrs.
Vermilloe's sister-in-law, Mrs. Rice, came in regularly to
wash linen for those who could afford to pay.

Like most sailors, Williams spent freely on his return to land, compensating for months of danger, hardship and lack of female company. There was little incentive to plan for the future. Not for him the subservience and diligence of a Marr, the months of servitude which might in time be rewarded by a small gratuity and the chance of a settled home. When the money was gone there was always the pawn shop or gambling at whist, cribbage, putt and all fours. And when no resources remained, there was another ship, another voyage. In the meantime London had plenty of amusement to offer; a bear baiting, a public hanging; an evening squiring a female acquaintance to the Royalty Theatre in Wellclose Square; nights of riotous tippling in the notorious 'cock and hen' clubs typical of the easy-going conviviality of the age, where young men and prostitutes met to drink and sing songs until the early hours. And when these amusements palled, the present seemed wearisome and the future bleak, there was always the solace of more drink. Drinking, gambling and debt; these were links in a chain which bound many of the poor to their misfortunes. The links were extremely hard to break and there is no evidence that Williams tried to break them.

From the account of Williams's first examination, given in *The Times* of 24 December, it is obvious that the case against him was no stronger than it was against a dozen other suspects who had been taken into custody; indeed there is an inference that he was unlucky not to have been released.

The seafaring man named John Williams underwent a very long and rigid interrogation. The circumstances of suspicion which were alleged against him were that he had been frequently seen at the house of Williamson the publican and that he had been more particularly seen there about seven o'clock on Thursday evening last; that on the same evening he did not go home to his lodgings until about twelve, when he desired a fellow lodger, a foreign sailor, to put out his candle; that he was a short man and had a lame leg; that he was an Irishman; and that previous to this melancholy transaction he had little or no money; and that when he was taken into custody he had a good deal of silver.

These suspicious circumstances having been proved against him the magistrates desired him to give an account of himself. He avowed that he had been at Mr. Williamson's on Thursday evening and at various other times. He had known Mr. and Mrs. Williamson a considerable time, and was very intimate there. On Thursday when he was talking to Mrs. Williamson she was very cheerful and patted him on the cheek when she brought him some liquor. He was considered rather in the light of a friend than a mere customer of the house. When he left their house he went to a surgeon's in Shadwell for the purpose of getting advice for the cure of his leg, which had been for a considerable number of years disabled in consequence of an old wound. From thence he went to a female chirurgeon in the same neighbourhood in the hopes of getting his cure completed at a less expense than a surgeon's charge. He then went further west and met some female acquaintance, and after visiting several public houses, he returned to his lodgings and went to bed. The circumstance of desiring his fellow lodger to put out his candle arose in consequence of his finding the man, who was a German, lying in bed with a candle in one hand, with a pipe in his mouth, and a book in the other. Seeing him in that situation and apprehending that the house might be set on fire by his carelessness, he told him to put out his light and not to expose the house to the danger of being burned to the ground. He accounted for the possession of the money found upon him as the produce of some wearing apparel he left as pledges at a pawnbroker's. He never made any mystery of his having been at Mr. Williamson's on Thursday evening; on the contrary, he told the landlady and several other people that he had been with poor Mrs. Williamson and her husband a short time before they were murdered, and remarked how cheerful Mrs. Williamson was.

The Times reports that 'under all the circumstances of the case' the prisoner was remanded for further examination. He was committed to Coldbath Fields Prison, where Sylvester Driscoll, the Irishman who had been arrested on the day following the murder of the Williamsons, was still confined.

An Excise Officer had corroborated Driscoll's story of how he came to possess a gallon of brandy and a quart of whisky; nevertheless, the magistrates were in no mood to discharge anyone, however slight the evidence might be, and Driscoll remained behind bars.

Meanwhile, the magistrates at the Whitechapel Public Office were pursuing their inquiries into the activities of the Portuguese. The two sailors Le Silvoe and Bernard Govoe, picked up over a week earlier, were still separately confined in Coldbath Fields Prison. Now, a friend of theirs called Anthony was brought up for examination. Someone had informed against him and it was then discovered that Anthony had left the neighbourhood and entered on board a West Indiaman which lay off Deal. An officer was dispatched to the ship and Anthony was identified and brought back to London to face the Whitechapel magistrates. The only suspicious circumstances alleged against him were that he was a friend of Le Silvoe and Bernard Govoe and had been seen with them about the time that Marr and his family were murdered; that the next or succeeding day he had enlisted on board the West Indiaman; and that the woman with whom he was living lied when questioned by her acquaintances, and still more so when examined by the officers. So the unfortunate Anthony joined his fellow-countrymen in Coldbath Fields Prison.

There was no real evidence against any of the three. They were Portuguese and they had been seen in Ratcliffe Highway shortly after the Marr murders. These two facts were sufficient to place them in peril. The magistrates had become infected by the prejudice of the mob. They were desperate and worried men, obsessed with the need to seem busy, and in their timidity, reluctant to release any suspect once he had been brought before them, for fear of letting loose a murderer. It seems that, to them, any activity, however unprofitable and ill-directed, was better than none.

The Irish fared no better than the Portuguese. Michael Harrington, William Austin and William Emery were picked up in Poplar on no better grounds than that the first looked and dressed like the man seen by Turner rifling Mrs. Williamson's pockets, and the second was short and lame. Emery was arrested with them, presumably because he was keeping doubtful company. He and Harrington stated that during the whole of the previous week they had been on board the *Astel,* East Indiaman, at Gravesend, where they were entered as seamen, and that they lodged with a Mr. Smith at No. 25 Angel Court, St. Martin's le Grand. Austin said that he was also a shipmate with the other two prisoners and had only been discharged the previous Saturday from King's Bench Prison, where he had been confined for about ten days.

It was obviously important to check the identity of the prisoners. On this occasion, however, it seems that the magistrates were short of officers, probably because they were out scouring the East End in search of tall or lame Irishmen, and a gentleman from the public gallery obligingly volunteered to visit St. Martin's le Grand to check part of the alibi. He set off immediately, no doubt with visions of public fame, if not of a substantial reward, but he had cause to regret his impetuosity. The address was that of a common lodging house, typical of the thousands which had sprung up in eighteenth-century London. It contained as many families as rooms, while the single lodgers, poor, illiterate and transient, paid one penny a night, or little more, for the privilege of lying together, sometimes fifteen or twenty in a bed. In these conditions the landlord could seldom vouch for his tenants, or the tenants know the name of their landlord. The landlord was not called Smith but there was a lodger who admitted to that name, although he disclaimed any knowledge of Harrington or Emery. After a dispiriting half-hour, the inquiring gentleman returned to Shadwell with his report. Since no satisfactory alibi was forthcoming the three Irishmen were remanded for further examination.

Meanwhile yet another gang, this time of seven, had been taken into custody, all apprehended in a house near Williamson's. In the possession of one of them were found two shirts, stained with marks which resembled blood, and a waistcoat with similar marks, the latter bearing on it the evident imprint of a pruning knife. All were found in a damp state as if they had been recently washed. The man in whose lodgings they were found stated that the marks were the stains of hop vines, as he had been employed as a hop picker during the last season in Kent. The seven men were, however, remanded in custody until the shirts and waistcoat could be inspected by a 'chemical gentleman' in order to ascertain whether the stains were those of an animal or vegetable substance. This is the first reference during the whole of the investigation to any scientific examination of evidence. Presumably the report of the 'chemical gentleman' was satisfactory, as the seven unfortunates were released next day, as were Harrington, Austin and Emery 'after confirmation of their story by the most satisfactory testimony' and a further man, Patrick Neale, taken up on suspicion at Deptford. All were discharged with an apology for their detention, and a congratulatory compliment on the removal of the suspicions attached to them. The magistrates were by now probably uneasily aware that they had yielded too easily to the prejudice of the mob. They found it prudent to declare 'their high satisfaction and approbation of the conduct of the Hibernian inhabitants of the Wapping district in their exertions to forward the view of the police in bringing the sanguinary wretches who have hitherto escaped to a just and exemplary punishment'.

It was Tuesday, Christmas Eve; and now the Whitechapel magistrates finally bowed out of the case with a piece of information as absurdly irrelevant as any that had come their way. A Hertfordshire magistrate arrived to report 'a very extraordinary circumstance which he thought might throw some light on the late shocking events'. A man named Bailey, a bricklayer's labourer from Norfolk, had been taken up on suspicion of felony. On searching the prisoner's room a considerable quantity of valuable plate was found, together with some blood-stained linen. This circumstance excited a suspicion that Bailey was concerned in the late murders and he accordingly underwent a stringent cross-examination. He denied all knowledge of the murders, declared his ignorance of any persons connected with them, and his unwillingness to impeach innocent persons. That same evening he was remanded in custody in Cheshunt, and the next morning, when the constables went to bring him up for further examination, he was found suspended from a beam by a silk handkerchief and quite lifeless. *The Times* states that 'the unfortunate man did not evince any intellectual derangement but that there was little doubt that the property found in his possession

was stolen from some gentleman's house in the neighbourhood'. This is very probable, but it is difficult to see why the
Hertfordshire magistrate should have connected Bailey with
the Marrs' or Williamsons' murders since nothing substantial
was stolen from either house. By now, however, any information, however irrelevant or incongruous, was received and
reported. Not only the London magistrates, but the whole
country was desperate for action. Even as far away as Portsea
and Portsmouth rewards for the apprehension of the murderers
were being raised by public subscription. They raised the total
amount offered to nearly £800, an unprecedented sum in those
days.

And then, still on Christmas Eve, it seemed that at long
last the vital break had come. Seventeen days after the murder
of the Marrs and four after the last hand-bill had been issued
describing the maul in detail, the weapon was identified – on
whose initiative it is not clear. And it is far from apparent
why it should have taken so long to trace a weapon clearly
stamped with the owner's initials. It may have been the landlord of the Pear Tree, Mr. Vermilloe, who recognised the
description. Certainly it was he to whom the final reward for
the maul's identification was paid. He was at that time a
prisoner in Newgate Prison for debt, and it was to the prison
that Capper bore his carefully packaged exhibit. Mr. Vermilloe
recognised it. He said that it belonged to a German sailor
from Hamburg named John Peterson, who had recently
lodged at the Pear Tree, and had left his chest of tools in
Vermilloe's keeping when he returned to sea. Most of the
tools were marked with Peterson's initials and Vermilloe,
although he would not commit himself to a positive identification, was almost certain that this maul had been among them.
He had used one of the mauls to chop wood, and had himself
broken the tip.

It must have been with satisfaction and profound relief
that Capper bore the maul and his good news back to Shadwell
Public Office. At last his efforts and those of his colleagues
seemed likely to be crowned with success. They had worked
indefatigably. They had sat at all hours examining suspects.
No information brought to them had been ignored. No clue
unexplored. All they had received for their pains had been

open criticism or muttered abuse. One might almost suppose that the mob held them personally responsible for the deaths of the Marrs and the Williamsons. But now success was surely in sight. The murder weapon, still stained with blood and matted with hair, had undeniably come from the Pear Tree. They already had in custody a suspect from the Pear Tree. The inference was obvious and inescapable. Markland thought it right to acquaint the Home Secretary with their tentative optimism and, at the same time, to remind Ryder of the zeal with which he and his colleagues were pursuing their inquiries:

Shadwell 24 Dec. 1811
7 o'clock.

Dear Sir,

The whole day has been spent on examining men brought to this office on different suspicions; we cannot yet say that we have sufficient clues to lead to a discovery: there is one man who we are going to examine this evening on whom suspicion is rather strong: should anything transpire you shall have the earliest information from

Dear Sir
Yrs very sincerely
Geo. Markland.

That evening, shortly after seven o'clock, John Williams was brought up into the crowded courtroom of the Public Office. The candlelit interrogation and the examination of witnesses was typical of its kind. It demonstrates some of the defects and injustices of the system, and the almost unmitigated power of the magistrates to conduct an inquiry in the manner they chose. Their function was primarily inquisitorial. Their only judicial function was the committal of the prisoner for trial if the case against him was sufficiently strong, and it was they who decided on the strength of the case. There were no rules of evidence. The magistrates asked any question which seemed to them likely to elicit the truth, or which took their fancy. Prisoners were allowed, even encouraged to incriminate themselves. Hearsay evidence was admitted. Overt prejudice by witnesses, partiality, insinuations and malice went unrebuked. Irrelevant and uncorroborated information was freely given and often accepted.

The prisoner was not represented by a lawyer or friend, nor was he permitted to be present to hear the evidence. Consequently he was often unaware of the strength of the case building up against him.

Nor were all the proceedings in open court. A magistrate could order a witness to be brought to his house, and could there interrogate him in private. He could visit a witness in prison, as Capper had visited Vermilloe. It is probable that only a small minority of the magistrates were corrupt. Most were honest and conscientious, anxious to get at the truth. But truth was too often an early casualty in the undisciplined and prejudiced courts over which they presided.

The Morning Post published on Christmas Day, reported the proceedings extensively. John Turner again described the man he saw. He stated:

> While he was going downstairs he was sure he heard a man walking slowly in the sitting-room, and that his shoes creaked, and that he was confident the man could not have nails in his shoes. When he got to the door he only saw one man in the position, and dressed in the manner, described in his examination before the Coroner.
>
> The prisoner was here brought forward and the magistrates particularly questioned the witness, whether he thought the prisoner at the bar was the man? The witness could not state that he was, but said that he had seen him two or three times in Williamson's house. He did not know whether he was in the house on Thursday night last.

It is interesting to follow the working of the magistrates' minds by observing the order in which they called their witnesses. Clearly they hoped that Turner, their key witness, would identify Williams as the murderer. But whether or not he did, some confirmatory evidence would be desirable. The killer of Williamson and Marr must have been blood-stained, and might well have sent his blood-stained clothing to be washed. So, hopefully, they called Williams's laundress.

Mary Rice was examined. She washed for the prisoner for more than three years. She knew his stock of linen perfectly well, but had not washed for him for the last fortnight.

The magistrates here rigidly examined the witness.

Q. Have you not seen blood on his shirts?

Yes, I have. On one of them.

Q. Have you seen any blood on his shirts since last Saturday week?

Yes, I have. One of his shirts was bloody about the collar, like the mark of two fingers.

Q. Was there no other part stained?

I took no particular notice; his shirt was torn at the breast.

Q. Did you not take notice of the shirt being torn?

Yes, but judged the prisoner had been quarrelling – he might have had the shirt torn.

Q. When was it you had this shirt without being torn?

Last Thursday week.

Q. Will you swear there were no other marks of blood on the shirt?

There was a little blood on the arms and several spots on other parts of the body; but, taking no particular notice at the time, I washed it and kept the shirt in order to mend it.

Q. Have you washed out all the stains?

I think I must, for I boiled it well in hot water.

Q. What linen have you generally washed for the prisoner?

Four linen shirts and some stockings; but never any white handkerchiefs. The prisoner used to wear black handkerchiefs.

(The prisoner wore a white neck handkerchief on his examination.)

To be meaningful, this passage needs to be read with other newspaper accounts of Mrs. Rice's evidence. The *London Chronicle* makes it clear that the washerwoman (who was Mrs. Vermilloe's sister-in-law) was speaking of two shirts she had washed for Williams. The first – 'which was very much torn about the neck and breast, and had a good deal of blood on it about the neck and arms; she supposed he had been fighting . . . was before the murder of Mr. Marr, but the second was four or five days afterwards'. This 'was also very much torn, and marks of blood on it, which appearances she attributed likewise to fighting. . . . She remembered the prisoner's fighting in her house with a lodger of hers, and that then he had a shirt torn to rags, but this was three weeks back.'

The examination of Mrs. Rice brings out several points. It shows the crude nature of the interrogation of witnesses, the readiness of the magistrates to ask leading questions, and their extraordinary naïvety in assessing the evidential value of a torn and bloody shirt. It shows too, that they were clearly confused between the two crimes. Mrs. Rice had washed Williams's bloody shirt four or five days after the murder of the Marrs, but before the murder of the Williamsons. It could have no relevance, therefore, to the crime on which Williams was taken up. And, apart from the likelihood of a murderer sending his bloody shirt to his own washerwoman, what was the significance of the tear? Williamson struggled with his assailant; and the killer's clothes on this occasion must have been blood-stained, and might well have been torn. But the Marrs were annihilated with ferocious suddenness, and it is unlikely that any of that pathetically unaware household put up a fight. The evidence of Williams's shirt points clearly to a tavern brawl some time before the murders at the King's Arms.

Mrs. Vermilloe, the landlady of the Pear Tree, was next examined. The *Morning Post* reported:

Q. Is your husband in confinement?

Yes, he is in prison for a debt of £20, and has been for seven weeks.

Q. Is there a chest of tools in your house?

Yes. It belonged to a person now gone abroad. She had never looked into it; knew it contained two or three mauls; one of them her husband sometimes used, and it lay in the yard.

Q. Did you ever notice the marks on the mauls?

Yes, on one or two. They were marked J.P., and belonged to one of her lodgers who had gone abroad since February last. His name was John Peterson.

Q. Did you ever know the mauls were missing?

Not till Monday, when there was enquiries made.

Q. Could you identify the maul if you saw it?

I don't know.

The magistrates here ordered the fatal maul to be produced. The witness was extremely agitated and burst into tears. After some pause and a chair being handed to her she recovered from her fright.

Q. On your oath will you say that this is not the maul?

I don't know.

Q. Will you swear it is the maul?

I can't say.

Mr. Markland – Is the maul similar to the one you have seen in your house?

Yes, it is something like it.

According to the *London Chronicle* reporter other material points came out during Mrs. Vermilloe's cross-examination. She said that she had known the prisoner 'for some years'. There had been two or three mauls in Peterson's tool chest three weeks ago, but within that time they had disappeared. 'The box which contained them was always unlocked, and anybody in the house might have access to it. It was in the same room where the prisoner's sea-bed was deposited.' When the maul was produced Mrs. Vermilloe 'shrunk back with horror and consternation. It was with great difficulty she could be got to look at it steadily'. But then the washerwoman jumped to her feet:

Mrs. Rice interposed, and said, that her little boys could speak positively as to the identity of the maul, as she had frequently heard them describe a broken-pointed maul with which they used to play in the square before their aunt's door.

The boys were sent for. During the absence of the messenger, the prisoner begged to account for the manner in which the shirt, given to the laundress on Friday night fortnight, became torn and stained with blood. He said he had been dancing with his coat and waistcoat off, at the house where he lodged, about half past eleven o'clock at night; and his sport being stopped by the watchman, he had retired thus undressed to the Royal Oak to treat his musician. In the Royal Oak he met with a number of Irish coal-heavers playing at cards, and they insisted on his playing with them. He consented, after much entreaty, and lost a shilling's worth of liquor. He was then for retiring peremptorily, when a scuffle ensued between him and one of the party, who seized him by the shirt collar, which he tore, and then struck him a blow in the mouth, which cut his lip, and from that wound issued the blood which stained his shirt.

The magistrates told him to confine himself to the shirt found bloody on Thursday week, to which caution he paid no apparent attention.

The *Morning Post* reported the examination of the next two witnesses as follows:

Michael Cuthperson and *John Harrison*, the prisoner's fellow lodgers at the Pear Tree, stated that the prisoner came home on the morning of the murder about one o'clock. Cuthperson was in bed but not asleep. The watchman was going past one o'clock. He was positive that the prisoner said, 'For God's sake put out the light, or else something will happen' – but was not certain whether it was the same morning as the Marrs' murder[1]. Harrison went to bed about twelve and awoke when the prisoner came home, but did not take notice of the prisoner. They all slept in the same room.

The maul was then produced. Harrison thought it was like one that the children had played with in the yard.

It was then that the eleven-year-old William Rice made his appearance and came excitedly into court. His evidence was important. Children, and particularly boys, are usually excellent witnesses. They have a keen eye, a retentive memory for anything which interests them; and, being untroubled by the irrational doubts and divided loyalties which can afflict their elders, usually give their evidence simply and without self-consciousness. William was such a lad. When he took the stand Mrs. Vermilloe burst into tears so vehemently that she had to be taken out of the court. Mrs. Vermilloe's histrionics must have added to the drama of the occasion, but they would hardly have made the task of the magistrates any easier. But William was unaffected by his aunt's distress. The magistrates eyed him sternly but benevolently and, before showing him the maul, cunningly asked William to describe it. This he did, mentioning the broken tip. The weapon was then produced. The child carelessly took it up, tried to carry it, and looked on it with what the *Morning Post* described as 'the most composed innocence'. The magistrates asked him if this was the same hammer with which he and his brother had played. He said it was. He had not seen it for about a month, but he was positive that this was the maul with which he had played at being a carpenter – 'and he dared to say that his brother would say the same'.

William Rice was the last witness examined. It was very late by now, the heat of the crowded courtroom was oppressive and the magistrates, conferring softly together, decided that it was time for the hearing to be adjourned. At this point the prisoner attempted to speak, but the *Morning Post*

[1] Either the witness or the reporter was confused. From the first examination of Williams it is apparent that the candle incident related to the night of the murder of the Williamsons.

reported that 'the first question he asked was of such a
tendency that he was desired to desist'.

What did John Williams say to provoke the magistrates to
silence him? Did he shout out an accusation against someone
who was considered above suspicion? Was he provoked into
abuse or defiance by tiredness, the lateness of the hour? By
frustration that he was ignorant of the strength of the case
building up against him? We shall never know. He was taken
back to Coldbath Fields Prison. The courtroom cleared.
Carriages were summoned, horses brought by grooms to the
door. The poor of Wapping made their way home through the
darkness in companiable groups, talking over the evidence,
speculating fearfully on the future. The magistrates went home
to their late dinners in the comforting knowledge that they
had finished a good evening's work. And tomorrow was
Christmas Day.

In the year 1811, *The Times* was published as usual on
Christmas Day. It cost sixpence halfpenny – the equivalent
of forty pence today – and for this the reader was offered
four pages, each containing five columns of print. Of the
twenty columns published on 25 December 1811, eleven were
taken up with advertisements; one and a half were devoted
to an angry letter from *Publicos* denouncing, with a wealth
of Latin, a Christmas production at Westminster School of
Terence's *Adrian;* a further one and a half columns covered
dispatches from James Monroe in Washington; there was a
brief dispatch from Wellington in the Peninsular, and a
column describing a dinner given in Dublin by the Catholics of
Ireland to the friends of Religious Liberty. There were only
two news headlines. One, captioned *Nottingham, December
22nd,* led a quarter of a column of print about the activities
of the Luddites. The other, *Murders in New Gravel Lane,*
covered two whole columns, setting out the evidence given
before the Shadwell magistrates on Christmas Eve. Perhaps
it was as well, for otherwise the various authorities all over
the country who were avidly collecting clues and examining
witnesses would have had no means of knowing what had
happened at the central point, Shadwell.

The Times contained no reference at all to Christmas in
its news columns, and only a few references in its advertisements. T. Bish (Contractor) offered lottery tickets as Christmas
presents with the prospect of a £20,000 win; his slogan:
'the tickets are few, the prizes numerous'. A bookseller of
Paternoster Row begged leave to announce 'to the Nobility,
Country and Public in General, that he has recently printed
the following little Books for the amusement and instruction
of Youth. . . . The History of Little Ellen, or the Naughty
Girl Reclaimed: a story exemplified in a Series of Figures,

6/6d. coloured . . . .' There were plenty of patent medicines offered, and tucked away discreetly in a corner at the bottom of the back page:

> Currie and Co continue, with unabated ardour, the eradication of those disorders which are the consequence of illicit indulgence. In professing the cure of these complaints they hold out no inducement to vice, but sensible as all men must be of the existence of such calamities, they offer their assistance as regularly educated Surgeons of London and of the Royal College of Edinburgh. In all cases of Syphilitic infection, and in every complaint of Debility, whether arising from destructive habits, long residence in a warm climate, free living or any other cause, the patient may rely on a speedy restoration to vigorous health.

More topical, however, was a prominently displayed advertisement in Christmas week:

> Guns, pistols, Blunderbusses etc. – To be SOLD, for about half the first cost, several beautiful DOUBLE and SINGLE BARREL GUNS, by Maston, and all the best makers; excellent Air Guns, Holster Pistols or Muskets and every other bore, House Pistols and Blunderbusses, with or without bayonets; house cutlasses and swords, and pocket pistols of every sort, from two to fourteen barrels the pair. The whole are warranted, and a trial allowed, or exchanged within twelve months. A great quantity of the best Dartford gunpowder, also flints and every kind of shooting tackle.

In 1811 Christmas was still a religious rather than a commercial feast. There were no Christmas cards, and although it had from ancient times been the custom to decorate houses with ivy and bay leaves, no one in England had yet adopted the German tradition of lighting the greenery with candles. The old-fashioned Christmas feasts described by Addison and Smollet (a century before Dickens 'invented' Christmas) still survived in rural parts, and country squires who had recently set up houses in London tried to keep up something of the tradition of hospitality. The emphasis was on vast quantities of food and drink, though this year public-spirited men had contributed their share towards the defeat of Napoleon by undertaking not to drink French wines. Prisoners were not forgotten. By direction of the Lord Mayor those in the City were to receive 'one pound of beef, a pint of porter, and half a threepenny loaf each, pursuant to annual custom'. For one lad, though, it was all too much. The *London Chronicle* records:

Gluttony. – Tuesday morning a journeyman weaver, at Bethnal Green, engaged, for a trifling wager, to eat 4lbs. of fat bacon raw, 4 lbs. of boiled potatoes, and half a quartern loaf, and to drink two pots of porter, and a pint of gin, within one hour, which he completed six minutes under the time, but was soon after taken with violent sickness, and is not expected to survive.

To the poor and starving cooped up in the slums of Wapping and Shadwell this Christmas brought nothing but fear and misery. The Bill of Mortality for the London parishes for the last week of 1811, with its catalogue of *ague, cowpox, eaten by lice, flux, French pox, gravel, grief, jawlocked,* and *tissick* is a poignant and grotesque record of the afflictions of the age. It was published to warn the Court and nobility of any dangerous epidemic or infectious disease, and they could hardly have been reassured by the figures that year of sixty-eight deaths from consumption and ten from smallpox. Most of the dead were the commonplace victims of disease, poverty, ignorance and neglect. It was the footnote to the table which struck cold to the heart this Christmas Day: 'Murdered – three at St. Paul's, Shadwell'.

Panic was still very near the surface. In Greenwich it broke out. *The Times* reported:

Greenwich was thrown into great consternation during divine service on Christmas Day; but it was in the Church the panic spread most effectually. While the clergyman was reading the Litany, the alarm drum beat to arms. The congregation were struck with amazement and horror, and everyone trembling for his friends and home, apprehensive the murderers were in the neighbourhood. Scarcely had the first moments of surprise and enquiries passed when the Sexton stood up in the Church, and after solemnly demanding silence with an 'O YEZ! O YEZ!', said, 'This is to give notice, that the commander of the River Fencibles[1] desires every man will repair to his post, there to do his duty.' The horror now was at its height; the only doubt was whether the French had landed or assassins were murdering and robbing in the town. All flew out of the Church, and in the scramble several were hurt, but none seriously. It was found that a large party of Irishmen, who had been drinking freely, had quarrelled; but whether with the town's-people or among themselves was difficult to ascertain; for it appeared, that they did not much care with whom they quarrelled, so that they could get in a little fighting, and that they had been knocking down and insulting every person they met. The River Fencibles having assembled, seized about fifteen of the ringleaders, whom they conveyed on board a tender, and the others found it prudent to sneak out of the way.

Such vulgar panic left Whitehall unmoved. The Home Office disdained to acknowledge its existence. A murder or two, more or less, in the turbulent East End raised no eyebrows. As for the current stories in the newspapers of multiple massacres, they were so wild as to be almost certainly exaggerated, or even totally false. The word went round the Department that the whole thing was an elaborate hoax, made up by journalists starved for copy. Crimes on such a scale were inherently implausible; and the Home Office, at least, was not going to be taken in. This, at all events, is what was being rumoured about Ryder's apathetic Department. 'It is said,' *The Times* complained on Boxing Day, 'that at the Secretary of State's Office an affectation prevails of discrediting the published accounts, and treating them as insertions to amuse or terrify the public.'

However that may be, the Department opened as usual

---

[1] The River Fencibles comprised a sort of Home Guard to man the Martello Towers in case of invasion. Service was popular as a means of avoiding regular service in the Navy.

on Christmas Day and Ryder found a job for his eighteen clerks. Whatever his staff may have been saying, he at least was beginning to take his responsibilities more seriously. For two weeks he had been badgered by correspondents from all over the country to do something effective about the reform of the police, and feeling was running high in London. For an ambitious politician action of some sort was imperative. Ryder talked to Beckett, the Under-Secretary, and was persuaded, as ministers have been before and since, that anything precipitate would be a mistake. First it would be prudent to find out the facts: how many watchmen were actually employed in the various parishes in the Metropolis, how many additional parish patrols had been recruited, and how much were they all paid? So the order went out – the Home Secretary wanted a fact-finding circular to be sent immediately to the seven Public Offices.

Then, somewhere down the line, the purpose of the inquiry was lost. Perhaps it arrived during the office Christmas party; no one saw, or cared to find out, the point of the inquiry. But one of the older clerks remembered that the information had already been obtained – in 1804 wasn't it? A quick check of the letter book confirmed the date. The returns must be somewhere in the office. But Christmas Day was no time to hunt in the registry for papers seven years old. It was surely more sensible to spread the work and ask the magistrates' clerks to send in a duplicate. So a circular duly went out to the seven Public Offices, dated 25 December 1811, referring to a letter of 19 November 1804 and requesting, 'for Mr. Ryder's information, with the least possible delay, a Duplicate of the returns made by the Office to the letter above-mentioned'. The magistrates' clerks, accepting that requests from Government departments were necessarily arbitrary and incomprehensible, and taking the sensible view that it was less exhausting to comply than to argue, searched their files and wrote out in their careful copperplate the names and addresses of watchmen long since forgotten and some, no doubt, dead. It was not until the replies began to come in on Boxing Day that a second circular had to be hurried out, requesting information about the numbers currently employed. Both requests were signed by Beckett, but the second circular did not withdraw the first; so the magistrates obediently forwarded two sets of returns, one of them seven years out of date. As far as the investigation of the murders was concerned, the up-to-date information was as useless as the old.

The *London Chronicle,* sensitive to the public mood, devoted the whole of its leader on Christmas Day to the subject, *Police of the Metropolis.* The recent murders 'called loudly for some serious revision' of the system. The watchmen and constables were not to be blamed as individuals. They were victims of a system ludicrously inadequate for a great metropolis 'where characters of every cast and degree of human depravity, and where villainy, in every form and shape is to be found. . . . Where the very improvements and advantages of civilised society serve to add fuel to the passions; where beings are to be found whose moral feelings have never been brought into action, and who know not God, and who fear not eternity, who have been brought up in the principles of the first murderer, Cain, their hands against everyone.' The writer recalled fears canvassed when the Public Offices had been set up in 1792, each with its tiny quota of police officers, that the police were 'already sufficiently inquisitorial and intermeddling, and that there could be no extension of its powers without some compromise of the liberty of the subject'. The risk must now be taken, and taken urgently. 'Is a man to retire with his family in tranquillity to their repose, or are their beds to be haunted at night with images of midnight murderers, and their hours of rest contaminated by dreams of blood?'

Many Londoners were asking such questions, and they were coming up with immediate, practical answers. If neither Government nor magistracy would protect them they would protect themselves. Ever since the week-end, when the full shock of the Williamsons' murders had sunk in, men had been arming themselves with swords, pistols, cutlasses, any weapon on which they could lay their hands. It was a spontaneous reaction, in line with a long tradition in un-policed England, where self-help was often the only help in times of trouble. Already some 500 voluntary associations existed for the mutual protection of their members, and an association formed in Barnet in 1784 was held out as something of a model; it employed several 'police officers' to patrol the district in order to drive thieves off elsewhere. The following notice was typical of many which were being nailed to the doors of churches and public houses in London:

TO THE INHABITANTS OF LONG-ALLEY, AND PLACES ADJACENT

In these Times, so alarming to every peaceable Inhabitant of the Metropolis. – When MURDER stalks abroad with Fury, equal to the Banditties of the Forests of Germany. – When the late ferocious and horrid Massicrees, plainly indicate that among us are Monsters, not to be surpassed even by the most barbarous Nations. – When the list of Robberies, daily announced from our Police-Offices, are so numerous, that they bid defiance to our Laws; and when we find a Coroner declaring 'Our houses are no longer to be deemed our Castles!!' we are imperiously called upon to be personally the Guardians of our Families and Properties.

A Meeting, for the above Purposes, will be held at MR. BULL'S the CASTLE, Long-Alley, on Friday next, at Seven o'Clock in the Evening, precisely, to adopt some Measures, for carrying the same into effect, when it is earnestly requested the Inhabitants will attend.
Dec. 24, 1811.

On the morning of Christmas Day the inhabitants of Shadwell assembled to form their own association. They passed a resolution thanking the vestry for their promptness in offering a reward following 'the late horrid Murders in New Gravel Lane', declaring the watchmen to be 'entirely inadequate', and establishing a patrol of 'thirty-six able-bodied men of good character' to be divided into two companies of eighteen men each. They were to be armed with pistols and cutlasses, and were to be paid twelve shillings a week; absentees were to be summoned before the magistrates. Both companies were to be on duty every night, relieving one another at midnight. One of the trustees appointed to supervise the arming of the patrol was George Fox, who lived opposite the King's Arms, and had helped Anderson to break in after the alarm was given. Fox was a local stalwart, much respected in the community. He was a steward of the Universal Medical Institution in New Gravel Lane, a charity which gave advice and medicines to the poor at a dispensary or in their own home 'with the benefit of cold, warm and vapour baths', and which did much to alleviate the wretchedness of the sick poor. It was natural that he should now play a leading part in the community's defence.

The Shadwell magistrates, however, were not idle on Christmas Day either. In the morning a City Alderman named Wood called on Capper, and according to the *London Chronicle* he 'stated information which was of great importance'. The same afternoon the two of them carried a grisly parcel to Newgate Prison, containing the maul and the ripping chisel found at the Williamsons; and for the second time they interrogated Vermilloe about them. Mrs. Vermilloe was there already, consoling her husband for his Christmas in prison. Now both of them, reported the next day's *Times,*

. . . underwent a very minute examination: the result of which has afforded a clue towards tracing the murders home to the offenders. Mrs. Vermilloe, who was so much affected by the sight of the maul on Tuesday night that her evidence was very inconclusive, gave to the worthy Alderman, in an unembarrassed manner, the decisive information tion as to the identity of that blood-stained instrument. It turns out that the prisoner in custody has gone by another name besides Williams; and that, instead of being a Scotchman, as he represented himself to be to the Magistrates of Shadwell Office, he is a native of Ireland. Other matters came out, which prudence requires to be withheld from publicity, until the further examination of the prisoner shall take place before the Magistrates of Shadwell Police Office. Mr. Alderman Wood and Mr. Alderman Atkins called yesterday at the Office in Shadwell and remained in conference with the Magistrates there for two or three hours upon this subject.

Mrs. Vermilloe's change of attitude at this meeting is interesting. She had spent the morning with her husband, and they must have spoken of little else but the murders. He probably convinced her where the interest of both of them lay. The initials punched on the maul, together with William Rice's evidence, proved conclusively that the weapon had come from Peterson's chest of tools. To persist in equivocation might only expose them to suspicion. Besides, there was a substantial reward at stake, and Vermilloe saw no reason why at least part of it should not come his way. There was no need to volunteer information, but to deny facts which were plain to everyone could only antagonise the magistrates and jeopardise their chance of reward. Under the influence of her husband, Mrs. Vermilloe conquered the repugnance which the maul aroused in her and confirmed the identification.

The Times reporter was interested in the maul; the *London Chronicle* man, meanwhile, had ferreted out something about the ripping chisel:

> The conference was private and continued until four o'clock in the evening. Mr. Vermilloe gave testimony to the instrument called a *ripping hook,* being found among the chest of tools deposited in his house. We must here remind our readers that this said ripping hook, about two feet in length, was found by the side of Mrs. Williamson (*sic*), and it is the same which Mr. V. has deposed that he knew perfectly well the instrument. Mr. Vermilloe has likewise given information of another man whom he conceives must be concerned in the late inhuman murders.
>
> The Magistrates immediately forwarded directions to the different officers to go in pursuit, and late last night every exertion was used to find out the man alluded to; and we have the pleasure to state, no doubts are entertained of his detection.
>
> As far as can be officially learned, there were only two men concerned in both of the atrocious murders. The fact of Williams having been seen running up the alley by the side of Williamson's house, after the alarm was given, it is said, is likely to be proved by a person of the name of Johnson, at the next examination of Williams.

Here was progress. Mr. Vermilloe had given a tip-off about another man besides Williams. Presumably he also lodged at

the Pear Tree, or at all events had access to Peterson's tools.
Vermilloe would have no difficulty in identifying him, and
the prospects of his detection were said to be first class.
Already bands of police officers were scouring London for
him. There were believed to be two men concerned in the
murder of the Williamsons. Assuming John Williams to have
been one of them, the other must be the tall man Turner
had seen bending over Mrs. Williamson's body – the same
man who, according to Johnson, had been running up
New Gravel Lane towards Ratcliffe Highway soon after the
alarm was given, and who had called out to his shorter companion (Williams?): 'Come along Mahoney (or Hughey) come
along.'

It was a little too easy. The mysterious man Vermilloe spoke
of had yet to be found, and how reliable, anyway was the
prisoner's word? Further, if as expected Johnson identified
one of the men who had been seen running up New Gravel
Lane as Williams, then he must have been the shorter of the
two; and on Johnson's own account this shorter man was
addressed by his companion as Mahoney or Hughey. Neither
of these names could have been mistaken for John or Williams.
Perhaps there was a simple explanation: Williams was now
said to have been born in Ireland, and not Scotland, as he
claimed; so his real name might be one of those which Johnson
had heard. Yet even if this were true it would still leave
another fact unexplained. Given that there were two men
concerned in the Williamsons' murder, and that they were the
same two who were seen running up towards Ratcliffe Highway, what became of the footprint discovered on the clay
bank behind the King's Arms? What of the open window, and
the blood on the sill? Whoever escaped at the back of the
house would surely never have been so stupid as to double
round to the front, where the crowd was gathering to watch
Turner's dramatic descent. So perhaps there were three
murderers? Or could it be that the two men Johnson saw
had had nothing to do with the matter after all?

Aaron Graham, meanwhile, had been spending part of his
Christmas Day on the case, investigating the activities of yet
another Irishman, this time with the suspicious name of
Maloney. Could this be one of the men Johnson had seen?

Early in the morning he received a letter from Captain Taylor, of the frigate *Sparrow,* lying off Deptford. Taylor reported that Maloney had joined the ship a few days earlier, and that he answered the description of one of the murderers – he did not say which. Graham sent Police Officer Bacon to arrest the man and fetch him to London. They returned in the evening. Being Christmas Day the court was closed, so Graham interrogated the prisoner in his own house next door. He was not satisfied with Maloney's story, and had him locked up for the night in a watch box.

The weather that Christmas was fine but cold. The temperature barely rose above freezing point all day, and at eleven o'clock at night there were four degrees of frost. A raw chill from the river settled over Wapping, matching the mood of countless terrified families huddling for warmth and security in the dismal jungle beneath the shadow of the great dock wall, only one thought in their minds – was Williams the only murderer? How soon would he swing? Would he hang alone or with others? What a spectacle that would be, the greatest hanging since Patch was turned off, the greatest ever.

The magistrates, though, in their superior, guarded houses, could begin to relax. With John Williams safely locked up in the Coldbath Fields Prison, Maloney confined in a tiny watch box, Driscoll still behind bars as a precaution, and Vermilloe ready to talk his way out of Newgate, they might surely settle down that night to a well-earned Christmas dinner and banish, for an hour or two, the dark horror of the past fortnight. Perhaps some relaxed; but one, at all events, could not get the case out of his mind. All day, whenever he had ventured out into the streets, he had been accosted by angry, anxious people demanding to know why nothing was happening; and even now, at eleven o'clock, armed men muffled in great-coats patrolled the frozen streets. The pressure on a magistrate was becoming unbearable, particularly a magistrate who happened also to be an artist, a poet, a novelist and a dramatist.

Joseph Moser, of Worship Street Public Office, was all these. At sixty-three he had long turned from painting to the composition of 'many political pamphlets, dramas and works of fiction, which,' a scrupulous contributor to the *Dictionary of*

National Biography had to admit, 'enjoyed but a temporary popularity'. However, his duties as a magistrate he performed with 'zeal and ability'. This zeal Moser now displayed in a letter to the Home Office ostentatiously headed:

Spital Square, 25th Decr. 1811
11 o'clock P.M.

Dear Sir,

I received your circular letter this evening and, as you will see, have not lost any time in sending to you, for the information of Mr. Secretary Ryder, the 'Duplicate of the returns made by the Office of Worship Street of the number of Watchmen and Parish Patrole employed in this district, agreeable to a letter of J. King Esq dated 19th of November, 1804', which is, I believe, the paper required, and which I am very glad to transmit as the minds of the people here are in a state of very considerable apprehension inasmuch as I cannot go out of doors but I am assailed with enquiries whether the Murderers are taken? I have had several suspicious persons brought before me but have, upon examination, discharged them. I have written to the Mayor of Norwich respecting a man named Bonnett,[1] whom I sent our officers to Chesunt to bring to town, but when they arrived there they found he had just hung himself in the Cage. This man I strongly suspect had some concern in the late Murders. Though the alarms in this district are, as I have observed, great, yet everything is perfectly quiet. Our officers patrole the streets and examine the public houses every night, and of course, report to me, but at the same time I could hope that, in order to repress anxiety, we were able to make more effectual exertions: yet even these will require some caution in their operation, or they may increase the alarm that they are intended to repress.

I have with honour to be
With great respect,
Dear Sir, your very obedient
Humble Servant
JOSEPH MOSER

[1] *Alias* Bailey – p.96

Next day – Boxing Day – the cold weather continued, and it began to sleet. The Shadwell magistrates ordered the fires in the Public Office to be well stacked up for another long day's hearing – the last, surely, before the committal of Williams on charges of multiple murder? Five witnesses had been summoned to attend, and a sixth, almost certainly a key witness, was eagerly awaited from Marlborough. In addition a woman named Orr, who lived next door to the Pear Tree, was volunteering an extraordinary story that purported to connect Williams with yet a third ripping chisel. Partly as a result of Vermilloe's help, it seemed, the clues to the whole mystery were now fast falling into place. That morning *The Times* reported:

> The mystery which has so long concealed the perpetrators of these crimes, seems now, ere long, likely to be removed. A trend of important circumstances have been discovered within the last eight and forty hours. In the course of yesterday morning, information was received at Shadwell Police Office, from Marlborough in Wiltshire, that a man of very remarkable appearance was detained in custody by the Magistrates of that town, under strong circumstances of suspicion. The description given of him was that he was remarkably tall, and answered precisely the appearance of the man who was seen to run up Gravel Lane, along with a shorter man, just after the alarm of murder was given. His apparel had been examined and upon one of the shirts were found a considerable number of blood stains, and the shirt itself was very much torn about the breast and neck. Other circumstances have transpired which tend still further to clear up every doubt of his identity. A private correspondence has been discovered between him and the man already in custody, which clearly connects them with the shocking transactions. The Magistrates despatched Willans and Hewitt down to Marlborough from whence they are expected to return this evening with their prisoner.

The magistrates' patience must have been severely tested while they waited for this next villain – for here, beyond doubt surely, must be the tall man seen running up New

Coldbath Fields Prison, 1814

'Ignominious exposure of the Body of that inhuman Murderer, John Williams, alias John Murphey, on the last day of the year 1811'

Gravel Lane towards Ratcliffe Highway just after the murder of the Williamsons? Every suspicious circumstance pointed to it: his build, appearance, the bloody and torn shirt, above all, the 'private correspondence' with the prisoner. Meanwhile routine examinations must proceed. The police officers who searched the Pear Tree had picked up yet another suspect who lodged there. Was this the result of yet another tip-off from Vermilloe?

John Frederick Richter, a young foreign seaman, who resided at the Pear Tree Public House, where also John Williams lodged, was brought in custody to the Office by Butler and Holbrook.

The circumstances of suspicion lodged against him were in consequence of a pair of blue trousers having been found under his bed, in a damp state, with the appearance of mud having been imperfectly washed away from the knees downwards. The prisoner, when called upon to explain this circumstance, said that the trousers in question were left behind at the Pear Tree public house, by a man who had gone to sea. As nobody claimed them, he appropriated them to his own use. He knew of no mud upon them. None had touched them while in his possession; and although he acknowledged having brushed, he denied ever having washed them. He was then strictly examined with respect to his knowledge of Williams. He said he had known Williams about twelve weeks, but not intimately. He never drank with him out of the house, and only now and then held intercourse with him in the Pear Tree Public House. There was a chest of tools in the house belonging to a foreigner named John Peterson. There were several mauls amongst other tools, none of which he had seen in the last three weeks. He was then shown the maul which was found in Mr. Marr's house, which he said was exactly like the one he had seen amongst Peterson's tools. Peterson had marked his tools with the initials J.P., and upon looking at the same initials about this instrument, he verily believed it was the same he had seen at the Pear Tree. He did not know that Williams was an Irishman from his conversation but he had heard other persons say so. He remembered that Williams had large whiskers three or four days before he was taken up, but when he saw him last he did not take particular notice of any alteration in his face. On the night of the murder of Mr. Williamson and his family,[1] he heard a knock at the door a little before one o' clock, and he was afterwards told it was Williams. He never heard Williams ask his landlady for a loan of sixpence. He did not think Williams was a mariner from his appearance, but he had heard that he was employed on board the *Roxburgh Castle,* Indiaman. He had also heard that the Captain of that vessel had observed, that if Williams ever went on shore again, he would surely be hanged. This was in allusion to his bad character on board the ship.

The witness seemed, through the whole of his examination, to answer the questions put to him with great unwillingness, and appeared as if he wished to hold back information within his knowledge. The Magistrates cautioned him to be careful about what he said, and encouraged him not to be at all afraid of speaking the truth from any apprehension of the consequences. He still, however, proceeded in his taciturnity upon some interrogatories tendered to him.

The *Morning Chronicle* brought out other points from Richter's evidence:

On being minutely questioned respecting his knowledge of two persons – a carpenter and a joiner (whose names, though known at the Office, were for obvious reasons suppressed) as acquaintances of Williams, he said that about three or four weeks ago he saw them drinking at the Pear Tree public house with Williams, and since that time had seen them there without Williams. On the night of the murder of the Marr family, a few minutes before Williams came home, there was a knock on the door, and

---

[1] This appears to be a reporter's error in confusing the two cases. The *Morning Chronicle,* in the passage next quoted, leaves no doubt that the reference is to the night of the murder of the Marrs, and this seems inherently more probable.

he (the examinant) went down to open it, when he found
the key had been taken from the inside of the lock. He
called to the mother of Mrs. Vermilloe, the landlady, to
come down and open the door. Hearing her coming down
he went up to his own room; and when there, heard her
in conversation with a man whose voice he thinks was that
of one of the two men before mentioned. A few minutes
afterwards Williams himself came in. This was almost
half-past one o'clock.

About eleven o'clock on the day after the murder of the
Marr family the examinant went from curiosity to examine
the premises, which he entered and saw the dead bodies.
From thence he returned to the Pear Tree, where he found
Williams in the back yard, washing out his stockings,
but he did not tell Williams where he had been. On being
asked by the magistrate why he did not tell Williams,
the examinant answered – 'he did not know, he could not
tell'.

Richter was remanded in custody, being unable to account
for the mud on his trousers, and their damp condition. Next:

Cornelius Hart and *Jeremiah Fitzpatrick,* two Irishmen,
the carpenter and joiner alluded to by the last witness
(and suspected to have been concerned with Williams in
the murders) were then put to the bar. Hart said that he
had known Williams only about a fortnight; and never
drank any beer with him, and only two glasses of gin. The
magistrates asked the witness what was the reason for
calling on Williams at the Pear Tree a few nights before
Marr's murder, and was answered that the witness had
been out drinking, and had spent all his money, and his
wife would not open the door for him, and he came to
Williams in consequence.

Richter was called back to contradict Hart in his statement, that he had never drunk any *beer* with Williams,
but he said that it might perhaps be gin. Richter added
that he had seen Hart, Fitzpatrick and Williams in company
on the Sunday following the murder of Mr. Marr. One of
them afterwards called again to enquire after Williams,

but he did not desire that his calling should be concealed. Williams was in the habit of keeping very bad hours.

Fitzpatrick said that he had become acquainted with Williams about three weeks since, when they drank some beer together. This was the first time witness had anything to do *with the set*. Being asked what he intended by the word *set*, he said he meant Williams. Some time afterwards, he, Williams and another man, went to the Union, in New Gravel Lane (two or three doors from Williamson's) where they had some Sampson, or strong gin. The witness owned that he had called upon Williams between the murders of Marr and Williamson, but denied that he had ever expressed a wish that it should be concealed. On the night of Mr. Marr's murder the witness went to bed at half-past eleven.

The magistrates adjourned for tea, then resumed their examination in the evening. *The Times* reported:

John Cuthperson, a fellow lodger of Williams, touched on a point of material importance. He stated that on the morning after the murder of Mr. Williamson, when he got up, he saw a pair of his own stockings lying behind his chest, very much dirtied with fresh mud. He took them downstairs into the tap-room, where he found Williams. He asked him who had dirtied his stockings in that manner? Williams said: 'Why, are they yours?' 'They are mine,' the witness replied. Some little dispute then ensued as to their right ownership, when Williams took them into the back yard, and after washing the dirt off, returned them to the witness.

A woman of the town attended, and advised that two or three evenings after the murder of Mr. Williamson, she was standing in Shadwell, and overheard one man say to another as they passed, 'damn Turner, we will soon do for him, for if it had not been for him the murder would not have been found out.'

According to *The Times* the magistrates treated this woman's evidence 'very lightly'; but during the day's examina-

tions evidence came to light which reflected on the standard
of veracity of one of their earlier witnesses:

Cornelius Hart, who was examined in the morning, and
disclaimed all acquaintance with Williams, and denied
positively that he had called on him the day he was apprehended; and desired that it might not be said he (Hart)
had called, was contradicted indirectly. It appears that
although he did not call himself, he sent his wife to enquire
whether Williams had not been taken up on suspicion of
the murder; and told her to impose silence on the landlady
of the public house, with respect to the enquiry on his
(Hart's) part.

It was growing late when the last witnesses were called.
The man from Marlborough had not yet arrived, so there was
time to hear Mrs. Orr. This woman, the *London Chronicle*
reported, kept a chandler's shop near Sir William Warren's
Square, next door but one to Pear Tree Court and actually
adjoining the Pear Tree.

Mrs. Orr stated that on the Saturday before Marr's
murder, about half-past one in the morning, she was
getting up linen when she heard a noise about the house,
as if a man was attempting to break into the house. She was
frightened, and asked – 'Who is there?' A voice answered
which she knew to be Williams's, 'I am a robber!' She
answered, 'Whether you are a robber or not I will let you
in, and I am glad to see you.' Williams entered, and seated
himself down until the watchman was calling the hour
past two o'clock. Williams got up from his chair and asked
the lady whether she would have a glass. She assented, but
as he would not go out for it she went to the Pear Tree
public house, but could gain no admittance. She returned,
when Williams enquired how many rooms there were in
her house, and the situation of her back premises? She
replied that there were three rooms, and that her yard
joined Mrs. Vermilloe's house. The watchman came into
her house, which Williams resisted for some time. The
watchman told Mrs. Orr that he had picked up a chisel

by the side of her window. Williams ran out unobserved at this information. Soon afterwards he returned. The watchman was going, when Williams stopped him and desired him to go to the Pear Tree and get some liquor. The house was then open. While the watchman was gone for the liquor Williams took up the chisel and said, 'Damn my eyes, where did you get this chisel?' Mrs. Orr did not part with it, and retained the instrument till Monday last. Hearing that Williams was examined, she went to Mrs. Vermilloe's and showed her the chisel. Mrs. Vermilloe looked at it and compared it with the tools in Peterson's chest, when it was found to bear the same marks. She declared it was taken out of her house. Mrs. Orr instantly delivered the chisel to the magistrates of Shadwell Office, as being a further clue to the villainy.

Mrs. Orr says she knew Williams for eleven weeks. He frequently nursed her child and used to joke with her daughter. He once asked her whether she would be frightened if he came in the dead of night to her bedside? The daughter replied, 'No, if it was you Mr. Williams I should not.' Both the mother and the daughter thought Williams an agreeable young man, and of a most insinuating address, and never thought he could be the man who would attempt to rob or murder.

Finally Sylvester Driscoll was brought up from Coldbath Fields Prison. The magistrates told him that they were now satisfied with his account of the spirits found in his possession, but until he could give an adequate explanation of the blood on his trousers he would have to remain in custody. Driscoll was accordingly committed until the following Tuesday.

That concluded the examination on Boxing Day. And what, at this stage, did the case against the prisoner amount to?

Williams lodged at the Pear Tree, and for several weeks he had had free access to the tools in John Peterson's chest. One of these tools, the maul, had come from that chest; and it had been identified as the weapon with which the Marrs were murdered. There was evidence that Williams had not arrived home until after midnight on the night of Marr's murder. Richter put it as late as half past one. He had frequently been seen drinking at the King's Arms, and admitted to having been there on the night the Williamsons were murdered. That night he arrived home at midnight or later, and desired one of his room-mates to put his candle out. Next morning he had washed out a pair of muddy stockings, evidently borrowed from Cuthperson. It was said that he had been so hard up before the murder of Williamson that he had to borrow sixpence from Mrs. Vermilloe and had needed to pawn his shoes; afterwards he had a pound in his pocket, together with some silver. Mrs. Rice had washed his torn and bloody shirts. Mrs. Orr had come along with an extraordinary story linking Williams with yet a third ripping chisel.

After considering the evidence, the three Shadwell magistrates sent a brief note to the Home Secretary:

You will have perceived from the papers the examinations of Williams, which have taken place at this Office; they are pretty accurately given, and as such we think it unnecessary to give it now in detail. A further examination will be had tomorrow, and tho' many circumstances arise against him we are not yet certain that he will prove the Man – being so fully employed, you must excuse this short Note.

This letter is interesting. It confirms that the newspaper reports of the proceedings were correct; an important point since the actual depositions have been destroyed. And it clearly states that, by the close of Boxing Day, the case was still far from proved. As they talked over the evidence together, the magistrates must have been struck by its weakness and inconsistencies. They had questioned John Williams and had studied his demeanour in the dock. We are not told how he struck them, but it is significant that, at the close of his final examination, they were far from convinced that he was their man. But tomorrow was another day; another examination. And they awaited with confident hope, the arrival of the man from Marlborough.

That night the magistrates settled fresh tactics. They arranged to assemble at the Shadwell Public Office at ten o'clock on the following morning. Mallett, the Clerk, was instructed to see that the maul and all three ripping chisels were available. John Williams and Richter were to be brought from their cells in Coldbath Fields Prison, the former probably for the last time before his committal for trial. And now virtually everybody concerned in the case was warned to attend for the next day's hearing. Mrs. Vermilloe was summoned from the Pear Tree, this time with two of her lodgers – Harrison and Cuthperson. Inquiries had established the names of Williams's favourite public houses, and the landlords of two of them were requested to present themselves. One, Robert Lawrence, of the Ship and Royal Oak, would be able to speak about the fight that Williams claimed had resulted in one of his bloody shirts. The other, Mr. Lee, landlord of the Black Horse, New Gravel Lane, lived opposite Williamson, had seen Turner's descent, and had been among the party that broke into the King's Arms and found the bodies; and it was at the Black Horse that Unwin had conducted the second inquest. Finally, two men who were believed to be friends of Williams were summoned to attend: Jeremiah Fitzpatrick was called again, together with a new witness – John Cobbett, a coal-heaver.

It is apparent that, at this stage, the magistrates were devoting all their attention to John Williams. They probably felt that it would be more profitable to concentrate on their prime suspect rather than to complicate the public inquiry by introducing others against whom suspicion was less strong. Some of these were in custody – as was Sylvester Driscoll; nothing would be risked by delay. Besides, they still awaited the man from Marlborough. It would be expedient to defer the examination of all the possible accomplices until he had been brought to town. And if the proceedings on the morrow went as expected there was every hope that Williams would assist them by betraying his confederates, either at his committal or during his subsequent confinement. In a case of gang murder, to catch one was invariably to catch all. The important task at the moment was to deal with Williams.

There were two men, in particular, who must have been grateful that the magistrates' attention was so firmly fixed elsewhere. One was the carpenter, Cornelius Hart, who had worked for Pugh and carried out the alterations to Marr's shop window. He had denied any familiarity with Williams, but was afterwards proved to have sent his wife on a surreptitious errand to the Pear Tree to inquire whether Williams had been arrested. Another, who was the subject of much gossip in the neighbourhood, was a tall, stout man, who was said to be lame. So far there had been no mention of him in the newspapers, but in Wapping he was known as Long Billy. In the House of Commons, more than a month later, the Prime Minister and the Home Secretary both named him: William Ablass.

Next morning the three magistrates took their seats early on
the raised dais under the Royal Arms. The court was already
crowded. The seats, like boxed-in church pews, which were
reserved for important visitors, were crammed to capacity;
in the well of the court a packed mass of humanity moved
restlessly, as yet another spectator edged himself into the
crush. It was clear that this interrogation of Williams would
be vital, that a large number of witnesses had been summoned,
and were now waiting to be called. All the exhibits had been
assembled, and the blood-stained maul and the three chisels
(or was one an iron crow?) prominently displayed.

Outside the public office the mob stamped their feet on
cobbles white with a first sprinkling of winter snow, eager for
the arrival of the coach which would bring John Williams from
Coldbath Fields Prison. Inside, those nearest the door strained
their ears for the sound of wheels. The magistrates whispered
softly together. It was already past the hour when the prisoner
was due to arrive.

But when, at last, the court heard the subdued buzz of
excitement which heralded an arrival, and the door finally
opened, it revealed not the expected figure of Williams,
ironed and manacled, but a solitary police officer. He marched
up to the magistrates and delivered his news. The prisoner was
dead, and by his own hand. When the exclamations of surprise
and disappointment had died down the magistrates demanded
details. They were soon given. The discovery had been made
when the turnkey went to Williams's cell to prepare him for
his appearance before the bench. He found the prisoner
suspended by the neck from an iron bar which crossed the cell,
and on which the inmate could hang his clothes. The body
was quite cold and lifeless. The coat and shoes were off.
There had been no warning. Williams had appeared tolerably

cheerful when the turnkey had locked his cell the previous night, and had spoken with confidence of his hope of a speedy release.

The magistrates softly conferred together above the hum of speculation from the court. Their decision was quickly reached. The interrogations would proceed. There was no pretence now that this was a disinterested investigation. Williams had pronounced sentence on himself. The day's business would be to hear the evidence which would formally confirm his guilt. As *The Times* put it next day, 'The magistrates proceeded to examine the evidence on which they intended to found his final commitment.'

Mrs. Vermilloe, the landlady of the Pear Tree, and obviously a key witness, was called first. On Tuesday she had broken down on being shown the maul, and had been unable positively to identify it as having been in Peterson's chest. Then, on Christmas Day, she had given 'decisive information' as to its identity. On that occasion, however, she had been interviewed privately in Newgate prison with her husband. Clearly it was desirable that she should affirm the maul's identity in public. But now, away from her husband's influence, she again equivocated. The *London Chronicle* reported:

> *Mrs. Vermilloe* was very closely questioned by the Magistrates as to her knowledge of the fatal maul, which she declared she never missed until Monday last. She could not be at all positive that it was one of those which belonged to John Peterson. She seemed unwilling to identify it, and was asked by the magistrates whether, when she heard her husband in Newgate stated it to be the same, she had not exclaimed, 'Good God, why does he say so?' She at first denied using the expression, but on a witness being called who overheard her, she confessed that she employed it, or something like it.

Was Mrs. Vermilloe simply terrified? Had she been threatened? Or had she something to hide? It was important to know when she had first had suspicions of Williams, and what aroused them:

The first time she had any suspicion that Williams was concerned in either of the murders was when a young man named Harris (*sic*) who slept with Williams, showed her a pair of stockings belonging to him, which had been tucked behind a trunk in an extremely muddy state, even to within about an inch of the top. On further examination of them she saw evidently the marks of two bloody fingers upon the top of one of them. She then called in a man named Glass to look at them. He, believing the stains to be those of blood, advised Mrs. Vermilloe to turn Williams out of the house.

This news created something of a sensation. Why had she not disclosed so important a matter on her first examination? the magistrates demanded. The witness hesitated. Had she been intimidated by Williams?

She admitted that she was afraid that he, or some of his acquaintances, would murder her.

Q.   You need now have no such fear. You know his situation. You have heard that he has hanged himself?

(Much affected and shocked) Good God! I hope not.

Q.   Why do you hope not?

(After hesitation) I should have been sorry, if he was innocent, that he should have suffered.

What did Mrs. Vermilloe know? What was she holding back? She was probably not an intelligent women and was obviously much under her husband's influence. He had impressed upon her the importance of saying nothing which might jeopardise their chance of reward. Besides, she wanted to oblige the gentlemen by telling them what they wanted to hear – if only she could be sure what it was. She wanted, too, to protect the reputation of her house, even in front of those who might not have agreed that it had a reputation worth preserving. One thing was now clear to her. John Williams was dead. Nothing she could say or conceal could help him now. And so, in her ignorance and fear, confused by repeated questioning and often on the verge of hysteria, she hesitated, prevaricated, and made confusion worse. The magistrates pressed her yet again about her first suspicion about Williams, and now she told a different story. It was not, after all, Harrison's discovery of some muddy stockings.

The discovery of the maul marked 'J.P.' was the first thing that made her suspect Williams of the murder of Mr. Marr's family. The witness then related the circumstances of the discovery beforementioned of the ripping iron, at Mrs. Orr's window, which somewhat confirmed her suspicions.

The questions then put referred to the connections and associates of Williams, to which she replied that he had none, excepting now and then a few shipmates. He was in the habit of going to all the public houses, and behaving with great familiarity, but she never knew that he had any friends. When he returned from the East Indies, in the *Roxburgh Castle,* three months ago, he deposited £30 in her husband's hands, which was not all expended at the time of the murders.

The stockings and shoes Williams is supposed to have worn on the night of the murder of Williamson were now produced. The stockings appeared to have been washed, but the stains of blood had not quite disappeared. The shoes had likewise been washed.

Williams was in the habit of wearing very large whiskers, and Saturday night last was the first time she perceived that he had cut them off. After this period she closely watched him, and she thought he seemed to be afraid to look at her. The subject of the two murders was often mentioned in his company, and though before very talkative, she observed that Williams always slunk out of the way into the passage, and seemed to be listening to what was said. One day it was remarked to him that Williamson's murder was a very shocking affair. – 'Yes,' he said 'very shocking,' and he then turned off the conversation.

The witness was opening up, more at her ease. So the magistrates made yet another attempt to get her to identify the maul:

The maul, the ripping iron, and the two chisels were now brought before the witness that she might, if possible, identify them. But she shrunk away from the fatal instrument in horror. All she could say was that she had seen a maul something like it in her husband's house.

The magistrates tried another line:

Q. How long has Williams been at home?

About twelve weeks. He came home on 2nd. October.

Q. Have you ever heard of the circumstances of a Portuguese being stabbed at the end of Old Gravel Lane between two and three months ago?

Yes.

Q. Was Williams at home at this time?

He was.

Q. Did you hear anyone say that Williams was concerned in stabbing this man?

I can't positively say I did.

Anything, it seems, was now good enough to blacken the character of the dead man, but they could get little out of Mrs. Vermilloe on that score. She did, however, offer three more points that might be material to the case:

Since the arrest of Williams, a carpenter, of the name of Trotter, had called to enquire after him, and said he would soon be cleared. On the night of the last murder Williams had told the witness that Williamson was going the next day to pay his brewer. Williams's name, she had heard, was John Murphy.

Mrs. Vermilloe stood down and was followed into the witness box by Robert Lawrence, the licensee of one of Williams's favourite public houses, the Ship and Royal Oak. He said that Williams used to sit at the bar with great familiarity, but he never cared for the man. His daughter, however, knew Williams well. The girl, a 'very interesting female'

according to an impressionable *Morning Post* journalist, was
duly called:

> She knew Williams before Marr's murder. He gained her
> good opinion. After Marr's murder he used to say, 'Miss
> Lawrence, I don't know what is the matter with me. I feel
> so uneasy.' Once he came into the house greatly agitated,
> and said – 'I don't think I'm well, for I am unhappy and
> can't remain easy.' Miss Lawrence answered, 'Williams,
> you ought to know best what you have done.' He replied,
> 'Why, last night I ate a good supper off fowls, and had
> plenty of liquor.' Miss Lawrence immediately said, 'Good
> eating is not the way to make you unhappy,' on which he
> retired.

Miss Lawrence had been serving behind the bar when the
scuffle broke out between Williams and the Irish coal-heavers,
which accounted, according to Williams, for one of the torn
and bloody shirts that Mrs. Rice had washed. *The Times*
reported:

> On Friday week in the evening he came into their house
> with his coat off and said he wanted to find the police
> officers. He was then very tipsy. Some people in the tap-
> room began to play tricks with him. A snuff box was
> handed around with some coal ashes mixed among the
> snuff, of which he partook when it was given to him. He
> was going to strike the person who gave it to him, but was
> prevented by somebody's interposition. There was no
> fighting, nor was Williams struck. Nor was his mouth cut
> as he had represented for the purpose of accounting for the
> blood on his shirt. He was taken away, but returned half
> an hour afterwards and behaved very peacefully. Witness
> had not seen Williams since Saturday week, when she
> desired him not to come again to their house.

Williams's explanation that his shirt had become torn and
bloodied in a pub brawl clearly referred to the shirt which Mrs.
Rice testified she had washed before the Marrs' murders. He
was apparently unable to account, when asked, for the state
of the second shirt, probably because, on the washerwoman's

evidence, it was far less extensively bloodied. Miss Lawrence's testimony was intended to prove Williams a liar by discrediting an explanation which he had not, in fact given. It is probable, however, that by the end of her evidence no one in court, including the magistrates, was clear about which particular bloodied shirt was now in question.

And so, gradually, the prejudice against Williams was building up, despite the confusion and inconsistency of much of the testimony. Now came another key witness – John Harrison, the sailmaker, who had shared Williams's bedroom at the Pear Tree:

He stated that he never saw anybody in company with Williams but the carpenter (Hart). He had heard that this was the same man who had been working at Mr. Marr's house. Williams came to the house at about half past twelve on the night Mr. Marr and family were murdered. In the morning when witness heard of it, he told Mrs. Vermilloe, the landlady. He then went upstairs to Williams and told him also. Williams replied in a surly manner, 'I know it.' He was then in bed and had not been out that morning. Witness said he might possibly have overheard him telling Mrs. Vermilloe. That morning Williams walked out by himself. Witness had been reading the newspaper containing an account of the murder of Mr. Marr, and when he found the muddy stockings behind the chest something like suspicion struck him. He brought the stockings downstairs and showed them to Mrs. Vermilloe and several other people. From this circumstance and from the general conduct of Williams he was thoroughly persuaded he was concerned in the murder. He had told witness that he was well acquainted with Mr. Marr. One day he was walking from the City with Williams. He said that Mr. Marr had money to a considerable amount.

When he showed him the muddied stockings he took them into the backyard and washed them, at first in a rough manner in cold water; and when witness afterwards saw them they were quite clean. As witness slept in the same room he had an opportunity of observing his conduct since the murders. As he strongly suspected he was concerned in them, he longed for an opportunity of searching his clothes for some marks of blood. He was, however, always baffled in his intentions for whenever he attempted to approach his bed he found him awake. He always seemed restless, continually turning about in his bed and much agitated. He had overheard him speaking in his sleep. One night since the murder he heard him saying in his sleep, 'Five shillings in my pocket – my pocket's full of silver.' Witness called out to him repeatedly, 'What is the matter with you and what do you mean?' but he got no answer from him. When he slept he did not seem to be soundly asleep but always disturbed. In the morning after the murder of Williamson he saw a pair of muddy shoes under Williams's bed. Witness had always an impression on his mind against the prisoner, and always wished for an opportunity of bringing forward some evidence against him.

Williams's other room-mate, John Cuthperson, told a similar story. On the Thursday before the Williamsons were murdered, he said, Williams had no money, and next morning he had a good deal. Williams was restless at night, singing in his sleep, 'fol de rol de rol – I have five shillings – my pocket is full of shillings.' Like Miss Lawrence, Cuthperson spoke of Williams's strange talk:

Williams talked in his sleep in a very incoherent manner. Witness frequently shook and awakened him. On being asked what was the matter he used to say he had had a most horrid dream. After the murder of the Williamsons, Williams one day claimed to the witness of his dreadful situation, being greatly afflicted with a disorder. The witness advised him to go to a surgeon, when Williams replied – 'Ah! It is of no consequence, the gallows will get hold of me soon.' The witness recollected Williams talking only once in his dream, and was crying, 'run, run.' He called to him three times and asked him what was the matter. He thought Williams awoke and answered him in a strange manner.

Mr. Lee, the landlord of the Black Horse public house, opposite the King's Arms, was the next witness. He recalled

that on the night of Williamson's murder he had been standing at his own door waiting for his wife and niece to come
home from the Royalty theatre, worrying for their safety,
his thoughts on the murders of the Marrs, when suddenly
he heard the faint voice of a man crying 'Watch, watch!' It
seemed to come from Williamson's house. He afterwards
supposed it was the voice of the old man crying out for relief
after he had been wounded. It was seven minutes later when
he saw Turner descending from the window by the knotted
sheets. He was among those who broke into the house and
found the bodies. The witness said that he now 'felt certain'
that more than one man had been concerned in the murders.
Asked to name Williams's friends, he was only able to think
of John Cobbett, who had been in bed at the Black Horse
at the time of both murders. He, like other witnesses, had had
occasion to notice Williams's familiar ways:

> He was accustomed to come into the bar and sit down.
> He had seen him push against his wife and shake her
> pockets as if to ascertain what money she had. On one
> occasion he took the liberty of pulling out the till and
> putting his hand into it. Witness remonstrated with him
> and said he never suffered anybody to meddle with his till
> but his own family. He never thought very seriously of this
> matter until he heard of Williams being apprehended.

It remained to call three more witnesses – a prostitute and
two men who were believed to be friends of Williams. The
girl was Margaret Riley. She said she had seen two men 'run
out of Gravel Lane, one of them, as well as she could see, with
large whiskers, the other lame.' She thought that one of the
men brought before the magistrates on Tuesday was like one
of them. This amounted to very little. But the next witness,
said to be a friend of Williams, gave him – if his testimony is
to be believed – something of an alibi for the murder of the
Williamsons.

> *John Fitzpatrick* proved that he left Williams in company
> with Hart, the joiner, at the Ship and Royal public house
> at about quarter past eleven before the murders were

committed. This was corroborated by the testimony of Miss Lawrence.

The final witness was believed to be Williams's only intimate friend, the coal-heaver John Cobbett; and from the little of his evidence that has been reported it seems likely that, under effective cross-examination, he could have shed more light on the mystery than all the other witnesses put together. *The Times* reported:

> *John Cobbett* said that he had known Williams perfectly well. He got acquainted with him at a public house in New Gravel Lane, where they used to drink together. He had also been with him frequently at Mr. Williamson's, and they had drunk together. But he knew none of his acquaintances. He wished very much to have been able to get something out of him concerning the murders. Indeed, Williams asked him to come and see him during his confinement, but he was never able, in consequence of his being so much employed on board ship.

And the *London Chronicle:*

> *John Cobbett*, the coal-heaver, being called, pointed out a man named William Ablass, commonly called Long Billy, who was lame, as an intimate friend of Williams. The witness and those two were drinking at Mr. Lee's on the night of the murder of Williamson. Trotter, the carpenter, once said to the witness, 'It is a very shocking concern, as you would say so indeed if you knew as much as I do.'

Whatever it was that Trotter knew remained his secret. His evidence – the evidence of the man who had assured Mrs. Vermilloe that Williams 'would soon be cleared' – was never sought. The Shadwell magistrates had had nearly enough. They had been examining suspects for more than a fortnight. There had been no time to take stock, weigh the evidence, assess the credibility of this or that witness. Working under extreme pressure in a constant glare of publicity, unaided by competent staff, Capper and Markland were left at the end with a blur of names and faces, foreign as well as English and Irish – Harrison, Cuthperson, Cobbett, Vermilloe, Trotter, Hart, Fitzpatrick, Ablass, Richter, Driscoll. They were also left with a circumstantial case against Williams and the incontrovertible fact of his death, apparently by suicide. Why look further? Their doubts on the eve of the suspect's death ('We are not yet certain that he will prove the man,' they had told the Home Secretary) had, by the end of the morning, totally vanished. The further evidence, beyond the power of Williams to rebut or even challenge, now emboldened them to assert his guilt as an established fact.

> We think it our duty to inform you [they wrote to the Home Secretary at the end of the hearing] that from what appeared in Evidence previously to the death of Williams, together with what has appeared on a very full Examination this morning, that Williams was the perpetrator of the late murders in this neighbourhood; and we have also to add that we have every reason to hope that he alone was concerned.

The only lingering doubt was whether the man awaited from Marlborough had been Williams's accomplice in the massacres.

Later the same afternoon Capper made his third visit that week to prison; not this time to Newgate, but, accompanied by Markland, to Coldbath Fields Prison, where the body of John Williams was laid out. The Coroner, John Wright Unwin, had been hastily summoned to conduct yet another inquest.

> *Thomas Webb*, sworn. I am surgeon to the prison. I was called to the deceased this morning. I had found him in his cell lying on his back on the bed where he had been placed by the person who cut him down. He was dead and cold and had been dead many hours. On his neck on the right side was a very deep impression of a knot, and a mark all round the neck as from the handkerchief by which he had been suspended. The handkerchief was still on the neck; I saw no other marks of violence on his body. I have no doubt he died of strangulation. He told me the day before

yesterday he was perfectly easy and satisfied, for that nothing could happen to him.

Francis Knott, sworn. I am a prisoner here; I saw the deceased alive and well yesterday about half-past three in the afternoon. He asked me if he could see his friends; I told him I did not know. This morning about half-past seven o'clock, Joseph Beckett, the turnkey, came to me in the yard and desired me to go up to the cell of the deceased and cut him down, for that he had found him hanging. I went up immediately, put my arms around his body, and cut the handkerchief, part of which was round his neck and the other part was fastened to the rail which the bed and clothes are hung upon in the daytime – the rail is six feet three inches from the ground. I laid him on his back on the bed. He was cold and seemed to have been dead for some time. He was ironed on the right leg. He was placed in what is called the re-examination cells and left, as persons in this situation always are; I had no suspicion of anything of the kind happening; he was quite rational and collected when he spoke to me.

Henry Harris, sworn. I am also a prisoner here. I was standing by my cell door about half-past seven this morning. Mr. Beckett came to me to desire me to help Knott with the man who had hung himself. I went up and found Knott standing at the door of the deceased's cell. Knott observed to me the deceased had hung himself on the rail. I went in and saw him hanging on the rail with a handkerchief around his neck, one end of which was attached to the rail. I assisted Knott in cutting him down. Never saw the deceased before to my knowledge.

William Hassall, sworn. I am clerk to the prison. I have been so upwards of three years. The deceased was committed here by Edward Markland, Esq. on the 24th December, and was in custody here for re-examination. He was placed in the re-examination cell and ironed on the right leg. I considered him secure. He was placed in the prison as persons for re-examination invariably are. I went up to him on the morning of the 25th to ask him his age – he told me he was twenty-seven years of age. I observed to him his situation was awkward – he said he was not guilty, and hoped the saddle would be placed on the right horse. I asked him his business – he replied he was a seafaring man, and said he was a Scotsman. Williams in person is about five feet eight and a half inches in height. He was dressed in a brown greatcoat, lined with silk, a blue undercoat with yellow buttons, blue and white waistcoat, striped blue pantaloons, brown worsted stockings, and shoes. He was by no means of an athletic make.

Joseph Beckett, sworn. I am turnkey here. I locked the deceased up about ten minutes before four yesterday afternoon; he was alive and well. I asked him if he wanted anything – he said 'No.' He has said during his confinement, he hoped the innocent would not suffer, and that the saddle might be placed upon the right horse. Between seven and eight this morning I unlocked the door of his cell. I discovered him hanging to the rail in his cell with his feet nearly, or quite, touching the ground, with a white handkerchief around his neck, which handkerchief I had seen him wear. I called upon Harris and saw him cut down.

Mr. Unwin, the coroner, then addressed the jury:

The miserable wretch, the object of the present enquiry, was committed here on suspicion of being one of the perpetrators of the late alarming and most inhuman murders, and that suspicion is greatly increased by the result which has taken place; for how much augmented is the suspicion of guilt against the man who, to escape justice, has recourse to self-destruction! All homicide is murder till the contrary shall be shown. The law ranks suicide in the worst class of murderers, and this is a case of most unqualified self-murder.

I have applied my attention to the conduct of those entrusted with the custody of this wretched man, as a subject interesting to the public mind, and I leave it with you; I think there is no culpability attaching itself to them.

It only, therefore, remains that we consign the body of this self-murderer to that infamy and disgrace which the law has prescribed, and to leave the punishment of his crimes to him that has said 'Vengeance is mine, and I will repay.'

Throughout the whole of the next day, Saturday 28 December, the Shadwell magistrates awaited the arrival of the man from Marlborough. They were not, however, entirely unoccupied. During the afternoon, the *Morning Chronicle* reported:

William Ablass, commonly called Long Billy, a seaman from Danzig, was brought up on suspicion of being concerned in the late murders with Williams. It was charged that on the night of the murder of Mr. Williamson, of the King's Arms, he was in the company of Williams, drinking, at 10 o'clock. He gave the following account of himself –

Between three and four o'clock of the afternoon of the 19th December he was walking down Pear Tree Alley with a friend, when he met Williams. They entered the Pear Tree public house and had some beer, which the examinant paid for. From thence Ablass and Williams proceeded to Williamson's, the King's Arms, where they took a pint of ale. Ablass had seen Williamson once before. Mr. Williamson and the maid were present. Williams employed himself reading the papers.

From thence he and Williams went to Ablass's lodgings, but not finding tea, as expected, ready, they took a pot of ale at the Duke of Kent public house, which was paid for by Ablass. They left that house about six o'clock and went to the Black Horse in New Gravel Lane and had four glasses of gin and water in company with a tall man dressed in a blue coat, whose name Ablass could not recollect. Much conversation passed, but none of it related to Marr's murder. They then left the house, and Williams and Ablass parted at the door, Williams taking a direction down the street. This was, as near as Ablass could recollect, between eight and nine o'clock.

The Captain of the *Roxburgh Castle,* in which ship Ablass and Williams had sailed from Rio Janeiro, and in which the former had headed a mutiny, enquired of Ablass what had become of his wife and two children? Ablass denied that he ever was married, but said that he had allowed a woman to pass by his name, and to receive a part of his pay. To the question how he had maintained himself since he had left his ship some months since, he replied that having expended his pay he had supported himself by pawning his clothes. He was quite positive that he was at home on the night of Williamson's murder, and could prove it by several witnesses.

A messenger was immediately despatched for persons to substantiate these allegations, who returned with a woman, who kept the house in which Ablass lodged, and a fellow lodger, both of whom stated distinctly that Ablass had come home in the first instance to see if tea was ready, and again at about ten o'clock. He remained in the witness's company until past twelve, when it was reported that the murder had been perpetrated. – Ablass, on hearing it, exclaimed that he knew the people of the house, and went out to make enquiries. He came back soon afterwards, confirming the melancholy news.

On this satisfactory testimony Mr. Markland, the Sitting Magistrate, ordered that Ablass should be discharged.

Others were later to be less satisfied than was Markland by this convenient alibi. The Shadwell bench, however, were looking elsewhere for Williams's supposed accomplice; and at nine o'clock that Saturday evening they eagerly resumed the hearing, when the man from Marlborough arrived, having spent fourteen hours on a cold journey. He gave his name as Thomas Cahill.

The circumstances have a familiar ring. When he was arrested the prisoner had been wearing 'a shirt a good deal torn about the neck and breast', and stained with fresh blood. He bore a 'striking resemblance to the man described in the handbills as being seen to run from the premises of Mr. Williamson'. He was a stout man, about five feet ten inches in height, with sandy hair and red whiskers. In fact, *The Times* declared, as if the fact were in itself incriminating, he bore 'a remarkably strong likeness to the late unhappy wretch Williams'. Moreover, the new suspect spoke with a strong

Irish accent, and it very quickly became evident that he was an accomplished liar.

The matter of the torn and bloody shirt had already been cleared up by the Marlborough magistrates, on evidence that the prisoner had been in a public house brawl in Reading. But where had he been, Markland demanded, on the nights of the murders? Cahill replied that he had been lodging with a man named Williamson, at 121 Ratcliffe Highway. A messenger was sent to the address, and reported that no such person lived there. Markland was not surprised. Already, he observed primly, he had 'some doubts of the purity' of the prisoner's character. The prisoner cheerfully removed his doubts. He admitted 'with a good deal of *sang froid*' that it was all a lie. He had never lived in London in all his life.

Mr. Markland. Then what am I to think? Can you expect that I shall believe a word you now say, after such a confession?

Prisoner. I don't know your worship. You may depend upon it, I am as innocent of the murder as the child unborn. I'll tell no lie at all. I said many things that were not true, knowing very well that I was innocent, and that I could *asily* get rid of this charge.

He was a deserter from a regiment of Irish militia, Cahill now claimed, and had been lodging in Romford Row, in Essex, at the time of the murders. Markland was sceptical.

Mr. Markland. What did you do with your military clothes?

Prisoner. I met a Jew between Romford and Romford Row, and I bought this top-coat now on me from him, and put it over my regimentals.

Mr. Markland. What day did you say this was?

Prisoner. Saturday, your worship.

Mr. Markland. Come Sir, I see you are beginning your old tricks. Do you mean to tell me that you bought the coat off a Jew on a Saturday?

| | Sir, that must be false. The lowest Jew will not sell anything on a Saturday. |
| Prisoner. | I took him to be a Jew. He was a dark man, and he sold old clothes. |

There could have been few Cahills in Hertfordshire or Yorkshire where Markland and Capper gained their experience as magistrates, and parts of the long interrogation, which are irrelevant to the case, reveal the total lack of comprehension between them. Cahill, obviously solicitous for three such credulous gentlemen, tried vainly to convince them that his story of a wife in Bath and his subsequent military misfortunes were all lies. He was obviously as nonplussed by his judges as they were perplexed to encounter such an audacious and unrepentent rogue.

A watchman named Ingall was next called, one of the thirty-five old men employed by the parish of St. George's-in-the-East. He declared that the prisoner could not possibly have been in bed at his lodgings at Romford Row from nine o'clock until seven on the night the Williamsons were murdered, since he had himself seen Cahill drinking in Mrs. Peachy's public house, the New Crane, which was near by; and the time was then about eleven o'clock. Mrs. Peachy was sent for, and told to cast her mind back to the night of the 19th December. Had any strangers been in the New Crane? The woman reflected, then remembered that an 'ill-looking man' had called in the tap room for a pint of beer and a penn'orth of bread. 'Now, Mrs. Peachy,' said Markland, encouraged, 'look round the room, and try if you can see the man who came that night into your house.' The woman pointed to Cahill. He was certainly 'very like' the man, but she could not be certain. Her daughter Susan, however, had no doubt whatever that Cahill was the man. At this, 'the prisoner evinced signs of the utmost astonishment, and undertook to to try to provide alibis to prove that he had been in his lodgings in Romford Row.' So, late at night, the court adjourned.

At the resumed hearing, at midday on Monday, the public examinations at Shadwell finally degenerated into farce. Because they expected a bevy of Irishmen and rumours were being spread about Papist plots, a clergyman, the Rev.

Thirwell, was added to the bench; and Story, the senior magistrate, made one of his rare appearances.

Ingall, the watchman who on Saturday had claimed that he saw the prisoner in Mrs. Peachy's public house on the night that the Williamsons were murdered, now said, on seeing Cahill in daylight, that he was quite sure that he was not the same man. Mrs. Peachy was similarly doubtful; but Susan Peachy remained unshakeable in her belief that the prisoner had indeed been at the New Crane. He had then worn a hat.

The prisoner was ordered to put on his hat.

Q. Is that anything like the hat the man wore?

Yes. It came more on his face.

The magistrates observed that at this moment the man looked uncommonly like Williams.

Q. Had the man whiskers?

Yes. They came down nearly to his chin.

Q. Might it not possibly have been some other man?

I think not.

Q. Did you ever see Williams?

No.

Susan Peachy, Ingall and Mrs. Peachy were all despatched immediately in a coach to view the body of that miserable culprit in Coldbath Fields Prison. On their return they all gave it as their opinion that he (Williams) was the same man they saw at the *New Crane* public house on the Thursday night the murder was committed in New Gravel Lane.

Cahill, a much relieved man, then produced his own witnesses. The first was an Irishman named Cornelius Driscoll, the keeper of the lodging house in Romford Row. This reference to Driscoll is interesting as it goes some way to explaining the report in *The Times* of Boxing Day that the man from Marlborough had been in private correspondence with one of the suspects in custody. Sylvester Driscoll was still held in

Coldbath Fields Prison. It seems likely that the unfortunate magistrates of Shadwell, already bedevilled by the complications of the case (it was odd that Cahill should have claimed that he lodged with a Mr. Williamson of Ratcliffe Highway) were now to be further confused by a coincidence of two more identical names. Driscoll claimed to remember that Cahill had been at home on the night of the Williamsons' murder, but was 'either so stupid, or affected so much stupidity, that no satisfactory answers could be elicited from him'. So the magistrates called his wife.

Q. What are you?

A poor woman, your honour.

Q. Who is your husband?

He is Cornelius Dixon.

Q. Why, he has just told us his name is Driscoll?

Oh, it's all the same, Sir.

The Rev. Thirwell – Are you a Roman Catholic?

Yes.

Q. Cross yourself.

Mr. Story. – That's her business, not our's.

Suddenly a sergeant belonging to the Sligo Militia jumped up in court. He said he had seen Cahill's name mentioned in the newspapers as a deserter. He was on leave, and wished to identify the prisoner; so he was 'immediately examined'. All that transpired, however, was that, whatever regiment Cahill had deserted – if indeed he was a deserter – it was not the Sligo Militia. The prisoner's next witness, John Martin, was called.

Q. Are you a Roman Catholic?

I have been the chief of my life in His Majesty's service.

Q. Of what religion are you?

Yes Sir, I have been in His Majesty's *sarvice* a long while.

Q. Do you go to mass, or to meeting, or where do you go?

I go to none Sir, at present.

Q. Are you a Papist? I don't speak of Papists by way of reproach.

I don't know what a Papist is.

Q. What is your business?

I am an old soldier, at least the remains of one.

So it went on. A succession of broken down old men and women shuffled in and out of the court, obediently crossing themselves at the insistence of the Rev. Thirwell, and saying what they had come to say: the prisoner had been in the lodging house when the Williamsons were murdered. Nevertheless, caution prevailed to the end. 'The magistrates committed him to the House of Correction, for further examination, with this special observation, that they considered him completely exonerated from any suspicion of being concerned in the late murders.'

With the collapse of the case against Cahill the belief was growing, at least among the Shadwell magistrates, that John Williams had indeed been the sole murderer of both the Marrs and the Williamsons; and with this belief went a powerful realisation that so monstrous a villain, multiple murderer and self-destroyer, must provide an example that would shock the nation – not least because, at the end, he had cheated the very majesty of the law.

A GRAVE AT THE CROSSROADS

Almost every condemned criminal, whether sentenced by public opinion or by a properly constituted court, who has succeeded in killing himself before the official date of execution has been described as 'cheating the gallows'. One might suppose that the advocates of capital punishment would appreciate a man who, recognising the justice of his sentence, and accepting that only a life can compensate for a life, saves society the trouble and expense of an official ceremony, and embraces his sentence so wholeheartedly that he executes judgement on himself. But society has seldom seen it in that light. The phrase 'cheating the gallows' carries the clear inference that suffering the full penalty of the law means suffering as and when the law prescribes; that a public offence demands public punishment, and that the concomitants of judical execution are an essential part of retribution. It is society, not merely individuals, that has been outraged. It is society that must be appeased. The sense of frustration and fury that followed Williams's unorthodox death was expressed in the House of Commons on 18 January 1812 by the Prime Minister, in referring to 'the villain Williams, who has lately disappointed the just vengeance of the nation by violently withdrawing himself from the punishment which awaited him'. And this note of public vengeance unjustly cheated was echoed by almost every writer of the time who dealt with the case. The crimes had been barbaric and horrible, almost beyond belief. It was essential that the victims should be publicly avenged. Few people had any doubt that Williams was now receiving his just deserts in the next world. But the punishment of God, if sure, is invisible, and the contemplation of hell fire does little to assuage a lust for revenge. Far more effective as a deterrent is the spectacle of punishment on earth.

It was never doubted at the time that the death penalty was the most effective of all deterrents; consequently the more people who witnessed it the greater its beneficial effect. John Williams, by his premature death, had robbed authority of its salutary example, and Londoners of one of their most dramatic entertainments. A hanging day was still virtually a public holiday, and a vast crowd would congregate to see the condemned dispatched. Few people in the early nineteenth century would have thought it justifiable to execute a man in private. The condemned had a right to a public death. How else could society guard against private vengeance, the knife in the dark, the secret executioner bringing death to the innocent in the secure privacy of a prison cell? Besides, if the populace had a right to their spectacle the condemned was entitled to his audience. Even into the late nineteenth century there were writers who could oppose private execution on the grounds that an Englishman had the inalienable right to confess his crime or profess his innocence in public.

Some of the worst horrors of public executions had already been mitigated. It was realised by the reformers that the scenes of violence, drunkenness and ribaldry which had accompanied the slow progress of the condemned from Newgate Prison to Tyburn robbed the act of execution of its proper solemnity; nor were they conducive to respect for the awful retribution of the law, or to a religious and penitent acceptance of their fate by those to be hanged. Many of the more flamboyant criminals appeared to gain courage from their public notoriety and went to their deaths beribboned and nosegayed as if for a wedding, casting coins to the mob. Others thought it fit to make their last appearance in a shroud. This may have been an indication of repentance, but was equally likely to have been a determination that the hangman should be cheated of at least part of his perquisite – the clothes of the condemned. For both the bodies and clothes of executed criminals became the property of the hangman. Relatives or friends could purchase them if they had the means, otherwise the bodies were sold to surgeons to be dissected. The bargaining between hangman and relatives was often hard, sordid and public, and sometimes resulted in undignified scuffles, when the body was almost literally torn apart. But the cadaver and its clothes were not the only perquisites of the hangman. He could also sell the rope, and in the case of a notorious criminal this could fetch as much as a shilling an inch. The rope which had hanged John Williams would certainly have fetched at least that sum, while such a smart young man would no doubt have made his last appearance in a suit well worth bargaining over.

Williams, however, would have been spared the three-hour torture of the ride to Tyburn. In 1783 the place of execution was transferred to Newgate, and it was on a scaffold hung with black, and especially erected for each hanging in an open space in front of the prison, that the condemned of 1812 were dispatched. John Williams himself, when home from his voyages, must often have witnessed such scenes. They were, after all, notable public events which emptied the factories and workshops, the coffee houses and taverns, and made an equal appeal to the fastidious aristocrat with a taste for the macabre or the lowest of the mob. One can picture Williams, female acquaintance on his arm, his remarkable yellow hair well-combed, dapper in his blue coat and yellow and blue striped waistcoat, as he pressed forward through the throng to get a better view of the scaffold, then waited for that exhilarating moment, that upsurge of mingled terror and sensuality, when the drop fell. For executions were now more humane. They were still unscientific, still frequently botched, but the adoption of the drop as a general mode of execution in 1783 meant that the accused had at least a reasonable chance of instantaneous death. The deaths from the carts at Tyburn were seldom as merciful; the hangman or relatives often had to pull at the legs of the delinquent in the hope of ending his agony, while every convulsion of the victim's limbs would be hailed with shrieks of execration or groans of pity.

But if the drop was more merciful it was also more effective, and there was now virtually no hope of bringing the executed back to life. This, although uncommon, was certainly not unknown. Criminals were sentenced to be hanged by the neck until they were dead, but it was the hangman who decided when life was extinct. By tying and placing the knot in a particular way, or by cutting down the condemned sooner than was usual, it was possible to make subsequent revival a

comparatively easy matter. A felon with money to bribe the
hangman, friends to care, could reasonably hope for a premature resurrection in a nearby tavern where the means to
resuscitation would be to hand. It was not a resurrection for
which Williams could have hoped. But if executions at Newgate were more expeditious and humane, the mob that
attended was the same mob who made hideous the long
purgatory from Newgate to Tyburn. They would gather from
early morning to gain their vantage points, rich and poor,
thief and gentry, men, women and children, whiling away the
time until the entertainment began with gossip and laughter,
ribald jokes, petty thieving or the hawking of merchandise.
There were some who came to pity, most who came out of
morbid curiosity, and some because few sights were so fascinating to them as a human being in the agony of death. The
removal of the scene of execution from Tyburn to Newgate
Prison may well, as a chronicler of Newgate states, have made
the performance shorter and diminished the area of display,
but the entertainment was still as popular. When Holloway
and Haggerty were executed in 1807 for a murder committed
five years earlier 40,000 people assembled near the prison.
Because of the pressure of the mob some of the spectators
tried to withdraw. This only increased the confusion, and
soon panic broke out in which nearly 100 people were trampled
to death or injured. At an execution in 1824 no less than
100,000 people assembled at Newgate. One may be sure that
the execution of John Williams would have rivalled this event
in general popularity.

Apart from the general disappointment there were others
as well as the hangman who had been cheated of their pickings.
The Ordinary of Newgate, to which prison Williams would
have been committed, could no longer hope for a lucrative
sale from the murderer's published confession which it would
have been his responsibility – and probably his pleasure –
to extract. The Ordinary of Newgate at that time was
the Reverend Brownlow Ford LLD. Dr. Ford was probably
no worse or better than the majority of Newgate parsons;
indeed he later professed to Jeremy Bentham a great interest
in prison reform, and, in 1805, he had submitted to the Home
Secretary a long list of suggested improvements in the system

of policing. But the early nineteenth century was no more successful than is the twentieth in recruiting the right people to jobs requiring exceptional dedication, compassion and mental stamina, but rewarded with low pay and negligible public esteem. A parliamentary committee which investigated the state of prisons wrote about the Reverend Brownlow Ford that 'beyond his attendance in chapel and on those who are sentenced to death, Dr. Ford feels but few duties to be attached to his office. He knows nothing of the state of morals in the prisons; he never sees any of the prisoners in private; he never knows that any have been sick until he gets a warning to attend their funeral, and does not go to the Infirmary for it is not in his instructions.' When a Mr. J. T. Smith wished to visit one of the condemned before his execution, and went to see Dr. Brownlow Ford, he found him at the public house in Hatton Garden, where he was known to reside, 'seated most pompously in a superb masonic chair under a stately crimson canopy while the room was clouded with smoke curling to the ceiling, which gave Mr. Smith a better idea of what he had heard of the Black Hole of Calcutta than any place he had seen'. But it is unlikely that Dr. Ford was negligent in his attention to the more notorious of the condemned. Their situation would have been too interesting, their confessions too lucrative. Some of his charges, while enlarging in most uncharacteristic language on the Sabbath breaking, drunkenness, or moral delinquency that had led to their present unhappy state, may have been consoled, or at least gratified, by his attentions. It was probably the first time in their lives that they had been the object of such concentrated spiritual concern. Impending death makes the dullest of us interesting to our fellows, and it is not surprising that fees were charged to those wishing to view condemned prisoners. A visit to the monster of Ratcliffe Highway would have been almost obligatory for the fanciers of violent death, while John Williams's confession, suitably amplified no doubt by Brownlow Ford, would have been a notable addition to the popular literature of the gallows. The account of the murders published in 1811 by Fairburn, must have seemed curiously incomplete without the customary confession and description of Williams's demeanour on the scaffold.

But if the drama could not now end in the murderer's public ignominy at Newgate, at least some reasonable alternative could be staged whereby the mob might be appeased and society's abhorrence of the murderer amply demonstrated. On Monday, 30 December *The Times* announced: 'Mr Capper attended on the Home Secretary on Saturday for the purpose of considering with what justice the usual practice of burying the culprit of a similar description in the cross road nearest the spot where the offence of suicide is committed might be departed from in this extraordinary instance of self-murder.' There is no record of what precisely passed between them at this meeting, but immediately after it Beckett wrote to Capper:

I have talked with **Mr. Ryder** of the matter you mentioned this morning. He agrees in the opinion that it might be advisable to bury Williams in Shadwell, and he sees no objection to the body being exhibited previously near the place appointed for interment, provided no risk is run of creating disturbance, if the magistrates should be of the opinion that by the help of the police officers of your office, and those who it may be desired to attend from the Thames Police Office, this danger can be prevented. You will be so good as to see the Coroner and arrange with him for the ceremony, which I understand you to say would take place on Monday.

The letter concluded by asking Capper to consult Story and Markland about the distribution of the reward money.

The ceremony to which Beckett referred was well recognised as a public mark of obloquy when an offender who had been condemned to death committed suicide while awaiting execution. It was usual to bury him at a dark hour at the intersection point of four roads, and to drive a stake through the body. There seems to have been no legal authority for the custom, and it probably arose from an old superstition that only by driving a stake through the body could the ghost of the dead and self-damned be prevented from returning to earth to plague the living. The significance of the crossroad may have lain in the fact that the sign of a cross implied sanctity; but the more usual belief was that the evil ghost, if he did succeed in breaking free of the impaling stake, would hesitate irresolutely at the four roads, uncertain which to take. The practice was certainly not unusual at the time, although it was even then being criticised; and the last burial of a suicide in London at a crossroad is said to have been in June 1823, when a man named Griffiths was buried in the early hours of the morning at the junction of Eton Street, Grosvenor Place and the King's Road, but with no stake driven through the body. Sometimes the body of the convicted offender was displayed to the public. In December 1793, a Londoner, Lawrence Jones, who had been convicted of robbery in Hatton Garden and ordered for execution on 8 December, was found dead in his cell by the turnkey who entered to prepare him to hear the condemned sermon and to receive the sacrament. Jones had succeeded in strangling himself most ingeniously by winding one end of his knee strings around his neck, knotting the other end to the ring by which his chain was fastened, and bracing both feet against the wall. His clothed and fettered body, the face covered with a cloth, was extended upon a plank on top of an open cart and was then hurled into a pit at the foot of Hatton Garden with a spike driven through the heart. It may have been this case which the magistrates had in mind when considering what should be done with Williams's body. But there was a difference. Williams had not been found guilty and condemned to death. He had not been committed for trial. He had not been given the most ancient and cherished of an Englishman's rights, the opportunity to plead before a jury of his fellows.

The magistrates at Shadwell were not the only people who had opinions on what should happen to Williams's corpse. That weekend Sir John Carr wrote from his home in Rayner Place, Chelsea, a letter to the Home Secretary in which excitement seems to have had a deleterious effect on punctuation:

Sir John Carr presents his compliments to Mr. Ryder and takes the liberty of suggesting, as no doubt can now be entertained of the guilt of the wretch whose atrocities have so justly excited the public horror and indignation, whether salutary example might not be presented to the lower orders by parading the body of Williams from the Coldbath Prison to Ratcliffe Highway where it is presumed the law is to take its course; (the corpse) to be covered with a piece of red cloth and placed with the face uncovered and upwards on a large board to be fixed upon the top of a cart with the murderous instruments placed on either side of the corpse before which the common executioner might be seated; the stake with which the body is to be pinned to be borne before by a proper officer and foot constables to keep the crowd at a safe distance from the cart, to have the date shown of the procession and the names of the streets through which it is to pass announced in the papers.

Beckett noted on the letter: 'Mr. Ryder's compliments to Sir J. Carr, and acquaint him that an arrangement of the sort mentioned by him has been already made.' And so, to quote *The Examiner:* 'the premature death of Williams having defeated the end of that justice with which it is probable from the very suspicious circumstances that have transpired, this wretched man would have been overtaken, the magistrates came to a resolution of giving the greatest solemnity and publicity to the ceremony of interring this suicide.'

About ten o'clock on the night of Monday 30 December, Mr. Robinson, the High Constable of St. George's parish, accompanied by Mr. Machin, one of the constables, Mr. Harrison, the tax collector, and Mr. Robinson's deputy, went to Coldbath Fields Prison, where the body of Williams was delivered to them. It was put into a hackney coach. The Deputy Constable joined it. The blinds were drawn, the doors firmly closed, the horses whipped into a brisk trot. The other three gentlemen thought it more seemly, as it must certainly have been more comfortable, to travel in a separate coach. It was left to the unfortunate Deputy Constable to clatter over the cobblestones to the Watch House of St. George's, with the dead eyes of the demon of Ratcliffe Highway fixing his in a dead stare whenever, by some extraordinary compulsion, he found himself gazing at the suicide's face. Knowing to what a height of hysterical and superstitious fear this single, somewhat inadequate young man had reduced London, it must be imagined that the journey was not agreeable. The Deputy Constable, with the body of John Williams clumsily rolling on the seat opposite him, must have tried not to think what might happen if a horse stumbled, the coach lurched to a stop, and he and his sinister travelling companion were exposed to the view of the mob. There was little chance that Williams's body would survive intact, and his own might well be in jeopardy. The journey must have seemed unnaturally long, and it was with relief that he would feel the darkened coach draw to a halt at the Watch House of St. George's, known by the name of 'Roundabout', at the bottom of Ship Alley. Here, ungentle hands were laid on the corpse, and it was cast into what is described as the 'black hole' to await the next day's ceremony.

On Tuesday morning, at nine o'clock, the High Constable with his attendants arrived at the Watch House. They were accompanied by a cart that had been fitted up for the purpose of giving the greatest possible degree of exposure to the face and body of the supposed murderer. On the cart a platform had been erected, made of wooden boards which extended from one end to the other, forming an inclined plane. On this the body rested, its feet supported on a crossbar and the torso retained in an extended position by a cord which passed beneath the arms, and was fastened underneath the board. All the contemporary accounts agree that the countenance was fresh and ruddy and perfectly free from discolouration. The hair, of a remarkable sandy colour, curled round the face. The body was clothed in a pair of blue cloth pantaloons and a white-frilled shirt open at the neck, with the sleeves tucked up to the elbows. It wore neither coat nor waistcoat. On both hands were some livid spots, and *The Times* reported that the arms from the elbows downwards were almost black.

The cart was suitably decorated. On the left of the head was fixed perpendicularly the blood-stained maul. On the right, also in a perpendicular position, was fixed the ripping chisel. Above the head the iron crow found beside Williams's body was laid in a transverse direction, and parallel to it a stake sharpened at one end. About half past ten the procession moved off from the Watch House. *The Times* ceremonially sets out the order of the parade:

Mr. Machin, Constable of Shadwell
Mr. Harrison, Collector of King's Taxes
Mr. Lloyd, baker
Mr. Strickland, coal-merchant
Mr. Burford, stationer
    and
Mr. Gale, Superintendent of Lascars in the East India
    Company's service – all mounted on grey horses.

Next came:

The Constables, Headboroughs, and Patrols of the
    Parish, with drawn cutlasses,
The Beadle of St. George's, in his official dress
Mr. Robinson, the High Constable of St. George's,
The Cart with the BODY; followed by
A large body of constables.

The procession moved off in an impressive and unnatural silence. The Home Secretary's fear that the enraged mob might seize and wreak vengeance on the corpse proved unfounded. All contemporary records mention the strange and unexpected calm. The frail body was guarded as if it might suddenly leap to life and fall upon its persecutors. But the drawn cutlasses, the phalanx of watchmen, were not required. No one sought to lay violent hands on Williams. There were no howls of execration, no screams of abuse. Why, one wonders, this unnatural restraint? It can hardly have been pity for the dead man. Few, if any, present had any doubt that here was the murderer of the Marrs and Williamsons. Few, if any, would have been repelled at this public display of his corpse, or indignant at the dishonour in store for it. Was it perhaps awe that kept them silent? Did they share the emotion which Coleridge confided to De Quincey some few months after the murder: 'For his part, though at the time resident in London, he had not shared in the prevailing panic; him the murders only affected as a philosopher and threw him into a profound reverie upon the tremendous power which is laid open in a moment to any man who can reconcile himself to the abjuration of all conscientious restraints if at the same time thoroughly without fear'. Was the silence one of speechless amazement that this frail body could have achieved so much horror? Or was the mob stunned into silence by wonder that the monster who had added self-murder to his heinous crimes, could wear such a human face?

The cavalcade passed slowly down Ratcliffe Highway to Marr's shop, and here it stopped. As the cart shook to a halt, Williams's head flopped to one side, as if he could not bear to look at the scene of the holocaust. One of the escorts climbed on to the cart and firmly placed the body so that the dead eyes seemed to be gazing into the house at the uneasy ghosts of his victims. After about ten minutes the driver urged the horse forward, and the parade started off again. Of all the processions which London has known in its long and often dark history there can be few as bizarre and macabre as this parade on New Year's Eve, 1811, of a corpse dead four days, through the drab streets of riverside Wapping. The body, dressed in its tawdry and prison-stained finery with the left leg still ironed, the crude cart with the hastily constructed platform, the one lumbering horse; all were in ghastly contrast to the ranks of pretentious authority with which this solitary corpse was escorted to its ignoble grave.

It was estimated that over ten thousand people witnessed the spectacle. Every window was patterned with faces, every pavement crowded, every doorway crammed. The cart rumbled on in the grey half-light down streets where Williams had walked in life, past the pubs where he had roistered, flirted with barmaids, danced and quarrelled. From Marr's shop it was led down Old Gravel Lane, by the London Dock wall to Cinnamon Street, and from there on to Pear Tree Alley, where it stopped for some time close to the Vermilloe's public house, where Williams had lodged. It then proceeded into Sir William Warren's Square for the purpose of turning round, since there was no passage for a cart into Wapping. The procession re-entered Cinnamon Street, proceeded through King Edward Street, along Wapping and up New Gravel Lane. Here it again halted for ten minutes outside the King's Arms. It was afterwards recalled that the dreaful silence which fell when the cart creaked to a stop was broken by one sharp and terrible sound. A hackney coachman who had halted his coach

VIEW OF THE BODY OF JOHN WILLIAMS

the supposed Murderer of the families of Marr and Williamson, and Self-destroyer, approaching the hole dug to receive it, in the Cross Road, at Cannon Street Turnpike.

near the top of the lane uncurled his whip, bent down from his seat, and with an oath delivered across the dead face three short-arm lashes.

From the King's Arms the procession made its slow way along Ratcliffe Highway and up Cannon Street to the turnpike gates at which four roads met, the new road north to White-chapel, Back Lane (also known as Cable Street) running from Well Close Square east to Sun Tavern Fields and Cannon Street. Here a hole about four feet deep, three feet long and two feet wide, had been dug ready. The hole was too small for the body, deliberately so. There was no intention that these ignoble limbs should lie in the semblance of innocent sleep, or be decently disposed as if laid out for Christian burial. Williams's body was seized, tumbled roughly out of the cart, and forced into the hole. Immediately one of the escorts jumped down beside it and began to drive the stake through the heart. As the blood-stained maul thudded on the stake the silence of the crowd was at last broken and the air became hideous with shouts and execrations. A quantity of unslaked lime was cast into the hole; it was then filled with earth, and the paving stones were immediately replaced and hammered down. *The Times* ends its report:

> The parties forming the procession then dispersed and those persons who had not had an opportunity of witnessing the awful ceremony advanced, and while regarding the grave of one who had proved himself such a disgrace to humanity, they seemed to entertain no other feeling than horror for his crimes and regret that he had not lived to receive at the hands of justice that ignominious punishment which the laws of his country prescribed, but which when compared with his guilt seemed an inadequate compensation to the enraged feelings of his fellow subjects.

But, however subdued their behaviour, the mob were still the mob, and the usual thieves and pickpockets were about their business. Humphrey, one of the Bow Street Runners, was not so enthralled by the parade of a corpse, however notorious, that he could not keep his eyes on the living. He detected two of his old acquaintances in the act of robbing a gentleman,

George Bignall, an accomplice of Scott, a notorious pickpocket, and Robert Barry, one of Bill Soames's gang. He arrested them both, and they were committed for want of bail until the next sessions.

After Williams's burial the newspapers reported that there had been found in one of his pockets after his death a piece of iron hoop 'sufficiently sharp to wound him mortally'. At first it excited surprise how he had come by it, since it had not been on him when he was first taken into custody, nor when he was put into the lock-up house. The officers at length discovered that it formed part of the iron fastening which secured the walls of the temporary lock-up in the Lebeck Head opposite the Shadwell Office. They compared the piece of iron hoop with the broken part of the fastening, and concluded that, during his very short confinement in the public house before he was removed to Coldbath Fields Prison, Williams had wrenched away part of the iron hoop and reserved it for his purpose.

And so darkness fell over Shadwell and Wapping. The little groups standing around the grave melted away; the lamp-lighter made his round; the Watch prepared to call the hours. People came out of their houses less fearfully, a great terror lifted from their minds. No one who had really studied the evidence could imagine that the story had come to its end. But to the ignorant, the frightened and the defenceless, the day's business had brought comfort and reassurance. Whatever further discoveries about the crimes might be made, had not the demon of Ratcliffe Highway amply demonstrated his guilt and been laid at last? For a week or two they would tread warily around the place where the slightly uneven paving stones marked the wretch's grave. Children, greatly daring, would leap upon the stones, then rush for cover, fearful equally of their mothers' wrath and the contamination of those awful bones. For months there would hang about these crossroads the tenebrous *ambiance* of superstitious awe. But it was a busy street, and was to become busier. The hurrying feet, the wheels, the clattering hooves of nineteenth-century London would pass in a never ending stream over the dreadful grave until, in time, no one could be quite certain where the corpse of Williams lay.

On the following Sunday there could have been few sermons

preached in East London which did not deal with the abominable murders and with the murderer's dreadful end. One,
printed in Fairburn's 1811 pamphlet, probably to replace the
condemned sermon or the murderer's confession, either of
which would have more appropriately ended the book, is
typical of its kind in its evangelical fervour, its exoneration of
authority and particularly of the Government, from any
blame, and its reliance on the sanction of hell fire and damna-
tion to frighten the unrighteous into virtue and respectability.
The text was taken from the nineteenth chapter of St.
Matthew's Gospel at the eighteenth verse, 'Thou shalt do no
murder'. The opening passages are typical of the whole:

O my beloved Brethren! with what tongue, in what
language, shall I address you, on the recent alarming and
aweful events? Robbery and Rapine stalk abroad at noon-
day; Murder, cold-blooded Murder, seeks us in our very
dwellings; and, to use the emphatic language of the Coroner,
'Our houses are no longer our castles; we are no longer
safe in our beds!' What words of mine, my beloved Brethren!
can paint the universal consternation? Cries and lamenta-
tions fill our streets, terror and dismay appear on every
countenance!

To reflect that, in the short space of ten days, seven of our
fellow creatures, who were enjoying health and spirits like
ourselves, and dreaming of no danger, should all have been
barbarously massacred, at their own firesides, by the hands
of the midnight assassin, is surely enough to appal the
stoutest heart, to shock the most hardened criminal!

Some persons have made these melancholy transactions
the groundwork of complaint against the Government, but
I cannot see with what justice. How, let me ask such persons,
how could the Government have prevented the commission
of these dreadful deeds? What human sagacity could foresee
them? What mere mortal precaution could possibly have
guarded against them? If Government really possessed the
power of preventing such enormities, is it not natural to
believe that such power would be more particularly exerted
to shield the sacred Head of the State, to preserve the
Lord's anointed? And yet we all know that our beloved and

revered King himself (whose sore affliction we now so bitterly bewail) has, in the course of his reign, had no less than three direct attacks on his sacred person! And to what was his safety owing? Not to the vigilance of his Government, not to the precautions of his Ministers, but, solely and wholly, to the superintending care of a gracious Providence! Maniacs and Murderers, as they are out of the pale of common humanity, are also out of the reach of human prevention. I know not what precautions could have saved the poor families, whose aweful fate now fills us with sorrow and amazement. That our system of Police is very defective, and that its negligence must be very great, is certainly proved by the daily depredations of pick-pockets and housebreakers. But, my beloved Brethren, I repeat it again and again, the best system of Police in the world could not have prevented the late dreadful occurrences. No, my beloved, it is not to office runners, it is not to the staff or to the man, that we must look for the prevention of such atrocities. It is to the all-seeing providence of GOD, – it is to the all-searching influence of his Holy Spirit, – it is to these, and to these alone, that every soul of us can look for security from similar horrors!

THE FRENCH KNIFE

The confident verdict of the Shadwell Bench, that Williams
was the sole murderer of both families, could have deceived no
one for long, possibly not even Capper and his colleagues. It
left too many questions unanswered. Who was the tall man
seen bending over Mrs. Williamson's body? Whose the two
sets of footprints in the Marrs' yard? Whose the noisy exit,
made by more than one pair of feet, through the empty house
in Pennington Street? Nor, despite what they had said in their
letter to Ryder, did the Shadwell Bench entirely relax their
efforts. They and the other magistrates began searching for
the second murderer. They were no doubt able to comfort
themselves with the belief that, if the killing were the work of
a gang, Williams was its organiser and its head. With the head
severed, the body, however malignant, could do little further
harm. The panic was subsiding. It was now a question of
justice rather than public safety that Williams's accomplices,
if any, should be brought to trial.

Reports of new evidence, fresh clues, further arrests, continued throughout January. On Monday, 6 January, *The
Times* reported that Cornelius Hart had been taken into
custody for the sixth time by the Whitechapel officers. One
of them had overheard Mrs. Vermilloe say that 'if Hart had
been examined as closely as she had, something more would
have come out'. However, the carpenter gave the same account
of himself at Shadwell as he had on the five other occasions
when he had been brought up before the magistrates, and
The Times reports that, 'as his story was confirmed by the
enquiries of the officers', he was again discharged.

Then, during the first week of January, the assiduous John
Harrison, prime favourite in the stakes for prize money, came
up with another clue. Although his story was uncorroborated
it was considered to be worth half a column in *The Times* of

6 January. It related to the missing weapon – the sharp knife or razor, with which the throats of the victims had been slit. If this weapon could be discovered and linked with John Williams, it would provide positive proof of his guilt; and Harrison's story was accordingly received with gratifying interest. He reported that about three weeks earlier he had asked Williams to return a borrowed pocket handkerchief of his. Williams had told him to go to the pocket of his jacket and get it for himself. Harrison had put his hand into Williams's pocket and had drawn out a new French knife, about six inches in length, with an ivory handle. He had asked Williams where he had got it and Williams had replied that he had bought it a day or two before. Harrison now recalled the incident and told the magistrates that he had never seen the knife since, although he had searched Williams's sea chest and every part of the Pear Tree in the hope of discovering it. *The Times* commented:

> At the Coroner's inquest on the bodies of the unfortunate persons murdered in New Gravel Lane, it was suggested by the surgeon that the throats of Mr. and Mrs. Williamson and the servant maid must have been cut with a razor, from the incized appearance of the wounds. It is now, however, pretty clear that these sanguinary deeds were perpetrated with the knife in question, especially when it is known that Williams never had a razor of his own, and always applied to the barber to be shaved; and moreover that no razor had been missing from the house where he lodged.
>
> This important piece of information respecting the knife never occurred to the witness during his numerous examinations, as necessary to be communicated to the magistrates.

Meanwhile, inquiries were being made into Williams's past. The magistrates believed, and with reason, that a man who could sever the throats of five human beings, one a baby, with the casual expertise with which he might butcher an animal, was unlikely to have had a peaceable or uneventful history. The worst character defect so far alleged against Williams was a tendency to make free with other men's tills, and, by implication, with their women. Surely some more heinous crime than insinuating manners and over-familiarity could be laid to his charge? People recalled Richter's evidence that the captain of the *Roxburgh Castle* had prophesied that, if Williams lived to go on shore, he would be hanged. This was a promising lead, and the evidence for the remarkable prognostication was accordingly sought.

The sea captain's story, given to an enterprising *Times* reporter and told in the issue of New Year's day 1812, is important for the light it throws on the past of other men than Williams, and for the close connection it reveals between some of the protagonists in the case.

The accounts given of Williams and his connections, on the authority of the Captain of the *Roxburgh Castle* shew that this desperado, and one at least of his companions, were known, previous to the recent horrid murders, to be men of very bad character; and the discharge of Ablass (the particular associate of Williams) out of custody, on the deposition of a woman so directly interested in his fate, is to be regretted. It is but justice, however, to state, as our belief, that this fact did not appear before the magistrates at the time of his examination.

Williams (as he has been called) shipped himself in the name of John Williamson, in August 1810, in the *Roxburgh Castle*, Captain Hutchinson, bound to the Brazils, as an ordinary seaman. The ship having been detained a long time at Rio Janeiro, proceeded afterwards for a cargo to Demarara, from whence she returned on the 3rd or 4th October last, at which time Williamson was discharged, and was paid upwards of £40, the balance of his wages. Captain Hutchinson supposes, as he possessed an address superior to his situation, wrote a good hand, and had gone to sea at an advanced age, that he must have been driven to that line of life by his former bad conduct. As sailors on a long voyage, under strict discipline, have not opportunities of doing much mischief, Captain Hutchinson cannot relate much of Williams's misconduct; but mentions his attempting to impose himself upon a man at Rio Janeiro, as second mate of the *Roxburgh Castle*, and by that means obtaining a small sum of money. It was this circumstance that drew from Captain Hutchinson the expression attributed to him, 'that if he lived to go on shore, he would certainly hang'.

Williamson always endeavoured to pass as a native of Scotland; but Captain Hutchinson, who is himself from that country, easily discovered him to be an Irishman, and supposes him to be from the County of Down. When paid his wages by the owners, he represented himself to them as coming from Campbelltown, in Argyleshire. Besides the fraud committed on the second mate of the *Roxburgh Castle*, Williamson was engaged in a mutiny.

Captain Hutchinson, in his late voyage, had altogether a very bad crew; and whilst proceeding from Rio Janeiro to Demarara, when off Surinam, they broke into open mutiny; upon which Captain Hutchinson anchored under the guns of the fort at Braam's Point; and applied to Captain Kennedy, of His Majesty's brig *Forester*, who by threats and persuasion, procured their return to their duty. Three of the principals in the business were sent into confinement in Surinam for 24 hours; one of these was William Ablass, the same person who was apprehended on suspicion of being concerned with Williams in the late murders. Williams on this occasion escaped punishment, having pleaded that he was led astray by his companions.

From the evidence adduced before the magistrates, it appears that two men were represented as having been seen running from the house of Mr. Williamson, when the murders were committed – one a man, six feet high, the other shorter. Williams (or Williamson) was five feet eight inches high; and Ablass is a stout man, about six feet. So far these two men answer the description of the fugitives. Further, Ablass states himself to be a native of Danzig, but speaks very good English. At his examination on Saturday last, before Mr. Markland, at Shadwell office, he acknowledged he had been drinking in company with Williams, at three or four public-houses, on the night of the murders at Mr. Williamson's. He said that he left his comrade, Williams, at half-past eight, when he went home, and sat up till twelve, and then retired to bed. Being asked by the magistrate if he could prove this, he said he could by means of his landlady. She was sent for and attended with another woman. Her story was, that the prisoner came home from half-past nine to ten o-clock, and went to bed at twelve. It was remarked to the magistrates at the time, that the woman who attended with the landlady of Ablass had been in the habit of coming to the counting house of the owners of the *Roxburgh Castle*, to receive a monthly allowance of Ablass, and always represented herself, and signed the receipt, as his wife. Ablass denied, previous to this woman coming forward, that he had any wife, and appeared not to wish to claim any intimacy with the witnesses. Upon being asked how he had supported himself for so long without employment, he said he had pawned his clothes, and lived upon the bounty of some good friends. Under these circumstances, and upon the word of these women (for we are informed that they were not sworn) Ablass was discharged.

John Harris (sic), the sail-maker, who was the first to communicate his suspicions of the guilt of Williams, served on board the *Roxburgh Castle* in that capacity. He had the best opportunity of studying the character of the man. Having been the only means of pointing out one of the authors of these barbarous murders, and bearing a character from the Captain the very reverse of that of Williams, he seems deserving of some reward.

Harrison's story of the missing French knife was particularly interesting to the Shadwell Bench, whose main efforts were still directed towards finding further proof of Williams's guilt. It now occurred to them that a thorough search of the privy at the Pear Tree might reveal both the missing knife and Williamson's watch, and they gave orders for the privy to be emptied and rigidly examined. This was the first time that any part of the Pear Tree was officially searched, despite the fact that it must have been apparent to the magistrates that the Vermilloes' public house lay at the very heart of the mystery. Their neglect of this obvious and essential step is an indication of their ignorance of the first principles of criminal investigation. It may have taken a passage in the *Morning Chronicle* of 30 December to remind them of their duty:

There was certainly something very particular, and indeed mysterious, in the manner in which Mrs. Vermilloe gave her evidence, difficult to be accounted for. The ruffians concerned in the perpetration of these most dreadful murders appear to have resided near the spot, and perhaps search warrants might have produced some unexpected discovery in the neighbourhood. This hint, if attended to, may not yet perhaps be too late in regard to one or two public as well as private houses, frequently mentioned in the examinations.

Accordingly on Saturday, 4 January, Holbrook and Hewitt were dispatched for this disagreeable duty. The Pear Tree had had its share of excitement but the news of this fresh activity brought the crowd round again. One can imagine the scene. Richter's sullen face watching from an upstairs window. The enterprising John Harrison, anxious as always to demonstrate his zeal in the service of the law, pressing forward to volunteer his assistance. The crowd of regulars from the tap-room, kept at a respectful distance by police officers and watching in hostile silence while Mrs. Vermilloe, truculent and apologetic by turns, resentful of this fresh intrusion, but mindful of the power of the magistrates and the hope of reward, led Holbrook and Hewitt to the privy. We are not told when it was last emptied although this evidence is, of course, vital when considering the significance of any articles found. The officers worked away, grateful, no doubt, that this duty had fallen to them on a cold morning in early January rather than in the heat of summer. They laid out their finds in the yard. The search was not unrewarding. They discovered a pair of old blue seaman's trousers, part of a seamstress's hussive and a pair of clasp scissors. The scissors were attached to the hussive, and the immediate reaction of the officers was that these articles must have been owned by either Mrs. Williamson or Mrs. Marr. The trousers, which had been pushed to the bottom of the privy with a birch broom were then washed. After the filth has been cleared away there appeared on them what *The Times* describes as 'the most evident marks of blood in every direction'. Hoping to identify these articles with Williams, the magistrates ordered Mrs. Vermilloe, John Harrison the sail-maker, and Margaret Jewell to attend on

Monday, 6 January, and to give any information within their knowledge. Next day *The Times* reported the result:

Mrs. Vermilloe stated that she had often seen the trowsers of the description produced before the magistrates, but she could not pretend to say that she had ever before seen the identical pair in question. Sailors, in coming from the East Indies, used to wear such trowsers on board ship and they generally had them on when first landing; but she thought they were too shabby for Williams to have worn on shore. He was always very smart in his dress, but particularly so when in the house.

John Harrison said that he had frequently seen the trowsers throwing about the lumber room in the Pear Tree public house where seamen, on landing, used to throw off their sea apparel and deposit their chests and other lumber. He could not, however, undertake to say that he had ever seen them worn by Williams. He might have worn them, but he had never seen them upon him.

Margaret Jewell said she knew nothing of the scissors produced. Her late mistress had always used a much larger kind; and had she ever had those in question she certainly must have observed them. With respect to the part of the hussive produced, she professed equal ignorance. Mrs. Vermilloe also declared that she had never seen the scissors before.

Holbrook and Hewitt deposed as to the finding of these articles; and both of them declared that the stains on the trowsers were those of blood. Hewitt produced a caulking chisel which he found in a drawer in the lumber room at the Pear Tree, with the letters J. P. pricked upon it in the same manner as those letters were marked upon the maul found in Mr. Marr's house. The other tools belonging to John Peterson were not marked in that way upon the iron, but only upon the wood. This new discovery still more strongly confirms the identity of that fatal instrument with the house wherein the suicide had lodged. The identification of the scissors remains doubtful until Catherine Stillwell, the grand-daughter of the late Mr. Williamson, comes forward. She is ordered to attend this day before the magistrates.

There is no further mention in the contemporary reports of Catherine Stillwell's evidence. One assumes that she was unable to identify either the scissors or the hussive; had she done so this further link of the Pear Tree with one of the murders would surely have been mentioned. The mysterious finds in the privy had done nothing to advance the case against Williams. The seaman's trousers, the hussive and the scissors were never identified. Why and by whom they were stuffed into the privy remain minor mysteries.

Meanwhile Aaron Graham had continued his patient investigations. It was apparent both to him and to Ryder that the case was still unsolved, and on Tuesday, 7 January, the Home Secretary ordered the maul and the ripping chisels to be taken from Shadwell office and deposited at the Bow Street Police Office, each exhibit carefully marked. This may well have been the first time Graham had had the opportunity of examining them closely. Then, later that week, on January 10th, the Home Secretary sent to Shadwell for the full depositions taken from all the witnesses. It is a fair inference that he passed them on to Graham. The search for the second murderer had been placed by the Home Secretary firmly in his hands. Events from now on moved quickly, and the story is best told from the contemporary records:

The Times, Monday, January 13th. Bow Street – Mrs. Vermilloe, the landlady of the Pear Tree public house, and Turner, the man who lodged in the house of Williamson, who was barbarously murdered, have attended at the Office within these few days, with several other persons by order of Mr. Graham, and have undergone private and strict investigations: which induced him to dispatch, Lavender, Vickery and Adkins on Friday evening to apprehend a man of the name of *Hart*, who it has been ascertained, worked in the house of Mr. Marr on the day the murders were committed; and was seen in the company of Williams between ten and eleven o'clock at night. The murderers are supposed to have entered Mr. Marr's house about twelve o'clock.

On Saturday, *Hart* underwent a private examination before Mr. Graham, after which he was ordered into close confinement, and a man to take care and sit up with him.

On Saturday the privy of the house where *Hart* lodged was emptied, in the presence of Vickery and Adkins, but nothing particular was found.

The Times, Thursday, January 16th. A most important discovery has been made within these two days which removes every shadow of doubt respecting the guilt of the late suicide Williams. It was proved before the magistrates of Shadwell Office that three weeks before the murder of Mr. Williamson and his family, Williams had been seen to have a long French knife with an ivory handle. That knife could never be found in Williams's trunk or amongst any of the clothes he left behind him at the Pear Tree public house. The subsequent search to find it has been unsuccessful. On Tuesday Harrison, one of the lodgers at the Pear Tree, in searching among some old clothes, found a blue jacket which he immediately recognised as part of Williams's apparel. He proceeded to examine it closely, and upon looking at the inside pocket he found it quite stiff with coagulated blood, as if a blood-stained hand had been thrust into it. He brought it down to Mrs. Vermilloe, who instantly sent for Holbrook and another Shadwell Officer to make further search of the house. Every apartment then underwent the most rigid examination for almost an hour and a half, when the officers came at last to a small closet where there was a heap of dirty stockings and other clothes, which being removed, they observed a bit of wood protruding from a mouse-hole in the wall, which they immediately drew out, and at the same instant they discovered the handle of a clasp knife, apparently dyed with blood; which upon being brought forth, proved to be the identical French knife seen in Williams's possession before the murders; the handle and blade of which were smeared all over with blood.

This fact completes the strong circumstantial evidence already adduced against the suicide. The bloody jacket also tends to confirm his guilt. It is pretty clear that that part of his apparel must have been stained with the blood of the unfortunate Mrs. Williamson, when the suicide was transferring her money, with his bloody hand, to his pocket.

The Times, Friday, January 17th. Mr. Graham pursued his private investigation in a room adjoining the Police Office. Mrs. Vermilloe, landlady of the Pear Tree, attended and gave her evidence at considerable length respecting a man of the name of *Ablass* who was apprehended on Wednesday evening and brought to the Office. The man has been in custody before, when he denied knowing Williams; it has since been proved that he was his companion. A boy has proved that he saw three men looking in at Mr. Marr's shop a short time before it was shut up on the night of the murders. *Ablass* is kept in close confinement, with a man to look after him.

The Times, Monday, January 27th. Mr. Graham went to the unfortunate Mr. Marr's premises on Thursday and examined some witnesses on the spot. The prisoners *Hart* and *Ablass* are still kept in close confinement, not being able to account to about a quarter of an hour of their time on the night of the murder at Mr. Williamson's. It has been ascertained that a man can walk at a quick pace in less than five minutes from Mr. Williamson's to the Pear Tree public house. On Saturday a man and woman who lived next door to Mr. Marr attended at the office and gave evidence respecting the horrible transaction. We understand it is their opinion that three or more persons were walking about at the time of the murders.

Parliamentary Debates, Hansard, Friday, January 31st. *Sir Francis Burdett:* 'What had they (the magistrates) been doing in the late examination which had taken place of persons who were supposed to have been concerned in the murder of Mr. Marr's family? . . . What was now the situation of that unfortunate person who was on confinement on suspicion of being concerned in the late murders, Ablass? What was he kept for? Why was he put in chains, immured in a dungeon and called upon every day to incriminate himself?' *The Home Secretary:* 'Ablass . . . had been asked some questions, which he declined to answer.' *The Prime Minister:* 'As to the severity which was asserted with respect to Ablass, there were circumstances of suspicion which led the magistrates to believe that he was on a given time at a given place; they did not require of him to criminate himself, though if he could have given a satisfactory account of himself during that period, the case would bear a very different complexion.'

The Times, Monday, February 3rd. On Saturday evening Ablass underwent another examination before Mr. Graham, and was discharged.

So, early in February, the case was drawing to its close, the key questions still unanswered. Was Williams the sole murderer of the Marrs and Williamsons or had others been concerned? Was Ablass discharged for want of evidence, or on account of political pressure? What did the case against Hart amount to? When was he released? What private information had Graham amassed after nearly two months of patient effort? What, at the end, did he secretly make of it all? By good fortune his final correspondence in the case with the Home Secretary has been preserved in the Public Record Office:

Sunday, February 2nd, 1812.

From some evidence which I obtained yesterday morning I judged it proper to discharge Ablass out of Custody in the Evening. I am now satisfied that there were two persons concerned in Williamson's murder and the Evidence on which I found my opinion induces me to believe that it was a shorter man than Ablass who accompanied Williams, if not in the actual perpetration of the deed, at least in assisting in or about the House at the time it was committed. Hart I have still in confinement, nor do I see how I can venture to release him yet. To speak plainly, I have the strongest suspicion that he was privy to, and in some way or other assisting, in the murder of Marr's family, although it will certainly be difficult and perhaps impossible ever to make it out. But I have proved the most material points of his own statement to be absolutely false. He told me, and still persists in it, that he never saw Mr. Marr after the Friday night (when he was known to be at work at Marr's house) whereas I have the Evidence of a Lady who was at the shop on Saturday (the night of the Murder) after nine o'clock when he came in and wanted to be allowed to finish the job (late as it was) which she understood from his conversation he had been employed upon. She has seen him since and is sure it was him that came into the shop while she was there. And what is very remarkable, he had a bag, or basket, of tools upon his shoulder which he does not account for, but which in my mind accounts in some measure for Williams's getting the maul so near to the place where he wanted it. To strengthen the suspicion, Hart is proved to have gone home that night exactly at the same time (one o'clock) that Williams did. On the following day (Sunday) he asserts that he was not out of Doors till late in the Evening and then only across the way to fetch some Liquor from the Pear Tree, instead of which two most respectable witnesses with whom he had worked a short time before, therefore could not be mistaken in his person, saw him about ten o'clock in the morning near to Marr's house, when he saluted them by putting his hand to his Hat as he passed them. On the next day (Monday) he states in positive terms that he was at work all day at the House, and for the landlord, of the Crooked Billet, who produces his Book to prove, and swears also, that he recollects Hart did not do nor was paid for a stroke, of work done for him on that day – and whether Williams did the murder alone or in company with another, I have the most satisfactory Evidence that two if not three men made their Escape precisely at the time of the murder through the passage of the House in Pennington Street. In short, if ever a man was held on strong suspicion Hart is justly detained at the moment.

This letter is one of the most curious documents in the case, and suggests that the patient and intelligent Graham had finally been reduced to a state of indecision and illogicality more appropriate to the Shadwell Bench than to a magistrate of Bow Street. It may be that his powers were failing him, that the first symptoms of his last illness were already taking their toll. Certainly he was under pressure from all sides, and must have been conscious that his reputation was at stake. But

Ryder can hardly have felt that the letter advanced the case, nor have failed to be struck by its inconsistencies and omissions, and by the irrelevance of much of the information it contained.

For more than a fortnight Graham had kept Ablass in chains, and securely guarded. Now he had been released, but the magistrate does not specify the evidence on which he judged it proper to discharge one of his prime suspects. He states himself to be satisfied that two persons were concerned in Williamson's murder, one shorter man than Ablass, and again he provides none of the evidence on which this important deduction was based. One of the murderers, a tall man, was seen by Turner. He could not have been Williams. If Graham was correct in believing that two men were concerned in Williamson's murder, and that one of them *who accompanied Williams* was shorter than Ablass then Williams was innocent. The logic is inescapable and it is difficult to see how it escaped the intelligent Graham. He could hardly have believed that Turner, who knew Williams, was mistaken in failing to recognise him under such momentous circumstances.

Graham was obviously convinced of Hart's guilt but his letter does not deal with the strongest evidence against the carpenter – the presence of Pugh's chisel in Marr's shop. The magistrate had obviously been intrigued by the problem of how the murderer got the other weapon, the maul, into the shop. But it is not clear from the letter whether Graham is suggesting that Hart left his bag of tools at 29 Ratcliffe Highway after his earlier visit of nine o'clock, or whether he accompanied the killer, bearing the bag on his shoulder, and then handed over the maul to the murderer or attacked the victims himself. It is hardly feasible that the tools should have been left ready earlier in the evening. Marr would almost certainly have removed them from the actual shop during the busiest night of the week; and the murderer could have had no assurance that they would be to hand when he wanted them. Both killings were done with extraordinary speed. The door on each occasion was fortuitously open, Marr's because he was awaiting the return of Margaret Jewell, and Williamson's because he had not yet locked up for the night and was probably expecting Anderson to return for a final pot of beer. The

murderer must have had the weapon in his hand, probably
concealed under his coat as he entered, and must have struck
with immediate and ferocious strength. It seems unlikely that
Hart would have encumbered himself with a bag or basket of
tools over his shoulder, or that if he did, he would have taken
them away with him while leaving the maul and the chisel
behind. Certainly Graham produced a formidable weight of
evidence to prove Hart a liar, but Hart's lies about his movements on the Sunday and Monday are not directly relevant to
what was happening late on Saturday night. Graham's oddly
defensive letter is more a justification for his continuing to
hold Hart in custody than a convincing case against the
carpenter.

And with this confused communication the investigation
came to an end. Graham, baffled and frustrated, made no
further efforts to find the second murderer. On 7 February
Beckett returned the depositions to Shadwell. Hart, like
Ablass, was released; and with so little public notice that the
date is nowhere recorded. Sylvester Driscoll, too, was finally
discharged and probably thought himself lucky to go free
with nothing worse than a severe admonition from Markland for
his imprudent conduct. Driscoll was an egregious and diverting
rogue to the last. During the latter part of his confinement the
cells in Coldbath Fields Prison were so full that the clerk of the
prison told him that he must be moved to the cell next to that
in which the dead body of Williams lay. *The Times* reports:
'The poor fellow exclaimed in a paroxysm of alarm. "Don't
put me there, for I'm sure I'll die in half an hour!" As his
terrors were invincible he was humanely removed to another
apartment.'

Every day Harrison and Cuthperson had been calling at the
Shadwell Public Office demanding the reward money, so that
they could return to sea. Beckett called Capper and Markland
to the Home Office to assist in drawing a plan for distributing
the rewards, and towards the end of February the money was
paid out. The schedule survives:

An Account of Monies distributed as Rewards to persons who gave information and evidence touching the late Murders of Timothy Marr and his Family on the seventh day of December last and of John Williamson and his Family on the nineteenth day of the same month and paid by the direction of the Secretary of State for the Home Department's Viz!:

Sarah Vermilye who first gave information respecting John Williams, the supposed perpetrator of these Murders, who in consequence was apprehended — £30

Robert Vermilye who identified the Maul found in M! Marr's house and with which the Murders there were committed — £30

John Harrison and Michael Gottlieb Solberg who gave strong circumstantial evidence against Williams - £30 each — £60

Margaret Jewell Servant to M! Marr — 5

George Olney Watchman who with Margaret Jewell prevented by their timely appearance Marr's property being plundered — 5

John Turner, Inhabitant in Williamson's house and who first by his descent from the Window gave information of the Murders in that house — 5

Shadrick Newhall Watchman who received Turner in his descent from the Window — 5

George Bleugh another Watchman active on the occasion — 5

Carried on £145.

Brought over £ 145:—

Mary Rice. Washerwoman who proved Williams's linen
to have been bloody ——. ——— } 5:—

Susannah Orr who gave strong evidence respecting Williams
on another occasion ——, ——— } 5:—

Benjamin Young. a Watchman. who supported the evidence
of Mrs Orr and found a Chisel at her door
afterwards identified by Mrs Vermilye —— —— } 5:—

Joseph Holbrook
George Partridge
Robert Brown
John Butler
Thomas Robinson
Ralph Hope
William Hewitt
& Robert Willans

Police Officers at Public Office. Shadwell who
were very active and dilligent on the occasion
of these Murders £10 each ——— } 80:—.

Charles Horton an Officer of the Thames Police Office
who found the Maul at Mr Marr's ——— } 10:—

Geo Story
Ia Markland

£ 250.—

Public Office
Shadwell
27th February 1812.

Note: All the newspaper reports appear to have
misspelt *Vermilye* as *Vermilloe* and to have
anglicised *Colberg* as *Cuthperson*.

A CASE FOR PARLIAMENT

The macabre exhibition of Williams's corpse and its interment beneath the New Cannon Street paving stones may have gone some way towards appeasing the sense of outrage in East London, but it did nothing to restore public confidence in the system of police. Thirty years earlier the Gordon Riots had caused a public outcry in London against the impotence of constables and watchmen to protect the capital against the fury of drunken mobs, but nothing had been done. Now the demand was renewed, and this time it was nation-wide. The horrors of Ratcliffe Highway, intensified in people's imaginations by their unique combination of circumstances – the dark December nights, the mean streets, the sickening brutality of the crimes, the suddenness with which the murderer struck and as silently vanished, the final ghastly parade of an eighth carcase – afflicted the whole population with a sense of insecurity out of all proportion to the events themselves.

Here was a spontaneous, country-wide reaction to which it is hard to find a parallel in all our history – for the nearest, perhaps, we have to look abroad to the shock experienced in the United States after the assassinations of the Kennedys and Luther King. The nature of the crimes and the importance of the victims were very different, but the national psychological reaction in each case was remarkably similar. In England then, as in America many years later, men felt that a society which failed to prevent the commission of crimes so heinous must itself be rotten at the core. 'The late acts of atrocity stamp our character nationally as a most barbarous set of savages,' W. Wynyard wrote to his friend John Beckett, the Under-Secretary at the Home Office, in forwarding his own ideas for improving the police. Many were saying the same thing. In Keswick, 300 miles distant from London, Robert

Southey expressed to a correspondent (Neville White) the very pith of this wave of anguish and self-criticism:

> We in the country here are thinking and talking of nothing but the dreadful murders, which seem to bring a stigma, not merely on the police, but on the land we live in, and even our human nature. No circumstances which did not concern myself ever disturbed me so much. I have been more affected, more agitated, but never had so mingled a feeling of horror, and indignation, and astonishment, with a sense of insecurity too, which no man in this state of society ever felt before, and a feeling that the national character is disgraced. I have very long felt the necessity of an improved police, and these dreadful events, I hope and trust, will lead to the establishment of one as vigilant as that of Paris used to be. The police laws cannot be too rigorous; and the usual objection that a rigorous police is inconsistent with English liberty might easily be shown to be absurd.

Southey stated the nub of the argument precisely, and the issue had not changed for fifty years. How was an efficient system of police to be reconciled with traditional English liberties? The only police force familiar to Englishmen, the French, was notorious as an instrument of armed terror; and few were prepared to press for reform at the risk of introducing tyranny. On 27 December, when the terror in Ratcliffe Highway was at its height, John William Ward could write to a friend: 'They have an admirable police in Paris, but they pay for it dear enough. I had rather half-a-dozen throats should be cut in Ratcliffe Highway every three or four years than be subject to domiciliary visits, spies, and all the rest of Fouché's contrivances.'

But could the old system survive the shock of the Ratcliffe Highway murders? The *London Chronicle*, in its Christmas Day leader, had called emphatically for a proper system of police. To the *Morning Post* the alternatives were stark: 'Either respectable householders must determine to be their own guardians or we must have a regularly enlisted armed police under the orders of proper officers.' Not all, however, saw the matter so simply. The *Morning Chronicle* reminded its readers how the police of Paris was 'most dexterously contrived for the purpose of tyranny', yet, nevertheless, believed that the 'stain on the character of our country' required a revision of the old system: 'We never think of taking down an old, shattered ruin of incumbrance, till we find it tumbling on our heads. This is the English beaten road of improvement. We always appear to improve less from choice than from necessity.' Public opinion was confused as well as shocked.

This prevailing ignorance explains why even now, in the weeks following the murders, while panic was still only slowly abating and householders everywhere were fixing chains to their doors and bolts to their windows, the idea of a regular police force gained little support. The great majority of those who cared enough to write to the Home Office preferred simpler solutions. Reform should start with the watchmen. They should be younger, and someone – perhaps a police officer from the Public Office? – should have a duty to inspect them during the night. The seats should be removed from the watch boxes to prevent their occupants from falling asleep. They should be armed with pistols and cutlasses and relieved of their rattles. Better men might be persuaded to serve if it were decided to change the 'degraded name of watchman for Warden of the Night'. The links between watchmen and prostitutes should be broken by arranging that any woman who showed the 'least sign of inducement should be sent to sift cinders, or if diseased, to a hospital – if this plan was adopted throughout the Kingdom it would do more for the preservation of the Army and Navy than 2,000 Doctors, besides being the means of increasing the population'. One ardent reformer even recommended that a watchman should be liable to imprisonment if, through negligence, he allowed a house on his beat to be broken into.

Other, more imaginative, ideas flowed in. One correspondent suggested that convicted thieves should be branded with the letter 'T', and if the crime were atrocious, with the letter 'V' also; suspects should be branded with the letter 'S'. Many people favoured the offer of bigger rewards. Someone suggested that criminals should be sent off to the army to fight wherever 'the battle raged fiercest'. George Greene, of Chelsea, was not afraid of tyranny. He recommended the police system that operated in St. Petersburgh, where 'every householder is obliged upon pain of imprisonment to give notice to the police officer of his quarter of every new inmate of his house, and the latter is obliged within the week to attend to have his name and residence registered'. A lighting contractor thought the remedy lay in better street lamps, and another recommended the erection of huge gas-lit beacons at 200-yard intervals, the outlines of which – reminiscent of the Eiffel Tower – he obligingly sketched. Garnet Terry, of Finsbury, applied the lessons of the murders in practical terms: 'Every house in which there is a male capable of bearing arms shall provide itself with a Hanger, Javelin or Pike, likewise a small Wicker Basket shield about twelve or more inches in Diameter with a strong wicker handle rising in a perpendicular direction from the centre of the concave side, this properly managed will be security against the blow of a maul or iron bar, and afford time for the thrust of the Cutlass, javelin or pike'.

Probably a vigorous Home Secretary could have pushed a radical Metropolitan Police Bill through the House of Commons in 1812. The mood of public opinion was receptive, and on 18 January, Ryder moved for a committee 'to enquire into the state of the nightly watch of the Metropolis'. If he needed any additional reminder of the state of public concern, he received it on the eve of the debate from a still terrified correspondent. The public should be excluded from the Chamber, *Pro bono publico* urged, and newspaper reporters admitted only on the understanding that the names of Members who spoke were not to be disclosed, for they would not afterwards 'be forgot by the miscreants who now put all law and religion to defiance; they would not hesitate a moment in disposing of the lives of those Gentlemen'. Happily *Pro bono publico's* fears proved to be exaggerated, and the distinction of those who took part in the debate testifies to the excitement and alarm that had now spread even to Parliament.

Introducing the motion, the Home Secretary said that although he did not consider it necessary to enter at any great length into the reasons for it, 'At the same time he felt himself justified in stating, that if the expediency of the measure rested upon the late horrible murders alone, by which two whole families had been completely exterminated, the atrocity of those crimes would in themselves have afforded sufficient ground.' It was true that no system of police could prevent the commission of such murders while there were persons vile and abandoned enough to commit them, but an improved nightly watch would be likely to diminish the chances. Those who had been abroad would know that even where there was a despotic, armed police, 'atrocities such as these were committed almost nightly, without exciting any of those deep impressions under which the mind of this country at present suffered'. The furore underlined the fact that few acts of this kind were committed here. Nevertheless, it was true that the law for appointing parish watchmen was being widely disregarded, partly because of the enormous growth of London. The Act required that the parish trustees should appoint none but 'able-bodied men' to guard the streets at night, but he knew of many instances in which those who were too old to earn their bread were appointed to be watchmen so that they would not be a burden on the parish. These were not the men to secure the lives and property of Londoners. It would be for the Committee to decide whether the system should be altered entirely, or whether it would be sufficient merely to enforce the present Act. But as far as he had thought about the matter at all, Ryder was rather inclined to the idea of enforcing the present system than of having recourse to anything new.

For the Opposition, the Home Secretary was followed by Sir Samuel Romilly, the penal reformer, who condemned the restricted terms of the motion. Anyone familiar with what had recently passed, and with the 'alarm and terror' which had spread throughout the Metropolis, must have expected much wider measures. The Committee ought to inquire not only into the state of the nightly watch, but also into the causes of the alarming increase of crime: for the past five or six years there had been a steady growth, and this, too, during wartime. It was a proved maxim that fewer offences were committed in a period of war than in peace, since many criminals enlisted in the armed services. But in this country of late, 'so far from being able to calculate on this solitary advantage, we were presented with a melancholy phenomenon of a protracted war and the continually increasing measure of offences against the peace and good order of society'. Moreover, the police had the strongest possible interest in multiplying crime since – unless they were 'men of the most refined principles of humanity and morality' – they would delay the detection of an offender until his crimes increased his value by increasing the reward for his arrest. 'Could it be endured with patience that such abuses should exist in the face of decency and commonsense? . . . His Right Hon. Friend had talked of other countries as affording greater and more frequent instances of atrocities than this: good God! where did those countries exist? He knew them not. He had never heard of them. He never remembered to have read of whole families destroyed by the hand of the murderer in any country but this.' The motion ought, Romilly urged, to be withdrawn, and submitted in a more comprehensive form.

So far in the debate little had been said about the details of the Ratcliffe Highway murders, but with the next two speakers came pointers to what was being said in high places in London more than a fortnight after Williams had been put underground.

William Smith, another Whig, supporting Romilly's proposal to widen the inquiry, went on: If the House 'attended to the nature of those horrible and barbarous outrages which for two months had kept the Metropolis in a state of perpetual alarm, and more particularly the atrocious murder of Mr. Marr's family (the authors of which had never yet been discovered), it would be evident that had the nightly watch of the Metropolis been in the best possible state those outrages and that murder could not have been prevented.' What could the watch have done? At best it could merely have driven the villains out of London into the surrounding villages, where people would have no protection.

So the authors of the Marrs' murders had never been discovered? The Prime Minister himself spoke next, and Perceval carried scepticism still further. 'The particular outrage that had excited such feelings of horror and detestation in the Metropolis, and the perpetrators of which, the Hon. Gentleman said, had escaped detection, was still wrapped up in mystery. It undoubtedly seemed strange that a single individual could commit such accumulated violence. The probability was that he was incapable of doing so; but on this subject no certain opinion could yet be formed. If this outrage was actually committed by the individual to whom he had before alluded (Williams), it was untrue to say that the culprit had not been found; but certainly he must repeat that it seemed strange to him that such devastation could be occasioned by a single individual. At the same time, as far as he had been able to trace the circumstances of the case, it appeared to be yet uncertain whether or not others were concerned in this horrible atrocity. But as the Hon. Gentleman had himself said, no state of nightly watch, however excellent, could have prevented such a crime. Indeed he hardly knew in what system of police a prevention could have been found. If such enormous guilt lurked in the human breast, no system of government could hinder it from endeavouring to effect its object. It might be close to us; it might be in our houses. The only security against such crimes was the manner in which the general sentiment of mankind hunted down the individuals by whom they were perpetrated.'

The Prime Minister was followed by another Opposition speaker, Abercromby, who supported Romilly's argument that the growth of crime had shown the police to be totally inadequate to its object. He accordingly moved an amendment to the motion to add the words, 'And also of the state of the police of the Metropolis'. Then came a touch of Panglossian optimism. Sir Francis Burdett, the wealthy, spirited radical and hero of the masses, a sort of latter-day Wilkes, declared himself convinced that if the system of nightly watch were improved there would be no need for any police whatever. The country should revive a law of Edward I, by which every householder was compelled in his turn to watch for the protection of others. The respectable part of the population would in this way be accustomed to the use of arms, so they would be available for national defence in the event of an invasion, or to repress riots.

The Prime Minister, unimpressed by this logic, accepted the proposal to widen the inquiry; and then, late in the debate, Sheridan rose to his feet to deliver a scathing attack on the Government's complacent and timid reaction to the emergency, and on the whole conduct of the magistrates' investigation of the Ratcliffe Highway murders.

Sheridan began with an all-out political attack on the Home Secretary, and Ryder's myopic view of what needed to be done.

After the alarms of the recent atrocities had spread throughout every part of the Metropolis; after the general and feverish anxiety of the public for redress and protection, down came the Right Hon. Gentleman to the House, and in order to remove at once, and effectually all alarm and anxiety whatever, solemnly proposed that a Committee should be appointed to inquire into the state of the condition of the nightly watch! This would have been at any time the meekest of all meek propositions; and at the present crisis it was not only the meekest, but he must beg the Right Hon. Secretary's pardon, if he added, the silliest proposition which could possibly have been made. . . . Why not go further and move for an inquiry into the state of the parish nurseries? (a laugh). The Right Hon. Secretary came before them brimful of information; he told them that the Act required able-bodied watchmen; and then he told them that the men employed were not able-bodied, because, forsooth, they were weak, old, and decrepit – very satisfactory reasons certainly why they could not be very active, young and vigilant! And then the Right Hon. Gentleman told them further that these sort of men were unfit for their situations, that the service, in short, wanted recruits; and that as at present, there was no watch to protect the city at night, that, therefore, they ought to proceed, with all due deliberation, to inquire into the state and condition of the nightly watch. To be called upon gravely to all this was bad enough; but to be called upon, with all the characteristic gravity of the Right Hon. Secretary, was scarcely supportable. The Right Hon. Gentleman knew the importance his manner could give to trifles – he was in the habit of throwing such an inflexible air of grave solemnity round all he had to offer to the House, that there was really sometimes danger lest they should attach to the matter what belonged to the manner merely.

Having thus put Ryder in his place, Sheridan went on to hit out at English xenophobia, a subject about which, as an Irishman, he held strong views.

When those horrible atrocities were first committed in the neighbourhood of Shadwell, they all remembered how eager vulgar prejudice was to fasten upon a foreigner – people grew all of a sudden thoroughly persuaded that there was evidence upon the face of those murders to show that they were perpetrated by a Portuguese, and by none but Portuguese: 'Oh, who would do it but Portuguese?' was the general cry. Prejudice, however, did not long stand still upon the Portuguese. The next tribe of foreigners arraigned and convicted were the Irish (a laugh) and it was nothing but an Irish murder and could have been done only by Irishmen! Beastly as this prejudice was, the Shadwell magistrates were not ashamed to act up to it in all the meanness and bigotry of its indignant spirit, viewing the murder in no less a light than that of a Popish plot. They commenced an indiscriminate hunt after the Irish people; and when they had them, in order to come at once to the plot, they began with the deep leader of 'Are you a Papist?' or, 'If you deny that you are, show that you don't know how to cross yourself'. Amidst this general suspicion of aliens and Irishmen, he wished to know whether the Right Hon. Gentleman had consulted with the head of the Alien Office? Had he consulted with the proper officers of the district? Had he consulted with the police magistrates of any of the divisions? Had he consulted with anyone likely to give him information upon the subject? If he had not, and he believed he had not, then was it to be the less wondered at that the Right Hon. Secretary for the Home Department had thought it sufficient, upon such an occasion, to be delivered of his solemn proposition for inquiring into the state and condition of the nightly watch!

Finally Sheridan poured scorn on the metropolitan magistrates, repeating openly what plenty of people had been saying privately for weeks.

Was there no jobbing in their appointment of some of those
police magistrates? . . . Were not many persons tempted
into these situations who were totally unfit to discharge
the duties attached to them? . . . For some of the police
magistrates he entertained the highest respect, and he
mentioned with pleasure the name of Mr. Aaron Graham,
who had rendered the public considerable services in his
conduct in the superintendence of the hulks. He thought,
too, that the magistrates of Bow Street Office had been
uniformly active and vigilant, but what should he say of the
magistrates of Shadwell? How should he attempt to describe
a conduct, in which folly and rashness were constantly
endeavouring to make amends for the grossest neglect of
duty? At one time we saw them mixing in the indiscriminate
cry of the mob, and greedily indulging in the prodigality
of seizing upon every man with a torn coat and a dirty shirt;
and at another, leaving Williams with all the means necessary to commit self-murder. Let one fact speak more
strongly than words could do to their general conduct. It
was now very well-known that Williams was not an Irishman, that not only no one circumstance came out to justify
that suspicion, but all that did come out proved him not to
have been an Irishman. However, the prejudice of the hour
would have him an Irishman, and as it was once bruited
about, it was generally believed. In the midst of the operation of this prejudice seven unfortunate Irishmen were
taken up on the strong suspicion of foul linen! They were
examined, and after having been made to cross themselves,
they were confined together in a close room below. The next
evening, some noise being heard, and perhaps no very
moderate one, the magistrates inquired into the cause of
this uproar, and they were told 'Oh! it is nothing but those
horrid Irish, who can never be quiet.' It turned out, however, that in this instance, at least, those Irishmen had no
great cause to be contented, for they had been confined in
this hole of a room for twenty-two hours without a bed to
lie upon, or a morsel of bread, or a drop of water to refresh
them! And what did the magistrates? They recollected
luckily the circumstance, and told their officers, 'Do for
God's sake give those fellows some bread and cheese, and

then bring them before us, and we will apologise for the trouble we have given them, and discharge them!'

This, he supposed, was what the Right Hon. Secretary would call vigour. But, giving them all due credit for such vigour, where was the vigour, the justice, the moral, or the decency, in that abominable spectacle with which they fed the worst appetites of the mob in the unseemly exhibition of the dead body to the multitude! Did they want to teach the people to prey upon carcases? Could it add to the sanctity of justice to make the passions of the mob hurry to riot upon a senseless carcase? Was there that certainty upon which alone justice ought to act to make such a spectacle fit? Should the people deal out the vengeance of the law by witnessing the formal procession of mangled limbs and putrid carcases? but what other was the true motive of this parade of the carcase and the maul and the chisel – what but a poor artifice to cover their own scandalous neglect? Why did they suffer that man to be alone? Why did they suffer him to be three days alone, though they knew that there was a bar across the top of his dungeon, and that he wore handkerchiefs and garters? The wonder really was that they did not give general orders to furnish the prisoner with a nightly supply of razors and pistols. But what could be said too extravagantly of their neglect and remissness, when it should be known that this wretch was suffered to possess himself with the sharp piece of iron, which was found in his pocket the morning after he hanged himself? Someone had said that all the watchmen of Shadwell had been discharged; and why, in the name of justice, not discharge all the magistrates too? He was himself pretty conversant with police affairs, and recommended a treatise, written in the year 1750 by Mr. Henry Fielding, a police magistrate, on the late alarming increase of crimes. He had hoped that the Right Hon. Gentleman would not think worse of the author for having been a poet and a dramatic writer. But to sum up his account of the vigilance of the Shadwell magistracy, he had merely to state they never once thought of searching the room of Williams till nearly two months after the murder, where they found the bloody trousers and the ivory hafted knife. He had formerly thought much upon the subject of the police, [Sheridan concluded] and as the Right Hon. Secretary had shown tonight that he had not as yet thought at all upon the subject, he begged that the Right Hon. Gentleman would begin to think of it with all possible dispatch, at least before he came again down to the House to move with great solemnity for an inquiry into the state and condition of the nightly watch.

A Committee of the House of Commons was duly appointed, with both Ryder and Sheridan as members; but one man, at least, had a better idea how the Members might spend their time. 'W' wrote to the editor of *The Examiner* recommending the appointment of a Corps of Honourable Members as the nightly watch. The Right Hon. C. Yorke should be 'transferred from the Board of Admiralty to a watch-box in Shadwell; for I remember, when a boy, that in his speeches to his constituents, wherein danger appeared his delight, he discoursed most heroically of wading though blood to defend his King and country.' As for the City Members, 'after having been stewed up for hours at a grand feast, consider the refreshing influence of a long round of watch; and how the duty will counteract the deadly effects of the dinner.' The West End should be patrolled by men of fashion, who would take the early watch and dine afterwards. 'Their presence will not be required at the House, except on a division; and those who speak early in debate may slip from their laurels . . . as the lights grow dim, *Old Sherry*, lighted up with claret, may sally forth, and put to flight the sons of darkness and disorder, by the illumination of his own lantern.' The Prime Minister, admittedly, could not be in more than five places at once, but next time he introduced a Bill he might 'add, as a *Ryder*, that the Secretary for the Home Department be instructed to know something of his duty.'

A few weeks later the committee published a report which is as uninteresting to posterity as it was agreeable to contemporary opinion. Predictably, it made some suggestions to improve the state of the parish watch and promote better co-ordination between the magistrates. Once more, however, Harriott – who died five years later after 'sufferings', the *Gentleman's Magazine* reported, 'of the most dreadful description, which even to his strong mind seem to have been beyond endurance' – deserves credit for a brave, forlorn attempt to persuade the Committee to think big. To him, the whole idea of the nightly watch was now thoroughly discredited. He urged that each of the Public Offices should have a strength of fifty policemen under the command of a chief constable. A waiting list of perhaps twice that number should be compiled as a police reserve. The Thames and Bow Street Offices would muster 200 more. The whole force should be made available wherever it was wanted in an emergency, and it should be directed by firm-minded magistrates – 'for firm and courageous, too, they ought to be, or they are not fit for police situations'.

Nobody listened. Harriott might just as well have flaunted the literary pretensions of the poetical Pye, Moser and Gifford for all anyone cared. A Bill based largely on the Committee's proposals was brought into Parliament soon afterwards. But by now the panic induced by the murders was dying down. And then, on 11 May, another murderer struck, reassuring the lower classes that it was not only they who were exposed to danger. John Bellingham, irritated that his letters kept being passed from one department of Whitehall to another with no more than an acknowledgement, carried a loaded revolver into the lobby of the House of Commons and shot the Prime Minister dead on the spot. Perhaps in his dying moments Perceval had time to recall his assertion, three months earlier, that 'no state of nightly watch, however excellent, could have prevented such a crime'.

It only remained to kill the Bill. In July, the House debated a petition from the Metropolitan parishes pleading that it was wholly inadequate, and would cost them an additional £74,000 in direct taxation. Ryder was no longer Home Secretary, and the Bill was without friends. The young Henry Brougham, afterwards a famous Lord Chancellor, delivered the obsequies. It was, after all, a dangerous little Bill, drawn up 'on sudden and temporary impulses and passions', that would have given police officers a power of an 'alarming description' under the authority of magistrates in the Public Offices who were no more than a motley collection of bankrupts, failed lawyers and – 'of poets in particular – yes, poets – not one of them that has not its poet'. The Offices 'were infinitely better stocked with poets than even the Treasury'. No more was heard of the Bill after that, but a great deal was heard by three more Parliamentary Committees (in 1816, 1818 and 1822) about the dangers to English liberty of a system of police; and when eventually Peel set up the Metropolitan Police in 1829, there came a second great outcry from the Churchwardens, Overseers and Trustees of the parish of St. George's-in-the-East.

John Williams's bones had been lying under the paving stones at the crossroads of New Cannon Road for eighteen years, and the stories about him had taken on an aura of myth and legend. Time had softened the sordid reality, and De Quincey had not yet immortalised Williams in print. A new generation of Churchwardens, Overseers and Trustees discovered that they were, after all, well content with their parish watchmen. What they expected of Peel's new 'Bobbies' we do not know; but early in 1830 the vestry resolved that their expectations had been 'altogether disappointed, inasmuch as the system is of too arbitrary a nature . . . from the laxity of its operation, offences have generally increased within the parish; burglaries have also become more frequent, the streets are in an intolerable state of riot and disorder at night, and so little confidence is felt by the inhabitants that private watchmen are employed at the exclusive charge of individuals; that the men attached to the police have frequently been seen drunk upon duty, and openly to associate and frequent public houses with prostitutes and other suspicious characters'. The vestry concluded by resolving that 'the present system is unconstitutional, and tends only to sap the foundations of our liberties'.

A contribution of £1,800 a year towards the cost of the Metropolitan Police was evidently too high a premium, eighteen years afterwards, to insure against the risk of a second John Williams.

THE EIGHTH VICTIM?

The confident verdict which early nineteenth-century justice pronounced on John Williams is a verdict on itself. But it is a little unjust to criticise the magistrates too harshly for their conduct of the case. As a force they were untrained, unco-ordinated and undermanned, and the men they had were totally inadequate for the job in hand. Yet even accepting the defects of the system, certain of their deficiencies and negligences seem incomprehensible. They neglected to make that thorough scrutiny of the maul which must have revealed the punched initials and which, by focusing their early attention on the Pear Tree, could have prevented the murder of the Williamsons. They took little account of the chisel found on Marr's premises, although they advertised for its owner and must have realised that it was almost certainly brought into the shop by the murderer. They did not search the Pear Tree until ten days after their chief suspect was dead. They wasted time and effort in the fruitless cross-examination of persons brought before them on totally inadequate evidence. They neglected to set up any organisation, however temporary and rudimentary, for the prompt exchange of information, and for the co-ordination of their separate activities. They wasted their own time and that of their officers by keeping suspects in prison unnecessarily because of a timid reluctance to let even the most unlikely suspect go once he had been brought before them. More seriously, once the identity of the maul had been established, they were so impressed by the fact that one of their suspects in custody had lodged with the Vermilloes and, therefore, had had access to the weapon, that they bent all their energies towards proving him guilty and failed to appreciate the wider significance of the identification. The immediate thorough searching of the Pear Tree public house;

the cross-examination of every person who lived there or had access to John Peterson's chest of tools; the examination of their clothes and razors; inquiries as to their movements on the nights of the murders: all these things should have been done. None of them were. Worst of all, the magistrates accepted Williams's apparent suicide as proof of his guilt, and in their eagerness to propitiate the mob, exposed the body of a man who had neither been committed for trial nor pleaded before a jury, to the ignominy reserved for a condemned murderer.

It is important to remember on what very slender grounds Williams was first taken up:

> The circumstances of suspicion which were alleged against him were that he had been more particularly seen there about seven o'clock on Thursday evening last; that on the same evening he did not go home to his lodgings until about twelve when he desired a fellow lodger, a foreign sailor, to put out his candle; that he was a short man and had a lame leg; that he was an Irishman; and that previous to this melancholy transaction he had little or no money, and when he was taken into custody he had a great deal of silver.

The Times report also states that there was a pound note in his possession. This preliminary evidence, slight as it was, all related to the murder of the Williamsons and Bridget Harrington. There was no mention at this stage of the murder of the Marrs and James Gowen. Interestingly enough, the Prime Minister in the House referred to the Marr murders as if they were unsolved. Williams was only accepted as the killer of the Marrs because he was accepted as the killer of the Williamsons. Yet the Williamson murder is the one in which the killer was seen and was clearly not identified as Williams. It was also the one for which, if Miss Lawrence's evidence is true – and she revealed herself as a hostile witness with no love for the prisoner – Williams had some kind of alibi.

Williams made no secret of his friendship with the Williamsons, nor did he deny that he frequented the King's Arms and had been there on the Thursday in question. But if being in the King's Arms was, in itself, suspicious, it is astonishing that half the male population of the neighbourhood were not taken into custody. Equally, it is hardly of great significance that Williams did not return to his lodgings until after midnight. The district was notable for its late hours, and shops and public houses were frequently open as late as twelve o'clock. Richter testified during his examination on Boxing Day that Williams 'was in the habit of keeping very bad hours'. In fact, if Williams did return to the Pear Tree after midnight –this is a point in his favour. The Williamsons were murdered soon after eleven o'clock and the King's Arms was only a matter of five minutes' walk from the Pear Tree. If guilty, Williams should have been home long before midnight. He would have had no motive for delay and every reason for getting himself off the streets and safely home before the general hue and cry was raised. The Pear Tree would have seemed his natural, and indeed his only refuge.

Williams's explanation of his protest to his fellow lodger about the candle rings true, particularly when one remembers the constant risk of fire in the old houses near the river. And Williams was a sailor on East Indiamen. The East Indiamen were built of wood and, because of the possibility that they might have to defend themselves, were armed. Fire at sea on a wooden ship with gunpowder on board and little possibility of escape was a greater terror than storm or enemy action, and the fire regulations were strict and were stringently enforced. All candles on deck had to be extinguished by nine o'clock and those below by ten. Williams's experience and training, both by land and sea, had taught him to dread fire. The sight of a lighted candle held by a man reading in bed after midnight would inevitably have provoked his protest. If, in fact, he had returned to his lodgings bloodstained, dishevelled and probably injured in the violent struggle with Williamson, a man considerably taller and stronger than himself, the most sensible way to avoid detection was to creep into bed, not to draw attention to his presence by arguing with a fellow lodger, particularly as the faint light from a candle held at a distance would hardly have presented much danger.

And there is the evidence of the pound note and the silver. Mrs. Vermilloe testified that the money Williams deposited with her husband was not yet completely spent. Williams was certainly in need of money. Why otherwise had he pawned his shoes? But this situation was not strange to him, nor indeed, to any sailor. He came home rich and was soon poor. If his answer to this dilemma had been robbery and murder, it is strange that he should not have resorted to those means when he returned from previous journeys. No evidence was ever adduced to connect the small amount of money in his possession with the Williamson murder. Had he stolen and subsequently sold Williamson's watch? It is surely inconceivable that the buyer would not have come forward. Was the pound note stolen from the King's Arms? If so, it must surely have been bloodstained. It seems much more likely that the money in Williams's possession came from the pawning of his shoes. The police officers who arrested him did not check the dates on the pawn tickets, but the fact that they were still in his possession was evidence of innocence. Williams was a vain young man, particularly about his appearance. If he had obtained money from the William-son murders, surely one of his first actions would have been to redeem his shoes?

Williams was only asked for an alibi for the Williamson murders and he stated that, after leaving the King's Arms, he had consulted a surgeon in Shadwell about the wound on his leg, had then gone on to a 'female chirurgeon' in the same neighbourhood in the hope of a cheaper cure, and had spent the rest of the night further west with some female companions and in visiting several public houses. He was not asked for the name of the surgeon or the female practitioner, and it is possible that he visited both too early in the evening for them to provide an alibi. But there was some corroboration of his story that he had been drinking. John Fitzpatrick and Miss Lawrence both testified that he had been drinking with Cornelius Hart in the Ship and Royal Oak at 11.15 p.m., a time which would give both men an alibi; while John Cobbett said that he had seen Williams with Ablass at Mr. Lee's public house. None of the witnesses strikes one as particularly reliable with the possible exception of Miss Lawrence. But insofar as there is evidence of Williams's whereabouts on the night of Thursday, 19 December, it corroborates his story that he had been drinking in several public houses.

Then there is the allegation that Williams cut off his distinctive whiskers. This was apparently taken as an attempt at disguise but it is difficult to see why, since only Susan Peachy came forward with the description of a whiskered man. And, if Williams were concerned and feared that his whiskers may have been recognised, to cut them off immediately after the crime was to invite speculation and suspicion. There were plenty of acquaintances to testify that he normally wore them; he could hardly hope that the ruse would succeed. The sullen Richter, when giving his reluctant evidence, testified that he could see little difference in Williams's appearance; and the truth may well be that Williams's decision to trim his beard was a perfectly innocent and routine procedure. It may be significant that Williams apparently had himself shaved when he was in Coldbath Fields Prison, since the Lawrence drawing made in his cell after his death shows him to be without a beard. Equally natural, surely, is Williams's surly 'I know it' when Harrison came dashing into his room to rouse him with the news of the Marr murder. The whole house must have been ringing with the news and Harrison himself admitted that Williams could have overheard him telling Mrs. Vermilloe. A guilty man would surely have made some attempt to feign horror, astonishment and surprise.

From the time of his first examination, prejudice against Williams built up and the magistrates did nothing to control it. In his evidence Harrison openly admitted that 'he had always an impression on his mind against the prisoner, and always wished for an opportunity of bringing forward some evidence against him'. Others were less blatant about admitting their prejudice but equally assiduous in indulging it. Mrs. Orr, who admitted that she and her daughter 'thought Williams an agreeable young man and never thought he could be one who would attempt to rob or murder', nevertheless produced the chisel left outside her window 'as further proof of his villainy'. Mr. Lee, the landlord of the Black Horse, told his story of Williams pushing against his wife and shaking her pockets, as if to ascertain what money she had, and described how, on one occasion, he had taken the liberty of pulling out the till and putting his hand in it. Lee naïvely admitted, however, that 'he never thought very seriously of this matter until he heard of Williams being apprehended'. Richter first started the story that Captain Hutchinson had prophesied that Williams, if he returned to land, would be hanged. The captain subsequently corroborated this but was obviously embarrassed at the need to justify his statement. He made the excuse that a seaman, being under strict discipline, had few opportunities for villainy, and the particular incident which the Captain recalled – that Williams, while on shore, had passed himself off as the second officer of the *Roxburgh Castle* and had succeeded in borrowing a very small sum of money – was surely a venial sin for the butcher of Ratcliffe Highway. It was no doubt typical of Williams's conceit that he should represent himself as an officer, and his pretension, combined with his quick temper, probably made him an unsatisfactory member of Captain Hutchinson's crew. But, on the evidence, his captain's prognostication of his end seems more like an outburst of irritation than a serious prophecy.

Nothing is known about Williams's early life. But, after his death and burial, much was surmised, all of it predictably discreditable. The *Newgate Calendar* declares:

It is generally believed that his real name was Murphy and that he had changed it to that of Williams in order to escape detection of some crimes of which he had formerly been guilty. Of his early life little or nothing is known with certainty. Whether he was in his native country at the time of the unhappy troubles of 1798 can now be only a matter of conjecture: but it is certainly not unnatural to suppose that a monster capable of committing the late atrocities must early in life have lost that inate horror of bloodshed which forms so striking a feature in the moral constitution of man. In the dreadful paths of rebellion probably it was that he was first tempted to imbrew his hands in the blood of his fellow creatures. And amidst those terrible scenes of midnight murder which that unhappy country then afforded might his sinful conscience have been seared to every feeling of repentance and remorse.

Assuming that Williams was, in fact, born in Ireland he would have been fourteen at the time of the 1798 rebellion.

There seems to have been a general determination that the monster of Ratcliffe Highway should be Irish. The Irish were an unpopular, despised and feared minority, a perpetual source of irritation to the law-abiding citizens of East London. Since Williams was not Portuguese, it was highly appropriate that he should be Irish. Again no evidence was produced; it was all innuendo, a blatant example of racialism and anti-Catholicism which had no relevance to the crimes. Sheridan attempted to refute the story in the House and an anonymous correspondent writing in *The Examiner* of 9 January 1812, under the pseudonym Julius Hibernious, dealt robustly with the allegation and, at the same time, attempted to discredit the evidence of the Corporal of the Guard.

To keep the natives of Ireland ignorant and barbarous at home and to calumniate them to the rest of Europe was the object of every succeeding Chief Governor of that country. . . . It is no wonder, therefore, that an immediate attempt was made to impress the public with the belief that the horrid murders in Ratcliffe Highway were committed by Irishmen. The honest Corporal of the Guard and the finding of the letter addressed to Mr. Nobody at Nowhere from his sworn friend Patrick Mahoney would no doubt some years ago have been promoted for a similar service to Ireland to the rank of Colonel. The ingenuity and cleverness displayed in the composition of that precious specimen of criminal correspondence would not have been lost upon men in power in that country. . . .

The *Morning Chronicle* of last week has furnished a second part to the honest Corporal's letter from Paddy Mahoney. The paragraph to which I allude exhibits as notable a vein of invention and, no doubt, as patriotic a purpose, certainly more circumstantial details and the advantage of novelty in substituting the name of Murphy for Mahoney. I shall merely remark upon the above that it comes before us in a still more questionable shape than the story which was boldly deposed to by the Corporal. We have not heard from any person in the several examinations that Williams deposed to his having gone by any other name or to his being an Irishman. He stated himself to be a Scotsman. A hearsay was inserted in some of the newspapers that he was an Irishman; but this appears to have been a sly touch in the Murphy and Mahoney style, and for the same purpose. I do not mean to say that bad men are not frequently produced in Ireland as well as in England: but until a regular deposition to the substance of the *Chronicle* story is laid before the public I and other Irish readers have a fair right to believe it a fabrication, and I shall continue to believe without any reflection upon Scotland, a country which I respect, that the murderer was a Scotsman and that his real name was Williams.

But the campaign of innuendo, calumny and vilification continued. *The Times* contrasted the conduct of the two seamen, Marr and Williams. Marr was sober, diligent, peaceable and obliging. Williams was idle, drunken, dissolute and quarrelsome. The agreeable young man with the open manners who was so readily received into Mrs. Orr's house, no matter how late the hour; who nursed her baby and teased her daughter; the young man whom Mrs. Williamson patted on the cheek and welcomed as a friend, was a monster hiding an insatiable blood lust beneath an agreeable face and insinuating manners. Certainly the sensitive and handsome face, shown in Laurence's portrait, was something of a problem to Williams's detractors. It is not a strong face certainly, but it can hardly be said to bear the marks of ultimate depravity. But De Quincey is equal to this challenge:

A lady who saw him under examination (I think at the Thames Police Office) assured me that his hair was of the most extraordinary and vivid colour, viz. bright yellow, something between an orange and a lemon colour. Williams had been in India; chiefly in Bengal and Madras; but he had also been upon the Indus. Now it is notorious that in the Punjab horses of a high caste are often painted – crimson, blue, green, purple; it struck me that Williams might for some casual purpose of disguise, have taken the hint from this practice so that the colour might not have been natural. In other respects his appearance was natural enough and judging by a plaster cast of him which I purchased in

London, I should say mean as regarded his facial structure.
One fact, however, was striking and fell in with the impression of his natural tiger character, that his face wore at all
times a bloodless ghastly pallor. 'You might imagine,' said
my informant, 'that in his veins circulated not red life blood
such as could kindle into the blush of shame or wrath or
pity, but a green sap that welled from no human heart.' His
eyes seemed frozen and glazed as if their light were all converged upon some victim lurking in the far background. So
far his appearance might have repelled, but, on the other
hand, the concurrent testimony of many witnesses and also
the silent testimony of facts show that the oiliness and
snaky insinuation of his demeanour counteracted the
repulsiveness of his ghastly face and amongst inexperienced
young women won for him a very favourable reception.

The young women must have been singularly naïve as well
as inexperienced to have been seduced into overlooking such
unprepossessing features as bloodless ghastly pallor, glazed
eyes and hair dyed like that of a high caste horse.

No evidence was produced to prove that any of the three
murderous weapons displayed so prominently on Williams's
bier was ever in his possession. Two of them, the maul and one
of the ripping chisels, came from the Pear Tree, and Williams
lodged there. But so did at least four other seamen, while
numerous others had free access to the pub. Richter, Cuthperson, and Harrison, all knew where John Peterson's tools were
kept. Hart was a regular visitor. Mr. Vermilloe used the maul
to chop wood; his nephews played with it, whiling away the
long hours while their mother was busy with the washing.
Vermilloe had a curious idea of what constituted safe keeping,
and it is apparent that anyone who lodged or visited the Pear
Tree could have helped himself to one of Peterson's tools. It is
significant that Mrs. Rice's small son William testified that the
maul had been missing for about a month, that is for a week
before the Marrs were murdered. William may have been
wrong. The evidence of a small boy about the passing of time
is probably less accurate than his identification of an object.
But the maul was an important toy to Mrs. Rice's children
who were probably not liberally provided with more ortho-

dox playthings; and they must have missed it. It is unlikely that William was wrong and his evidence, if true, opens an interesting possibility. If Williams had taken the maul, where had he hidden it? It was hardly an object to stow under his bed or in his sea chest. And if Williams were planning murder, why should he bother to steal the maul? He knew where Peterson's tools were kept, as did every other inhabitant of the Pear Tree. He could extract the maul when he needed it without the necessity of hiding it away in advance. The fact that the maul was missing for a week before it was used is one of the strongest indications that the murderer had access to, or had a friend living in, the Pear Tree, but did not himself live there. It also suggests that the maul and the chisel may initially have been taken for a purpose other than murder.

And then we come to the mysterious account of Williams's visit late on the night of the Saturday before the Marrs' murder to Mrs. Orr's. The more one examines this incident the more inexplicable it becomes whether one chooses to view it in the light of his innocence or his guilt. There is no reason to doubt the truth of Mrs. Orr's story; it is the interpretation of the facts which presents a problem. The magistrates accepted the facts at their face value. Williams was heard by Mrs. Orr when attempting to break into her house. Invited inside he had no alternative but to leave his incriminating weapon outside the window. Once within he settled down to chat with the old lady during which, with no attempt apparently at subtlety, he questioned her about the layout of her house and its relation to its neighbours, with the obvious intention either of robbing her and making his getaway, or of using the house and yard to gain entrance to some more promising property. He was stung into vehement and unreasonable anger by the arrival of the Watch and he tried to prevent Mrs. Orr from admitting the man. When she insisted he crept out to retrieve the chisel but was too late. The Watch had already discovered it. Mrs. Orr in her evidence put the official view. The chisel was 'further proof of his villainy'; and Mrs. Orr was suitably rewarded for her part in bringing the evidence forward.

But the story makes no sense. Why should Williams attempt to break into Mrs. Orr's house? He was known to her; she liked him. He had only to knock on the door and she would invite

him in. This, in fact, is precisely what happened. She might
not have welcomed even the agreeable and insinuating Mr.
Williams if he had come brandishing a chisel, but concealing
the weapon was hardly an insurmountable problem. It could
be hidden fairly easily in a sleeve or under his coat while he
slipped through the door. With the door firmly closed and he
and his victim alone there would be no further need of con-
cealment. And if she were not alone? In that case, it would
surely be more dangerous to attempt to break in and alarm the
company than to knock at the door as if on a casual visit. He
could, after all, always make an excuse for not joining the
company if in strength or in numbers they presented a threat
to his enterprise.

And if he came to Mrs. Orr's house as a murderer why didn't
he kill? He had gained access to her house. He and his victim
were alone together. And, if no handy weapon presented itself
and he yearned for the comfortable feel and strong assurance of
the one he had selected for the job, was that such a problem?
He could have made an excuse to leave her – perhaps offering
to fetch beer for them both – retrieved the ripping chisel and
knocked again for admittance. But he made no offer to fetch
beer. In fact, somewhat ungallantly, he insisted that his
victim should do so, thus risking a chance that she herself
would find the chisel. He could hardly have sent her out to give
himself an opportunity for robbery. Mrs. Orr never alleged
that any of her possessions were missing.

It is significant that the Watch entertained no suspicions of
Williams at the time, since the chisel was handed to Mrs. Orr
and the Watch then left her and Williams together to enjoy
each other's company. Williams now had both his victim and
his weapon conveniently to hand. Why didn't he kill? The
only reasonable explanation is that the Watch could have
testified to his presence in the house and could have identified
the weapon. That at least is plausible. What is impossible to
credit is the explanation of one writer on the crimes who would
have us believe that Williams sat in impotent fury chatting to
his victim because she had possession of the weapon and was
so disobliging as to refuse to hand it over to him.

Mrs. Orr was probably right in testifying that they talked
about her house and its environment, but she may well have

misinterpreted the significance of what could have been no more than casual chat. For why should Williams need to ask these incriminating questions? He had lived periodically at the Pear Tree for three years. He returned to this neighbourhood after all his voyages. The Pear Tree was literally at the bottom of Mrs. Orr's yard. He had only to look out of the window of his lodgings to see exactly how the land lay. He had been in Mrs. Orr's house before; it was not strange to him. Nor was it different from the many humble houses in the district with which he must have been familiar. It was thought suspicious that he resented the arrival of the Watch, but this was natural enough. He had no reason to love watchmen. Was it not one – and probably the same man – who had stopped his sport at the Pear Tree when he had been dancing with his friends so that he had had to resort to a public house to treat his musicians there?

But if we look at the facts closely an explanation presents itself. Mrs. Orr heard a noise as if someone were breaking in. Later, after some conversation Williams came in. It is at least possible that the chisel was deliberately left by the window by someone who had seen Williams enter the house and that it was found by the watchman because someone intended him to find it.

But the most surprising incident in the story is the description of the finding of the French knife. Nothing about this remarkable discovery rings true. Harrison claimed that he first knew of the knife when Williams invited him to search his coat pocket for a borrowed handkerchief. This story of the borrowed handkerchief echoes most suspiciously the earlier allegation of the borrowed stockings which Williams is said to have washed out after the Williamson murders. For a fastidious young man living in a common lodging house, Williams seems to have been surprisingly prone to acquiring his fellow lodgers' linen. But even if the story of the handkerchief is true, it is odd that he should have invited Harrison, who was certainly no friend, to rummage in one of his pockets, particularly if it held a knife recently bought for the purpose of committing murder. The knife might have been a mere casual and innocent purchase. Williams may have opened it and displayed its beauty to Harrison. One of them must have opened it. A clasp knife with a six-inch blade, strong and sharp enough to cut through three stout necks to the bone, could hardly have been kept safely open in a coat pocket. It would have cut the lining to rags and sliced off Harrison's intruding fingers. So Williams must have displayed the blade to Harrison when telling him about its purchase. It was an elegant knife with its handle of ivory, a suitable embellishment for a dandy. Probably Williams was rather proud of it. It is strange that no one else at the Pear Tree was favoured with a sight of this enviable acquisition.

But if this part of the story is odd, Harrison's claim that he had not mentioned the knife before during his examination because it had not occurred to him to do so is incomprehensible. This is the man who, from the start, had his suspicions of Williams, the man who crept to his side during the night in the hope of catching some incriminatory murmur from his lips as Williams turned and tossed restlessly in his sleep or sang his snatches of tipsy song; the lodger who went scurrying to Mrs. Vermilloe – but not direct to the police – with every fresh piece of evidence. He could not have missed the significance of the knife; indeed he admits as much. He claimed that he made a search for it in Williams's sea chest and in every corner of the Pear Tree, but he somehow forgot to mention it to the magistrates, despite the amount of less significant material which he thought fit to bring to their attention. He somehow failed to find it despite the diligence of his search, and the fact that he lived at the Pear Tree and could spend all his free moments looking around. The number of possible hiding places cannot have been large. How strange that so assiduous a seeker should have missed that closet with the tell-tale hole!

So the knife was found. It would be interesting to know who exactly directed the search, and what part if any Harrison played in it. The knife was found, and it was predictably covered in blood. But was it the weapon? *The Times* certainly had no doubt that it was, and its account displays the standard of deduction and logic which is typical of the whole conduct of the case: 'It is now pretty clear that these sanguinary deeds were perpetrated with the knife in question, especially when it is known that Williams never had a razor of his own and always applied to the barber to be shaved and, more-over, that no razor had been missing from the house where he lodged.'

But William Salter, the surgeon who examined the bodies, was specific that the weapon must have been a razor. Nothing less sharp could have cut through to the bone in one stroke without bruising the tissues. But Williams had no razor and he did own a knife; therefore the surgeon was wrong.

De Quincey too, had no doubt that the French knife was the weapon. His account is so inaccurate that one can only endorse the opinion quoted by W. Roughead that De Quincey 'was happily immune from a pettifogging intimacy with dates, names and trifling matters of fact, a tiresome and frivolous accuracy of memory':

It was now remembered that Williams had recently borrowed a large French knife of peculiar construction; and accordingly, from a heap of old lumber and rags, there was soon extricated a waistcoat, which the whole house could swear to as recently worn by Williams. In this waistcoat, and glued by gore to the lining of its pocket, was found the French knife. Next, it was matter of notoriety to everybody in the inn, that Williams ordinarily wore at present a pair of creaking shoes, and a brown surtout lined with silk. Many other presumptions seemed scarcely called for. Williams was immediately apprehended, and briefly examined. This was on Friday. On the Saturday morning (viz., fourteen days from the Marr murders), he was again brought up. The cir-cumstantial evidence was overwhelming; Williams watched its course, but said very little. At the close, he was fully committed for trial at the next sessions; and it is needless to say that, on his road to prison, he was pursued by mobs so fierce, that, under ordinary circumstances, there would have been small hope of escaping summary vengeance. But upon this occasion a powerful escort had been provided; so that he was safely lodged in jail.

And, if the French knife were the weapon, when, are we to suppose, was it hidden in that convenient hole at the back of the closet? Was it deposited there after the murder of the

Marrs, still wet with the blood of the child, to be recovered later, its efficiency proved, when Williams required it for the throats of the Williamsons? But a bloodstained knife left uncleaned for twelve days would hardly have sliced so efficiently through the Williamsons' stout throats. So was it perhaps a different knife that was used on the first occasion, and if so, what happened to it? If Williams threw it into the Thames why did he not dispose of the second knife similarly? Is it reasonable that Williams, bloody as he would have been, should have crept about the dark house after midnight in search of a hiding place? He couldn't be certain that the landlady or some other inmate of the house wouldn't watch his progress to bed. And why should the knife be so bloody? The instinctive action would be to wipe the blade clean, probably on the clothes of his victims, and when time and opportunity were right, to examine the knife for any incriminating traces of blood and wash them away. There was no shortage of water; the Thames flowed within a few yards of the Pear Tree. The murderer would either throw his weapon into the river, disposing once and for all of such incriminating evidence, or if he valued it too highly to bear to see it go, or had it in mind for further murderous use, at least he could ensure that it was clean. It was to be nearly 100 years before forensic scientists would be able conclusively to detect minute traces of human blood in the hinges of the knife. A quick swish in the river would have rendered the knife safe. Williams's shoes were produced in court. There is no record that the shoes were nailed, so they did not link Williams with the footprint at the back of the King's Arms. They had, however, been washed; and this fact was obviously regarded as suspicious. Would a murderer who took the trouble to wash blood from his shoes, have left the weapon itself still so incriminatingly stained? To secrete it uncleaned and clotted with his victims' blood in a house which was swarming with lodgers and visitors, where few movements can have gone undetected, and where he himself lived, would have been the act of a madman.

The description in *The Times* of the finding of the French knife immediately strikes the modern reader as suspicious. It struck a contemporary reader similarly. It would have been surprising had Aaron Graham accepted this story at its face value; and there is a brief but significant paragraph in *The Times* of 20 January:

> An officer belonging to Shadwell Public Office who found the knife and jacket of the late Williams underwent a private investigation on Saturday before Mr. Graham. The landlord of the Duke of Kent Public House also gave evidence upon the subject.

Someone, then, had been talking. There is no reason why the publican should have been questioned unless he had overheard some incriminating talk in his bar. Someone with money to spend on drink had been indiscreet. Perhaps the officer from Shadwell was able to convince Graham that this was just one more case of a rogue boasting wildly in his cups. There had been so many of them. But, if the talk were true, the inference was frightening, perhaps too frightening to contemplate. We hear no more of Aaron Graham's suspicions.

The sail-maker John Harrison's part in the mystery is difficult to assess. On the face of it, he was the murderer's accomplice, entrusted with the task of fabricating evidence against Williams and of deflecting police inquiries from the real killer. Certainly he did his job well and one suspects that he found it congenial and that there was enmity and resentment between the ex-shipmates. But Harrison, too, may have been a dupe, a credulous but honest fool who scurried to the magistrates with evidence which had been carefully planted for him to find. Yet this is hard to believe. It supposes a degree of subtlety on the part of the murderer which is scarcely in keeping with the crude barbarity of the crimes. And there is another point. Harrison described the French knife before it was found, thus preparing the ground for the subsequent discovery. If one rejects the evidence of the French knife it is difficult to believe that Harrison was honest. What is possible is that he genuinely believed in Williams's guilt and decided, or was persuaded, to fabricate the confirmatory evidence for which the magistrates were seeking, in the confident hope that they would pay handsomely for it. It is significant that following the discovery of the knife, *The Times* pressed for Harrison's zeal to be suitably recognised, and that he subsequently received thirty pounds – one of the highest rewards paid out.

As mysterious as the finding of the jacket and the subsequent discovery of the French knife is the allegation of the congealed blood in the inside jacket pocket. This was not submitted to 'a chemical gentleman' for his opinion, but, even if the magistrates had shown their earlier degree of scepticism, it is unlikely that the examination would have revealed anything useful. The blood may have been that of an animal – there were plenty of slaughterhouses in Shadwell, and no shortage, one imagines, of stray dogs and cats – but it was not until the turn of the century that scientists were able to distinguish human blood from that of other species. The bloodstained pocket was immediately accepted as further proof of Williams's guilt, despite the fact that the coat of a man engaged in such bloody murder would have been extensively bloodstained, particularly on the front and cuffs. Yet the front and cuffs of the blue jacket were apparently unstained, while the one inside pocket was stiff with congealed blood. The sleeves and front of the jacket could only have been preserved if the murderer had also been wearing an enveloping coat. The discovery recalled to mind – as it was no doubt meant to do – Turner's evidence of the murderer robbing Mrs. Williamson, then thrusting his hand into an inner pocket. But the tall man in the Flushing coat seen by Turner was not Williams. The 'stout man with a very large great coat on' seen lurking in the passage of the King's Head by Williamson was not Williams. Both men knew him well and could not have failed to recognise him. The facts are inescapable. If there was only one murderer, he was not Williams. If the blue jacket was worn by the man seen by Turner robbing Mrs. Williamson then it was not worn by Williams. If we reject Harrison's evidence of the finding of the jacket, and also his identification of the French knife, as inherently improbable and designed to further incriminate a man already dead, then the implications are clear.

If neither of the murder weapons was ever identified with Williams or seen in his possession, the evidence of the other bloodstained clothes – of which there is a superfluity – is equally circumstantial and inconclusive. The murders were almost incredibly brutal and bloody; the assailant, particularly after the violent struggle which Williamson put up for his life, must have been extensively bloodstained. Yet only one garment belonging to Williams was proved to have been bloodstained, and that on the uncorroborated evidence of the washerwoman, who could possibly have mistaken one shirt for another. Mrs. Rice testified that one torn and bloodstained shirt was washed by her after the Marr murder, but the shirt was merely spattered with blood 'about the neck and breast' and was certainly not sufficiently bloodstained to arouse her suspicions at the time. The stockings allegedly borrowed from Cuthperson had merely two bloody thumbmarks near the top. When challenged by Cuthperson about the ownership of the stockings Williams acted both reasonably and innocently; he washed them and returned them after 'some little dispute' as to their ownership. He would hardly have pressed his claim to bloodstained stockings which he had recently worn when committing murder. The stockings are of less importance, surely, than the damp and recently-washed trousers discovered under the bed of that taciturn and reluctant witness Richter. The seaman's white trousers found in the Pear Tree privy may or may not have been worn by one of the murderers. The fact that they were stuffed down the privy certainly suggests that they were connected with some bloody crime. But Mrs. Vermilloe was positive that the dandyfied Williams would not have worn them, particularly in the house, and even Harrison made no attempt to refute her evidence. The heavily bloodstained garments discovered by Mr. Penn and his Quaker friend in Ratcliffe Highway were never found or identified. One is left, therefore, with the evidence of one slightly stained shirt, and if that is taken as proof of Williams's guilt, what becomes of the evidence of the blue jacket? That could hardly have remained unstained if the shirt worn beneath it was spattered with blood. Professor Simpson gives his opinion that 'the assailant would be bound to have been bloodstained, mostly round the face, shoulders, arms and hands, from repeated blows. Blood and brain can be splashed for many feet by re-hitting bleeding wounds.' It is inconceivable that, had Williams or any person worn the blue jacket during the murders, only one inside pocket would have been stained.

But if Williams were innocent, why should he kill himself? Three possible reasons can be put forward. He might have decided that, with the identification of the maul, the evidence against him was so strong, and the local prejudice so intense, that he had no hope of escaping the gallows, or a public lynching, and that it was now a choice between execution before a violent and hostile mob or a more merciful death by his own hand. He might have been cursed with a personality given to sudden and irrational fits of despair and in the lonely small hours of the night, fettered and friendless, felt an irresistible urge to put an end to an unsuccessful and now discredited life. He was obviously a volatile and emotional young man; he may also have been unstable. Lastly he may have been involved, although innocently, with the murderers, perhaps by providing them with information for which they paid and have been overcome by remorse.

None of these reasons appeals to common sense. It was too early for Williams to give up hope. He hadn't even been committed for trial. There was still a good chance that he could convince a jury of his innocence, that someone would come forward who could confirm his alibi, or that the guilty would be arrested. The time for suicide is when all rational hope has faded. It is equally difficult to believe that he gave way to despair. He had seemed perfectly easy to the turnkey and to his fellow prisoners. At no time is he described as depressed or unhopeful. And it is equally difficult to see why he should kill himself out of remorse unless he were an active participant in the murders. If he had any suspicion who was responsible or had helped them, however unwittingly, he had only to turn King's evidence and tell all he knew, and he would almost certainly go free.

It was vital to the murderer to ensure Williams's death, whether or not he had been an accomplice, willing or unwilling. If Williams were guilty, it was highly unlikely that he would go to the gallows without making a confession implicating his accomplices. All the practised art of Dr. Ford would have been directed to that end. The Ordinary would have held out the certainty of everlasting fire for the wilful and obdurate, and the hope of salvation for the penitent sinner. And how best to demonstrate penitence than by making a good and full confession? A man would have a strong motive for silence only if he were indeed innocent; were disposed to appear so, no matter what the risk to his immortal soul, if only to cheat the Ordinary of the satisfaction of a full confession; or had made up his mind to sacrifice his hope of salvation to protect his friends. It is unlikely that Williams was capable of the last sacrifice. He was a man who made no close friends, and these crimes, in their sordidness and brutality, had no tinge of nobility. We can be sure that if Williams were indeed guilty and were condemned, he would talk, and it would be vital to prevent him.

His death was equally important to the murderer if he were innocent. He hadn't yet been tried and the evidence was circumstantial and ambiguous. At any moment some woman from the West End might appear to provide an alibi, some fresh discovery be made. Once Williams was dead and apparently by his own hand, the police activity would die down, the terrified mob would be satisfied and his guilt would be accepted as proved. A violent and ruthless man who had already killed seven people would be unlikely to hesitate over a final and necessary murder. The victim was accessible, fettered and defenceless. The gaoler was underpaid and could be bribed. The wage of a turnkey was one guinea a week and bribes were so common as to be almost regarded as a perquisite of the job. There must have been at least one man whose safety depended on Williams dying, and dying soon.

Williams's suicide was so convenient for his accomplices, if any, and so unexpected, that it was bound to excite comment at the time. The magistrates and the mob might prefer to take it at its face value as evidence of guilt: but there is a passage in *The Times* of 30 December which, without overtly suggesting that Williams died other than by his own hand, nevertheless hints strongly that the suicide was more mysterious than it at first appeared:

The suicide of the wretched Williams is an event, which is, certainly, to be regretted. If he was the murderer, or one of the murderers, it is a matter of lamentation that this additional act of desperation should deprive public justice of the means of proving his crime and inflicting the punishment which the laws of the country award for such atrocious offenders. It is to be regretted in another point of view: it is possible, we hope barely possible, that by self-murder he has saved himself from public execution; and may, if other clues are not discovered, save for the present whatever accomplice or accomplices he may have had in his bloody deeds. No doubt every mode of enquiry will be pursued by the magistrates and the inhabitants of the quarter where these shocking crimes have been perpetrated to get the best information possible on the subject; but in the consternation natural upon such atrocities some important particulars may slip the thoughts of the most active. We hope the lodgings of every person in the slightest degree acquainted with the self-murderer, or any of those who are or who may be suspected, will be searched with a scrutinizing assiduity. Activity of this sort now becomes the more necessary; for surely it would be a species of affront to British police and British law if such atrocities were to pass without the detection of the guilty.

A great deal, we understand, has been said conveying direct or indirect reflections on Atkins, the keeper of Coldbath Fields Prison; but it does not appear that such reflections are well founded. With regard to him personally we before mentioned that his health was so bad that his medical advisers would not permit him to attend the Inquest. As to the treatment of the prisoner in the jail, the magistrates desired him to be kept by himself, and he was accordingly put into a solitary cell for re-examination. There were three others confined in the prison on charge of suspicion for the same offence. An iron bar crosses every cell in the jail and serves the prisoners to hang their clothes upon, and their beds too when the floors are cleaned. An unfounded report has gone out that he was refused pen and ink, and that thereby his confession was prevented. We understand that so far from this being the fact, he was told that he might come down to the office in the prison and write what he pleased. After the first day when he went to the prison he expressed no sort of wish for pen, ink or paper.

Why should the Keeper of the Prison be criticised? The

presumption is because an important prisoner in his care was enabled to kill himself. This is a perfectly legitimate criticism and it is strange that *The Times*' correspondent should attempt to exonerate the unfortunate Atkins. The inference is that the 'direct or indirect reflections' on the prison-keeper relate to something worse than his carelessness in not checking that his prisoner had no means of doing away with himself. There is a suggestion in the passage that there was something suspicious about Williams's death, and that it was a cause of rumour and concern. The passage specifically refutes the rumour current at the time that Williams asked for pen and paper before he died. Williams asked for nothing. Is it reasonable to suppose that a man who was planning to kill himself and had made early preparation for the act by secreting away the half loop of iron, should not wish to explain his act? If he were guilty, and acting out of remorse, he would wish to clear his conscience. If he had been left to his fate by confederates, he would hardly die without naming them. If he were anxious to accept all the blame and to ensure the safety of his friends (which doesn't sound like Williams) he would be likely to have left a note stating that he and he alone was responsible for the murders. But he left no word. He felt no remorse. He displayed no anxiety. He was perfectly comfortable the day before he died 'because he knew that no ill could happen to him'. The fact that Williams had managed to procure the half loop of iron, if true, is proof of nothing except the natural desire of a fighting man in a perilous situation to avail himself of any weapon which came to hand. But Williams did not make use of the iron. He did not even make a half-hearted attempt at suicide by that means, although the hoop was 'sufficiently sharp to wound him mortally'.

There are other suspicious circumstances surrounding that notorious suicide in Coldbath Fields Prison. It was alleged that Williams hanged himself from an iron bar, six feet two inches from the ground. He himself was about five feet nine inches tall. Presumably then he stood on his bed to accomplish the deed. If he repented of his action as the handkerchief tightened about his neck and he began to experience the first horrors of strangulation, he could surely grasp the bar with his hands or feel with his feet for the edge of the bed. Neither of these actions would be possible if he died quickly, perhaps of vagal inhibition. But there is a suggestion that he did not die quickly. The *Morning Post* of 28 December states, 'His eyes and mouth were open and the state of his body clearly demonstrated that he had struggled very hard'. This is the only reference in the contemporary reports to a death struggle, but if true it provides one of the strongest arguments against suicide. If Williams did indeed struggle very hard why was it not possible for him to save himself? Professor Simpson advises that it is not uncommon for a suicide to bear marks of injury, if, in the final convulsions which proceed death, the body is dashed against a wall. But Williams is alleged to have hanged himself from a bar which ran across his cell. There is no suggestion that the evidence of a hard struggle arose from this type of injury.

And there is other evidence. A prisoner in an adjacent cell heard the violent shaking of chains about three o'clock in the morning. Was this Williams shaking his fetters in anger and frustration as prisoners sometimes did? Or was he struggling violently with someone stronger than himself, someone who held a hand over his mouth to stifle his cries while twisting a handkerchief around his neck? Or were there two men, one to silence and to throttle, the other to hold Williams's arms with such force that the *post mortem* staining showed them as blue from the elbows down? One must be careful not to read too much into this last piece of evidence. After death by hanging the legs and arms commonly show such staining, and there is now no way of knowing whether pressure applied immediately before death was to any degree responsible. There is nothing in the scant forensic medical evidence available to support the theory that Williams was murdered; equally, as Professor Simpson agrees, there is nothing to refute it. If a turnkey had been bribed to admit the murderers he would subsequently have kept silent. It was so much easier, and for him so much safer, to believe that Williams had killed himself. But there may well have been rumours. Was Sylvester Driscoll's frenzied panic at being lodged in the next cell no more than superstitious dread? Why did Graham think it necessary to order a man to sit up and watch over his prisoners Hart and Ablass, fettered as they were? Was it because Atkins, the prison-keeper, guessed that there was something very wrong about this particular suicide that he was too ill to attend the inquest?

No single feature of this mysterious case is stranger than the extraordinary abruptness with which the investigation ended. Few who had studied the evidence intelligently could possibly have believed that only one murderer was involved in both crimes, or could have found the case against John Williams either convincing or conclusive. The Prime Minister himself in the House of Commons expressed doubts as to whether Williams could have acted unaided. The exhibits were sent to Bow Street, and Aaron Graham was instructed by Ryder to continue his investigation. Two suspects, Ablass and Hart, were detained on suspicion; the Home Secretary defended his agent when Graham's detention of Ablass was criticised in the House. The preliminary evidence against both men was certainly stronger than that brought against Williams. Yet neither was committed for trial. Both were quietly released without either explanation or excuse. The inference is plain. The investigation ended, not because the case was solved, but because someone willed that it should end.

It is not suggested that the Home Secretary or the magistrates were either corrupt or indifferent, or that they conspired to suppress evidence. But it is suggested that they lost interest so suddenly and so completely in the case as to suggest that they feared what further investigations might disclose. It would not be the first time that authority has subjugated private justice to the public good, and sometimes the victims have been living. But Williams was dead. No exertions of the magistrates, no public or private inquiry, no determination to seek out the truth in the interests of justice, could help him now. Any man of honour would hesitate to condemn and execute an innocent victim, however expedient it might be to satisfy the mob's clamour for vengeance. But a dead victim, poor, friendless and with no known family, and one whose innocence was still only a matter of conjecture, of half-formed theories and unwelcome suspicions, could surely be left to rot in peace. It was as well not to give these theories and suspicions a name. The possibility that further inquiry might dredge up evidence that would cast doubt on Williams's guilt, which might even exonerate him completely, must have terrified all those responsible for the conduct of the investigation. They had exposed Williams's corpse to the ignominy reserved for convicted murderers and they had done so with the greatest possible publicity, and with the approval of the Home Secretary, who had subsequently been castigated for his compliance in the House of Commons. They were being criticised publicly and privately for incompetence; the whole future of the magistracy was in question. Their well-paid jobs were in jeopardy. The age was violent and it was imperative that there should be respect for law and for the guardians of order. Was this the time for the Home Secretary and magistrates to admit that the Ratcliffe Highway murders were still unsolved, to confess that Williams might even have been innocent, and that the suicide which was the strongest presumption of his guilt, might have been yet another murder, the murder of a fettered man in the custody of the law?

Probably no one expressed frankly either in writing or speech what was in his mind, but there may well have been a concensus, a tacit agreement, that it was now expedient that the Ratcliffe Highway affair which had provided so much disturbance, had occupied so much public time and had jeopardised so many reputations, should be allowed to fade from the public mind. There was obviously no credit or glory to be gained in persevering with the inquiry. Aaron Graham must have long realised that this was no second Patch case. He was already being publicly rebuked in the House of Commons for holding Ablass without trial. His fellow magistrates must have been hinting that this unnecessary zeal was putting the whole judiciary in disrepute, and that the case, if obstinately pursued, could bring as much discredit to Graham as the Patch case had brought glory. And Graham was the agent of the Home Secretary. He must have entered the case at Ryder's request; it would need only a hint from his master and the case would be dropped.

And there was another reason for closing the case. Harrison and Cuthperson were pressing for the payment of their reward monies so that they could go back to sea. The system for official rewards for information received was at that time crucial to criminal investigation, and depended – as indeed it does today

– on the informant's reliance that the promise would be honoured. If confidence broke down, the supply of information would dry up and the system of criminal investigation, already unorganised and inefficient, would collapse completely. And it was not only the sailors who were muttering about the delay. The Vermilloes must have been equally disgruntled. Soon, people in positions to make nuisances of themselves would begin to demand an explanation of this unusual reluctance on the part of the magistrates to reward their informants in a case of such importance. It was both easier and more judicious to pay out the money and let the local recipients go about their business and the sailors take their inconvenient knowledge back with them to sea.

Who then murdered the Marrs and Williamsons? There can be no doubt that both murders were the work of the same man, with or without an accomplice. Both displayed the same cruelty and ferocity, the same reckless disregard of danger. In both, one weapon was used which came from Peterson's tool chest at the Pear Tree. In both cases a tall man was seen earlier in the evening loitering near the scene. In both, the weapon (other than the razor or knife) was abandoned at the scene. In both the murderer or murderers entered by the front door and locked it behind them. Both victims were small but prosperous tradesmen. In both cases the killer or killers escaped through the back of the premises. In both cases the robbery, if that was the motive, was only partially completed, although no one could say with confidence what was stolen, as opposed to what was left, since no one remained alive in either household able to say how much cash had been in the house.

Despite the inadequacy of many of the records it is possible to deduce a great deal about the murderers, and to consider whom of the suspects best fits their descriptions. It is virtually certain that more than one man was involved in the murder of the Marrs. Two, possibly three, men were seen hanging about the shop earlier in the evening. There were two sets of footprints in the yard. The occupants of the house in Pennington Street adjoining that from which the murderers escaped, heard the sound of more than one pair of feet. Two weapons were used – the maul, and the sharp knife, or razor. In addition a ripping chisel was brought into the house and left unused on the counter of the shop, while the maul was abandoned in the upstairs bedroom. It is unlikely that only one person came armed with such an encumbering superfluity of weapons. The two sets of footprints were more suspect. It was winter, the yard would be muddy, and the searchers probably explored it in a crowd, keeping together for safety and comfort, and relying on the light of lanterns. The prints were never carefully scrutinised nor measured. Given the standard of police investigation at the time, it would have been highly unusual if they had been. But the evidence taken as a whole suggests that the murderer of the Marrs did not work single-handed.

It is less certain that the Williamsons' murderer had an accomplice. Turner saw only one man, and he resembled the tall man in a long coat seen by Anderson and Phillips earlier in the evening to be hanging about the pub – the man whom Williamson went 'to see about his business'. Turner was awake at the time of the crimes, he was close enough to the massacre to hear the cry of the servant girl and Williamson's last despairing words, and he crept downstairs in time to see the murderer bending over one of his victims. But two weapons were used also in the Williamson murders, the chisel and the razor. The inference is that one man was the actual killer in both cases. On the first occasion he had an accomplice with him; on the second the accomplice, perhaps because he had lost his nerve, or had gained nothing from the first terrifying crime, had refused or had not been invited to take part. A pointer to the possibility that more than one man was concerned in the second crime is the evidence of Turner that he heard the creaking of the murderer's shoes and that, in his opinion, they could not have had nails. The one set of prints in the yard were those of a nailed sole. But it seems unlikely that, if two men were concerned, they would have made their exits in opposite directions, particularly as this would have entailed one of them escaping into New Gravel Lane. It is equally unlikely that Turner would have failed to have sensed the presence of a second intruder. The man could not have ventured upstairs. He must, therefore, have been in the cellar with Williamson's body, only a short flight from where Turner stood. It is unlikely that he moved so quietly that Turner could have been unaware of his presence, particularly in that small house and under circumstances so appalling that nerves and senses must have been highly tuned to every sound.

Who, then, were responsible for these crimes?

We can deduce a great deal about the principal murderer. He was cruel, reckless and violent; probably he was what in modern psychological jargon we call an aggressive psychopath, a man incapable of experiencing either pity or remorse. He was a strong man and one who had tested his strength, confident of his ability to overpower the stout and vigorous Williamson. Despite the barbarity of the slaughter, Professor Simpson regards it as perfectly feasible that the killing was the work of one man. The murderer lived in the district but was not permanently of it. Had he been, surely this overwhelming cruelty and aggression would have demonstrated itself earlier. He was probably, then, either a sailor whose violence normally found an outlet in the hazardous ardours of sea life and in fighting the French, or a prisoner recently escaped from the hulks. If he were a sailor it is probable that he had been on shore long enough to have spent his accumulated pay. Almost certainly he had a criminal history. He was a man capable of organising and influencing others, possibly through the power of his strength and cruelty, a natural leader and one who bound men to him by fear. It is extraordinary that no one betrayed him, even with the temptation of an unprecedented reward. It is highly probable that he was a fighting man who had seen action. Both crimes were systematic killings, typical of hand-to-hand combat. In both there was a sudden sortie, overwhelming force immediately applied, casual and wholesale butchery, the seizing of a momentary advantage when doors were open and the coast clear. In both there was evidence of a preliminary reconnoitre.

All these facts fit Ablass. *The Times* describes him as a stout man, six feet high. He had a history of violence and had organised a mutiny. He had no satisfactory alibi, since the woman who vouched for him was the woman who passed for his wife. He had been at home for two months – long enough for him to have exhausted his pay. He had money for which he could not account, and his explanation that he was living on the bounty of friends and on pawn money is inherently implausible. Mrs. Vermilloe obviously had her suspicions of him.

There seems no reason why such a man should have included Williams in any enterprise. In fact, Ablass had reason to dislike Williams. Had not the latter managed to escape punishment at the time of the mutiny on the *Roxburgh Castle* by claiming that he had been led astray? This was not the confederate to take on an arduous enterprise, and with whom to share the spoils. Williams had nothing to contribute, not even physical strength. It is much more likely that Ablass would have seen Williams as the natural scapegoat if the enterprise failed. It is interesting that Ablass is the only suspect who was lame. It is tempting, therefore, to identify him with the lame man seen running up New Gravel Lane after the Williamson murders. But this man was the shorter of the two. The probability is that neither were concerned in the murder, although they may well have had good reasons for keeping out of the way of the police. If one or both of them had come out of the King's Arms they must surely have been seen by Lee, the landlord of the Black Horse on the other side of the street, who was watching for the return of his wife and niece from the theatre. He admitted that he heard a faint voice from the King's Arms crying 'watch, watch' although, surprisingly, he did nothing. Seven minutes later he saw Turner descending. If the killer had escaped into New Gravel Lane he must surely have seen him. The murderer could not have come through the front door since that was locked and the rescuers had to break in. To come through the side passage opening on to Gravel Lane would have precipitated him into the hands of his pursuers. Moreover, if these two men were the murderers, then Williams was certainly innocent. One of them was tall and the other was lame. Williams was neither tall nor lame. Ablass, though, emerged at the end as one of Graham's prime suspects, and the reports in *The Times* of 17 and 27 January (quoted on page 173) link his name with the murders of both the Marrs and the Williamsons. On 31st January, the Prime Minister was still speaking of the belief that Ablass 'was on a given time at a given place'. That place was either the King's Arms or Marr's shop. There is no reason to suppose that Ablass was ever able to rebut that belief.

And what of Hart? The strongest suspicion against Hart rests on the presence of the unused chisel on Marr's counter. It is possible that this was used as a way of gaining entry to the house. There would have been no difficulty in obtaining entry to the King's Arms, and the probability is that Williamson had not yet finally locked his door. But Marr, shutting up his shop at midnight, might be more reluctant to let in a stranger. In fact, both houses were fortuitously open, but the murderer could not have expected this. Hart had been working in the house; he could have explained that he had come to return the chisel. And there are other pointers to Hart. He had access to the Pear Tree, and he admitted, during his examination on Boxing Day, that it was to the public house that he went when his wife would not admit him to his own house a few nights before the Marr murders. But he did not lodge at the Pear Tree. It would, therefore, have been necessary for him to extract the maul some time before he needed to use it. He was a carpenter and could have borrowed for his own use both the maul and the chisel which killed the Williamsons sometime before the murders. He may well have known that Marr had money in the shop since he had been working there, and it is possible that the two had quarrelled. He would have been forced either to kill or acquiesce in killing because he was known to the family and could not leave the victims alive to recognise him. He was obviously suspected by Mrs. Vermilloe who knew far more about these crimes than she ever testified; and he sent his wife to inquire secretly whether Williams had been taken up.

However ambiguous and disingenuous some of Mrs. Vermilloe's testimony may have been, there is little doubt that Williams's landlady was convinced of his innocence and, of all the witnesses in the case, she was probably best placed to judge. She was obviously not a woman to defend him openly at the risk of antagonising the magistrates, drawing suspicion on herself, or jeopardising her chance of reward. But one of the most interesting features of the case is the way in which her belief in Williams's innocence is revealed in her actions, words and evidence, particularly in her involuntary protest 'Good God! why does he say so', when her husband positively identified the maul, and her obviously genuine shock when she heard that Williams had been found dead. This so impressed the magistrates that they pressed for a reason and she said after some hesitation, 'I should have been sorry if he was innocent that he should have suffered'. It was Mrs. Vermilloe, according to *The Times* report of 6 January, who said bitterly that if the magistrates had spent as much time questioning Hart as they had her they would have learned something about the crime. It was another carpenter, Trotter, who told John Cobbet, the coal-heaver, 'It is a very shocking concern and you would say so indeed if you knew as much as I do'. It was the same Trotter who visited Mrs. Vermilloe to tell her that Williams would soon be cleared. Graham seems to have been convinced of Hart's guilt. The evidence against him, had it ever been properly presented, would seem likely to have impressed even the Shadwell Bench.

After Williams's death Mrs. Vermilloe issued a statement, obviously prepared by a lawyer. It was printed in *The Times* of 20 January:

In consequence of a mis-statement in a morning paper respecting the woman, Mrs. Vermilloe, in whose house the late wretched Williams lodged, she has published a letter dated the 18th inst. in which she states that in justice to an unfortunate and persecuted woman, which she considers herself to be, she wishes it to be made public that the statement purporting that she had made a verbal confession of having participated in the late shocking murders of Mr. Marr's and Mr. Williamson's families is totally without foundation. She further states that she had nothing to confess, except what all the country knew – that it had been her misfortune to have had for a lodger a man charged with the most atrocious crimes.

The last sentence is interesting, particularly the use of the word 'charged'. One wonders whether it was at Mrs. Vermilloe's insistence that the sentence was so carefully worded.

And so, with the payment of the reward money, the case officially ended and the legend began. More than forty years later De Quincey published his *Postscript*. Under his pen the subtleties and mysteries of the case were finally obscured.

Horror was refined by sensibility; cruelty and barbarity were embellished with calculated sadism; a crude lust for plunder was heightened into the malignancy of embodied evil creeping stealthily towards its innocent and unsuspecting prey. De Quincey's account set the tone for subsequent writers on the case. They have been few, and the only mysteries they have pondered are Williams's motive – gain, revenge, homicidal mania, sexual jealousy, a desire to destroy other men's happy marriages born out of his own inadequacy have all been postulated – and whether he had an accomplice. The Ratcliffe Highway killings have been seen as a simple act of extreme barbarism holding little mystery or interest, since the perpetrator was caught and his guilt satisfactorily established. It is as if posterity has endorsed the verdict of the Shadwell magistrates and been as determined as they that the case shall be allowed quietly to die.

It now seems unlikely that we shall ever know the full truth. It may be that the violence which exploded with such devastating effect in Ratcliffe Highway in the dark nights of December 1811 had its fuse laid months earlier under the guns of Surinam, and that the log of the *Roxburgh Castle*, now lost or destroyed, holds the key to the mystery. But, despite the deficiencies of many of the contemporary records, two conclusions are inescapable. John Williams was virtually condemned and his memory vilified on evidence so inadequate, circumstantial and irrelevant that no competent court of law would commit him for trial. And whether he died by his own hand or that of another, it is at least probable that the corpse which was buried with such ignominy at the crossroads near St. George's Turnpike was the body of the eighth victim.

Much of that old Wapping survived until well into the present century.

An early casualty was the King's Arms, at 81 New Gravel Lane. In the eighteen-thirties the London Dock was extended, and the houses on the west side of the Lane were replaced by another huge dock wall; Williamson's public house was among the properties demolished to make way for it. Then Ratcliffe Highway lost its identity. The Rev. R. H. Hadden, curate of St. George's-in-the-East, wrote a perfunctory obituary in 1880: 'Ratcliffe Highway is no longer the *inferno* it once was. As a matter of fact, there is no Ratcliffe Highway now. We call it St. George's Street, East, by way of forgetting old associations.' But one association, at least, survived the change. Thomas Burke, a historian of East London, was able to identify Marr's shop as late as 1928; 'and very markedly,' he wrote, 'the ramshackle place fits the frightful scenes of which it was the setting.'

The erasure of old memories was accelerated on the eve of the Second World War when a local authority, insensitive to tradition, chose to re-name three of Wapping's prominent streets. In July 1937, Ratcliffe Highway, *alias* St. George's Street, became simply The Highway; in February 1939, the iconoclasts turned Old Gravel Lane into Wapping Lane; and a few months afterwards, New Gravel Lane was changed into Garnet Street. Then, in the following year, bombing completed the process of obliteration. On one of the terrible nights of September 1940, when much of London's dockland was gutted, the remnants of Marr's shop must have gone up in flames.

Now one can walk through the parish of St. George's-in-the-East to St. Paul's, Shadwell, and down to the deserted riverside wharves and jetties at Wapping, and hear little but the cry of seagulls and the distant roar of lorries hurtling along the

Highway. The sailors, the dockers, the lodging houses and most of the taverns have vanished. The last ship sailed out of the London Dock three years ago, and the great warehouses that once treasured their stores from the East Indies, of drugs and tea and indigo and spices, stand empty or ruined.

Yet it needs little imagination to recognise, even today, landmarks of the old Wapping. The layout of the principal streets – The Highway, Wapping Lane and Garnet Street – still conforms exactly with that of the earlier streets depicted on the endpapers of this book – Ratcliffe Highway, Old Gravel Lane, New Gravel Lane. A few names have survived every change. The great wall of the London Dock still casts its gigantic shadow over Pennington Street, and the corner with Artichoke Hill locates the site of the unoccupied house through which the murderers of the Marrs were supposed to have escaped. The square that contained Marr's shop, bounded on two sides by Artichoke Hill and John's Hill, on the others by Pennington Street and The Highway, can easily be traced. A block of flats named Cuttle Close fills the square now, and at its eastern corner a street sign, *The Highway, E.1.*, marks the site of number 29. Across the road Hawksmoor's distinctive tower presides over the once sadly bombed and now beautifully restored church of St. George's-in-the-East. Down by the river the Thames Police Station, hard by Wapping New Stairs, occupies the identical site of Harriott's Office. From time to time a modern Metropolitan Police launch, the *John Harriott*, drops anchor close by. The place where the pirates swung is marked on the wall of an old warehouse seventy yards to the west. One may still walk the precise route by which the corpse of John Williams was borne on its solemn progress to his grave at the crossroads of New Cannon Street and Cable Street. But the Pear Tree? Today Cinnamon Street, still cobbled as on the last day of December 1811, when that bier jogged along its length before turning round in Sir William Warren's Square, ends in derelict warehouses and a bombed site. Somewhere among the rubble may lie remnants of Mrs. Vermilloe's lodging house.

But few relics of the Ratcliffe Highway murders are now ever likely to come to light; and, by a strange irony, there is no trace of the last resting place of any of the victims. The church of St. Paul's, Shadwell, where the Williamsons were buried, was replaced by a new building in the following year. Its churchyard is cluttered with undecipherable memorials, and no sign of the Williamsons' tomb remains. The church-yard of St. George's-in-the-East was laid out as a public garden in 1886, when the gravestones were removed and placed against the boundary walls. On many the inscriptions have been eroded by time and the Marr memorial, if there, is unrecognisable. Nor were the remains of John Williams allowed to lie undisturbed. According to S. Ingleby Oddie, lately a Central London coroner, a gang of workmen employed in putting in new mains one hundred years later uncovered his uncouth grave. Two friends, Professor Churton Collins and H. B. Irving, a scholar and an actor, sharing a common interest in criminology, examined the bones. Churton Collins kept those from the right arm. Others, too, had their pickings. A scrap book now in the rectory of St. George's-in-the-East contains an undated entry about John Williams. It ends: 'His skull is at present in the possession of the owner of the Public House at the corner of Cable Street and Cannon Street Road.' It is perhaps fitting that John Williams's skull should have been treasured in a public house near the scene of his notoriety, and that his remaining bones, like those of the Marrs and Williamsons, should lie in a lost and unmarked grave.

BIBLIOGRAPHY

Unpublished Papers

H.O.42/118 – Correspondence from the Shadwell, River
Thames and other Public Offices in Middlesex with the
Home Office, December 1811
H.O.42/119 – Ditto for January 1812
H.O. 42/120 – Ditto for February 1812
H.O. 65/2 – Home Office Letter Book, containing correspon-
dence from the Home Office to the Middlesex Public Offices,
December 1811–February 1812

Newspapers and Journals

Issues of *The Times, London Chronicle, Morning Post, Morning
Chronicle, Courier, Examiner* and *Gentleman's Magazine* for
the period

Topographical

Broodbank, J. G., *History of the Port of London*, 2 vols. (1921)
George, Dorothy, *London Life in the Eighteenth Century* (2nd
ed., 1930)
Hadden, R. H., *An East End Chronicle: St. George's-in-the-
East Parish and Parish Church* (1880)
Mitchell, R. J., and Leys, M. D. R., *A History of London Life*
(1958)
Rose, Millicent, *The East End of London* (1951)
Sinclair, Robert, *East London* (1950)
Smith, H. L., *The History of East London* (1939)
Wheatley, H. B., *London Past and Present*, 3 vols. (1891)

Accounts of the murders of the Marrs and Williamsons

Burke, Thomas, *The Ecstacies of De Quincey* (1928)

De Quincey, Thomas, *On Murder considered as one of the Fine Arts*, and *Postscript*, De Quincey's Collected Writings, vol. 13 (1890). The essay originally appeared in Blackwood's Magazine for February 1827; the *Postscript* was first published in 1854.

Fairburn's *Authentic and Particular Account of the horrid Murders in Ratcliffe Highway and New Gravel Lane* (?1811)

Griffiths, A., *Mysteries of Crime and Police* (1898)

Jackson, W., *The New and Complete Newgate Calendar*, vol. 8 (1818) pp. 393–437

Knapp and Baldwin, *The Newgate Calendar* (1828), pp. 52–9

Lindsay, Philip, *The Mainspring of Murder* (1958), Chap. 1

Logan, G. B. H., *Masters of Crime* (1928), Chap. IX.

Pelham, Camden (ed.), *The Chronicles of Crime and the New Newgate Calendar* (1886), pp. 513–21

Radzinowicz, Leon, *A History of English Criminal Law*, vols. 2 and 3 (1950–56)

Roughead, William, *Neck or Nothing* (1939), pp. 245–77

Shearing, Joseph, *Orange Blossoms* (1938), Chap. entitled, *Blood and Thunder: An old Tale retold.* (A fictional account)

Wilson, Colin, *A Casebook of Murder* (1969), Chap. 4

Miscellaneous

Chatterton, E. H., *The Old East Indiamen* (1914)

Colquhoun, Patrick, *A Treatise on the Police of the Metropolis* (5th ed., 1797)

De Quincey, Collected Writings, vol. 10, *Literary Theory and Criticism* (1890): *On the Knocking on the Gate in Macbeth*

Harriott, John, *Struggles through Life* (3rd ed., 3 vols., 1818)

Lloyd, Christopher, *The British Seaman* (1968)

Malcolm, J. P., *Manners and Customs of London* (1810)

Oddie, S. I., *Inquest* (1941)

Parliamentary Debates, Hansard, vol. 21, cols. 196–222 and 482–9

Report on the Nightly Watch of the Metropolis, Parl. Papers, Reports (1812)

Simpson, Keith, *Forensic Medicine* (1950)

29 Ratcliffe Highway, St George's, Middlesex

Timothy Marr	Linen draper
Celia Marr	His wife
Timothy Marr junr.	Their infant son
Margaret Jewell	Servant to the Marrs
James Gowen	Shop boy
Wilkie	Former servant to the Marrs

The King's Arms, New Gravel Lane, St Paul's, Shadwell

John Williamson	Publican
Elizabeth Williamson	His wife
Catherine (Kitty) Stillwell	Their granddaughter
Bridget Anna Harrington	Servant to the Williamsons
John Turner	Journeyman, lodger at the King's Arms

The Pear Tree, Pear Tree Alley, Wapping

Robert Vermilloe (or Vermilye)	Publican
Sarah Vermilloe	His wife
Mary Rice	Washerwoman, sister in law to Mrs Vermilloe
William Rice	Her son
John (or Michael) Cuthperson (or Colberg)	Seaman, lodger at the Pear Tree
John Harrison	Sailmaker, lodger at the Pear Tree

John Peterson   Sailor from Hamburg, for-
                                         merly lodging at the
                                         Pear Tree

John Frederick Richter   Seaman, lodger at the Pear
                                         Tree

John Williams   Seaman, lodger at the Pear
                                         Tree

The Public Office, Shadwell

George Story ⎫
Edward Markland ⎬ Magistrates
Robert Capper ⎭

William Hewitt ⎫
Joseph Holbrook ⎪
Ralph Hope ⎬ Police officers
Robert Williams ⎭

The Public Office, Bow Street

Aaron Graham   Magistrate

The River Thames Police Office, Wapping

John Harriott   Magistrate
Charles Horton   Police officer

The Home Office

Richard Ryder   Home Secretary
John Beckett   Senior Under-Secretary

Coldbath Fields Prison

Mr Atkins	Prison keeper
William Hassall	Clerk to the prison
Thomas Webb	Surgeon to the prison
Joseph Beckett	Turnkey
Henry Harris	Prisoner
Francis Knott	Prisoner

Others

Spencer Perceval	Prime minister
James Abercromby Sir Francis Burdett Sir Samuel Romilly Richard Brinsley Sheridan William Smith	Members of Parliament
John Wright Unwin	Coroner
Walter Salter	Surgeon
Captain Hutchinson	Captain of the East India-man *Roxburgh Castle*
Mr Lee	Landlord of the Black Horse Public House, opposite the King's Arms
Robert Lawrence	Licensee, the Ship and Royal Oak Public House
Miss Lawrence	His daughter
Mrs Peachy	Landlady, the New Crane Public House
Susan Peachy	Her daughter
Susannah Orr	Widow
John Murray	Pawnbroker, neighbour to Mr Marr
Mr Anderson	Parish Constable, a friend of Mr Williamson
George Fox	Resident of New Gravel Lane
Mr Pugh	Master Carpenter
Cornelius Hart	Carpenter, Pugh's man

Trotter	Carpenter
Jeremiah Fitzpatrick	Joiner
John Cobbett	Coal heaver
William Ablass 'Long Billy'	Seaman, native of Danzig
Thomas Knight	Hackler, employed by Sims & Co, ropemakers
Le Silvoe Bernard Govoe Anthony	} Portuguese seamen
William Austin Michael Harrington William Emery	} Irish seamen
Thomas Cahill	Deserter
Sylvester Driscoll	Irishman who lodged near the King's Arms
Cornelius Driscoll (or Dixon)	A friend of Cahill